Understanding & Learning helped to create
employees, right across the company, put t
their activities, took responsibility to resol.
looked for ways to continually improve services. It is also a cathartic
process for employees which gets rid of any baggage people carry and
boosts morale.

The awards Orange Netherlands won for Customer Service were I am sure,
greatly due to U&L. I would recommend the methods to any company.

David Holliday, Former Chief Executive Officer, Orange, Netherlands

Richard brings a wealth of organisational change management and
leadership experience to the table. Through our engagement with his
company we evolved our delivery teams into an engaging, connected and
truly customer focused organization.

Understanding and Learning concepts and practices are now an integral
part of how we work with our employees and teams. Employee
satisfaction improvements along with leading business metrics improved
significantly following our adoption of Understanding & Learning
practices.

Ken Wilkinson, Director, EMEA Enterprise Support Services - Endpoint
Protection, Web and Messaging Security Products Symantec

'Understanding and Learning' makes the transition from just another
management book to a real practical team based engagement model. I
have had the privilege to see a team transformed applying the principles
of this book. The energy and enthusiasm created by the team based
environment is infectious allowing the natural human spirit achieve
greatness. Give it a go!

Nigel Paterson, COO, Veolia Water UK

I learned best practice change management at Sainsbury and then Tesco with Philip Clarke driving best ever service and cost to serve. I now use the techniques in this book because they are even more collaborative and productive. They focus on team achievement and contribution not just task and planning. Try it and you'll love it.

John Maddocks, Learning & Change Manager, Veolia Water UK

I really found the Understanding & Learning process inspirational. We are in an age where it is the norm for customer expectations and behaviours to continually change, primarily driven by digital and social improvements. Such transformational change requires a different way of thinking and management style and for me, that's where Understanding & Learning became so important when managing teams.

It worked so well that other teams who did not use the process became confused as to how we could work so quickly and implement so much at once. For me it is a management process that is fit for the digital age, ensuring teams are customer-centric and I strongly believe that it is a way of working required to remain competitive. It will definitely stick with me in my future roles.

Chris Cope, Digital Transformation Consultant at Capgemini

This is thought-provoking and will give you ideas on how you can transform any part of your business, be it through improving productivity, reducing costs, increasing customer loyalty or connecting your teams to work more effectively.

Kees van Ek, Principal Consultant, Atos KPMG Consulting, UK

If you want to make a real difference to your team or business read this book.

David Rance, Managing Director, Round, UK

The beauty of Understanding and Learning is its simplicity. The principles can be applied quickly and can be understood by everybody in your business very easily.

After a brief spell in an Understanding and Learning team, I wanted to join the team permanently. The passion, clarity of direction and collaborative environment created by Understanding & Learning meant that I couldn't imagine working in any other way.

Richard Bench, Digital Engagement Manager, Veolia Water UK

Richard has applied himself to his own philosophy of Understanding & Learning to achieve this comprehensive guide to implementing a leadership and organisation approach designed to compete in today's global environment. Creativity, customer relationships and team contribution will be essential to sustain western competitiveness in the future.

David O'Brien, Former Chief Executive Officer, N&P Building Society, UK

This book to my mind has two important attributes. The first is its obvious modest succinctness which allows immediate access to its position and the second bravery, in tackling two of the most difficult human abstracts, namely learning and understanding.

On reading this book one cannot avoid being gripped by Richard's enthusiasm for learning and his desire to understand experiences of learning and his innate passion for others to take these abstractions seriously as part of life.

Professor David Botham, Former Director of the Revans Institute of Action Learning & Research at University of Salford, Manchester, UK

This book will help me articulate the root cause of some of our issues and provide an action plan and aide memoir for improvement.

Carl Dawson, Senior Project Manager, BT Retail, UK

Having visited many contact centres, it is clear that front-line teams are still a huge untapped potential. In this book, Richard is a passionate and much-needed advocate of the steps we have to take to 'set our people free'. It advocates powerfully the need to measure the right things, which link into the factors that really motivate your people.

Paul Smedley, Chairman at the Professional Planning Forum, UK

Understanding & Learning changed the culture of our contact centre from ordinary to extraordinary. People smiled and the smiles were infectious. It was a great working environment. Everyone was free to contribute their best and our customers received first class service.

This book articulates the thinking behind the success and I would recommend the methods to anyone.

Mike Yeates, Former General Manager, BT Mobile, UK

I promise that when you read this book, you will not put it down. It is well written, and designed in an easily readable format. The ideas have 'shown me the light' and changed the way I approach managing teams forever.

John Shields, Customer Service Manager, TSC, UK

If you were shown a black hole which you knew you may, if lucky, only just be capable of leaping without being advised of the depth - would you jump?

Well think about it, this is the kind of pressure you place on people in work every day if they do not understand the direction the business is heading or their role.

Clarity through understanding - truly enhances business performance by providing the confidence to leap.

Karen E McCormick, Chief Executive Officer, Cheshire Building Society, UK

What I find fascinating is the evolution in mindset and language. First you learn and embrace it and then you consciously put it into practice until there comes a point when you are doing it subconsciously and the rest of the team are too. Sometimes you catch yourself saying something particular, which makes you smile!

Kathryn Betts, Improvement Manager, Veolia Water UK

Motivating people and creating teams with passion, energy and drive in a positive environment full of happy people is what I remember most about Understanding & Learning. They created an atmosphere that was totally unique; a place you never wanted to leave and never wanted the times to end. I would recommend the methods to anyone.

Gary Hudson, Business Customer Service Manager, O2, UK

This book never lets you forget that customers and employees are human beings in this technology age. The methods will help companies to create happy, contented employees and satisfied customers. Ultimately, this brings financial rewards for those companies who are brave enough to embrace the concepts.

Maria Grant, Managed Network Support Director, Azzurri, UK

I enjoyed the book and refer to it quite often. I agree with many of the theories. The chapter on understanding the customer was very close to my heart. Everyone will benefit from reading Understanding...keeping the human factor alive in the digital age as it provides a good insight and enhances the ability for teams to perform well.

I also like the focus on people development and the attributes of a good leader. All managers who need to improve customer satisfaction need to read this book.

Liz Mackinnon, Service Group Manager, Verizon Business, UK

It was somewhat of a revelation to read Richard's book and to really understand what he practices, as it suddenly occurred to me....if I hadn't met Richard I probably would have ended up being a manager I now know, I really wouldn't want to be.

Laura Davis, Digital Engagement Manager, Veolia Water UK

For people who are serious about people and the contribution that they can choose to make, this book shows the way. Understanding & Learning had an immediate impact and changed our business because it naturally facilitates the contribution of people. Our people became enthusiastic, engaged and the customers felt the difference - and we became more efficient!

Vince Muldoon, Former Customer Relations Director, Dutchtone, Netherlands

Understanding & Learning is fantastic, not only for the customer but also for team spirit and self-motivation. We now give the customer a unique experience and we make the emotional connection with them.

In our team, everyone helps one another because they want to and not because they have to. The book has been inspirational and the methods make all other initiatives look out of date.

Charles Hill, Customer Service Manager, Orange, UK

Understanding and Learning is more than a way of thinking, for me it is the key to delivering change and to improving our customer experience. I have found it instrumental in challenging myself and my colleagues in a positive way which motivates and encourages everyone to want to improve. The very nature of U&L is based on common sense and I often found myself smiling at the simplicity of the message but more so at the benefits it helped me to deliver.

I would urge to everyone to read this book and to explore the possibilities Understanding and Learning can help you to discover.

Derrick Williams MBE, Head of Customer Experience Planning, Veolia Water Central, UK

'Understanding...keeping the human factor alive in the digital age' is the best of this month's must-reads.

Often people need to be encouraged to think differently. In this book, Richard shows how managers can change the way they manage and make the day-to-day work of every agent more enjoyable.

Moreover, it should help stop staff churn and job loss within struggling contact centres.

CCF (The UK's No 1 customer contact magazine)

If you want to create an atmosphere where your teams feel valued and contribute their ideas every day, resulting in your customers also feeling valued, listened to and genuinely individually considered, this book provides you with the steps to reach it. It really works, and our teams have never looked back, well, maybe only to remind themselves just how very different it was before we started.

Jo-Ann Lyon, Head of Community Operations - Contact & Planning, Veolia Water Central

Great systems and processes alone will not create a great customer experience. Happy, motivated and enthused staff, prepared to put the customer first and go that extra mile, are what make the difference.

The methodologies outlined in this book have been used in a couple of my teams now with real results achieved. More engagement by staff to resolve their own problems, clearer communication paths and clarity of objectives within teams, all result in higher levels of employee satisfaction. Of course, with that comes an improved customer experience and more loyal customers!

Deborah Davis, Vice President, Risk Operations at PayPal, UK

Richard managed to turn the thinking of a typical stuck in his ways Finance Director into the realisable benefits of the Customer Experience and enormous engagement it delivers on all employees and stakeholders. I am now a true convert of embedding the principles into any new business I encounter.

Guy Chalkley, Operations Commercial Manager, Western Power, Australia

keeping the human

factor alive

in the digital age

ISBN 978 0 955 42890 6

First published November 2006
Revised October 2007
Second Edition April 2012

Printed and bound by CPI Anthony Rowe, Eastbourne

Published by Understanding and Learning Limited in conjunction with
Writersworld Limited
www.writersworld.co.uk/understanding.htm
www.understanding.co.uk/humanfactor.htm

keeping the human factor alive in the digital age

Richard Brimble,
Martin Clark and Chris Cope

This book is dedicated to ...

... those Directors who had the confidence and courage to employ me and then provide me with the opportunity to help them transform their company, improve their internal culture, and their customer relationships.

... those managers who took on board the thoughts within this book and challenged their own company to do things differently and creatively for the benefit of their customers.

... those customer-focused individuals, who enthusiastically contributed and provided feedback to ensure that the ideas in this book were practically applied within their company.

... the people I have worked with who have made the choice to think differently and take on the challenge to change things for themselves and for the teams that they are part of.

And finally,

... Julie, Chris and Steve who have always been there to offer love and understanding and give me the freedom and support to do what I love doing.

When I was apprehensive and cynical, you gave me trust
When I was going nowhere, you gave me direction

When I was in awe of you, you gave me friendship and inspiration
When I thought things would never change, you let me make the changes

When I was unsure of my ability, you gave me opportunity and confidence
When I was aggressive, you made me passionate

When I was confused and hurt, you listened and understood
Look how much you have given me

Thank you for changing my life more than I ever dreamed possible

Nicola Dolby, 02, General Manager

Contents

Understanding design...87

Understanding decision-making........................103

Foreword

I was first 'Brimbled' in June 1996.

I had just joined Cellnet, a UK cellular network operator, as Customer Care Director. At the time, Cellnet (later re-branded O2) was 60% owned by BT and 40% by Securicor. The two UK cellular networks (Cellnet and Vodafone) were not allowed to have their own service providers. As a result, BT had a separate mobile service provision operation named BT Mobile, Securicor had Securicor Cellular Services and Cellnet had its own 'arms-length' service provider called Call Connections. Together they managed over 80% of Cellnet's customers. My first decision as the new director was to relocate all the network customer care operations to Leeds in the north of England, which was where BT Mobile and the Call Connections customer care operations were based.

There was already a lot of tension between the service providers and the network, as well as between the service providers and the dealers, about who owned the customer relationship. Service providers were caught in the middle between the network and dealers and their future was thrown into doubt when the regulator allowed Orange and one-2-one, the new networks, to own the billing relationship with the customers.

So it wasn't long before I went over to meet the folks in BT Mobile to see what they did and to try to build a better working relationship. That's when I met Richard Brimble, their enigmatic General Manager of Customer Service. Richard didn't talk about what his people did; he was more concerned about how they did it. He enthusiastically explained his philosophy on contact centre operations; his emotional commitment to helping contact centre agents to become better people through valuing and trusting them, which in turn led to them valuing and trusting each other and giving them self-respect. In the mid-90s this was truly evangelical.

He believed passionately in self-managing teams; a far cry from the hierarchy of most companies - Cellnet included. He talked excitedly about metrics and how poor thinking and measures created the wrong behaviour, not just for the customer but also for the agents and the company. He explained the metrics that showed the difference between calls created by failures (therefore self-inflicted cost) and calls where customer value can be created. He waxed lyrically about the frontline teams continuously driving improvements to customer processes, and policies using feedback from customers. He showed me the chill-out areas where his teams could relax after the tension of dealing with customer queries in a non-customer-centric industry.

After more than two hours of Richard's passionate gesticulations I left and went back to the Cellnet office where my PA asked me, "How was it?" "I've just been Brimbled!" I responded.

Later that year Richard invited me to his team's customer service awards night, which was held in Bradford. The atmosphere was electric as team after team, individual after individual, went up for their awards. The room was full of happy people and I could feel the passion and energy. This was the reality of what Richard described to me that day in his office. People were being recognised for real achievements, not just by the management but also by their peers.

The emotion in the room was off any scale I had ever experienced and I got completely caught up in it. I am not ashamed to say that there were tears in my eyes. It was a defining moment for me.

I took Richard's ideas back into Cellnet and created a 'WOW the customer' culture, flattened the company structure, empowered the team leaders to drive change (including appointing two of them to represent customer care on the senior management product planning committee!) and set about making a difference to people's lives. We all had a great time doing it. The employee satisfactions statistics went off the scale. Customers were happy.

The culmination for me was the night when I presented the NVQ awards to my team members, many of whom had never received any qualifications in their lives. Once again the emotion was running high and I felt immensely proud, and at that moment I thought back to that night in Bradford and realised just how Richard must have felt. Most managers and executives seldom, if ever, experience anything like that level of job satisfaction. Yet there is no reason why this should be the case. I will certainly be forever grateful to Richard for helping me to experience that.

My work as a consultant has taken me into some of the world's leading companies to help them become more aligned around their customers. Becoming customer-centric is a journey that involves establishing a direct link between customer satisfaction and employee satisfaction. The customer only really joins you on the journey when they work with customer-facing people to drive improvements. That's how real customer loyalty starts and the customers quickly become raving fans when they discover that they, like the frontline people they work with, can really make a difference. Our model assesses all the capabilities across the company that collectively create the customer experience, and Richard's innovative thinking has been firmly baked into our capability assessment tools; so his legacy lives on.

We live in a world where we seem to have lost many core values that could make the world a better place, particularly respect and trust. One cannot blame young people for their attitudes. They did not create the world they are inheriting – we did.

Richard Brimble is a very special person whose beliefs and ideals are contained in this book. His unique style has influenced many people and his ideas have been used in both small and large companies, in several different industry sectors, to improve their bottom line performance. He has developed a reputation for thinking differently, being creative and helping people see things differently. Here he presents his concepts, insights and thoughts to business readers everywhere.

So if, like me, you want to make a real difference to people's lives, and therefore to the world in which we live, read this book.   When you implement the ideas and people say to you "Wow, this is fantastic, where did you learn all that?"   you too can say, "I've been Brimbled!"

David Rance
Managing Director of Round (www.round.co.uk)
October 2006

Preface

Six years ago when I published the first edition of this book, the fundamental challenge facing companies was to understand how to profit from individual and team potential, and to use that potential to drive collaboration, innovation, and excellence. The fundamental challenge today is still the same.

We all thought that the internet age would give companies unrivalled access to individual consumers. The ability for companies to connect with consumers online has been extremely important for profitability. However, there is a new not-that-well-understood revolution beginning to surface. The social media revolution has put consumers in control, as it has enabled them to share the good and bad experiences with national and international communities.

This has given consumers, whether in their own homes or on the move, the opportunity to comment and be the free marketers of individual companies. Ten years ago, we would not have thought that a capability would be in place where consumers could connect with thousands, recommending suppliers or solutions. These days the digital age, consumers trust not the marketing or the company's Chief Executive, but often people (their *virtual* friends) they do not even know. Consumers use their smart phone apps for solutions to problems or for advice before they make a purchase.

The technological revolution taking place today will change the way companies contact consumers forever. The social media tools available will change the way that companies communicate with their people. The next ten years might seem to be primarily about technology. However, the best companies will create an internal culture that encourages openness, trust and collaboration. This new open business approach will create potentially uncomfortable organisation dynamics for traditional-age thinkers.

Traditional companies will need to change. Inside some companies the traditional-age thinkers wish to control far too much. The traditional thinkers embrace secrecy and use methods of management that limit communication within the vertical silos. The by-product of this approach is a breakdown of trust between teams, preferring the safety of their silo when discussing issues or areas where understanding is not clear. Transparency and collaboration are now the order of the day in digital-age companies. They understand the new transparency, respond quickly and build trust with their consumers and their people.

The time to involve people and create an environment where teams understand and learn from one another has now arrived in the best companies. The technological revolution in our own personal lives will mean that traditional companies will die unless they make the choice now to change. If they don't change, the best people will not join them. The best people will leave and take with them the chance to build a sustainable business. Along with new technology, the missing ingredient in many companies is a fully embedded 'Understanding and Learning' process.

My motivation for writing this book was to share what some people consider to be a unique approach to company change leading to improved company performance. Six years after the first edition, the methods have been fully tested in at least two companies. I have refined the methods to make them applicable to not just the digital age but also the social media age. I appreciate the help from many of my colleagues and friends who today have chosen to think just a little bit differently.

During the last thirty years, I have worked with both large and small companies to improve their customers' experiences and their internal cultures. During this time, hundreds of people have encouraged me to share my experiences so that others can understand a better way of working and can learn new ways to address the challenge of how to profit from individual and team potential.

- In your company, are people making the most of their potential through collaborative teams?

- Are you having difficulty resolving conflicts between teams?

- Are company silos causing delays?

- Are good ideas lost in the management hierarchy?

- Are your training interventions bringing lasting change?

- Are customers emotionally connected to your brand?

- Are your customers and team players happy?

- Are you known for innovation and can you adapt quickly and creatively to customer requirements?

- How much time is wasted throughout the organisation discussing issues that are outside the individual teams' control?

I have worked with the cynical, the indifferent and the motivated, and have identified a way of working that has made a real difference to the success of the companies I have worked with. The central theme of this book is the importance of creating an environment where people can move out of their comfort zone and release their own potential - by understanding more and learning from their own and others' experiences to benefit themselves, the people around them and their customers.

With so much change still to come, we have the ability to make it easier being an employee these days. In some traditional companies, managers are still using twentieth century measures to help bring about improved performance. Recent research suggests that one out of two people in customer service operations are planning to leave their company, and according to a recent BBC survey, only a third of adults say they are happy in their work. In the private sector, not everyone is engaged and connected to their work, which in turn must undoubtedly be affecting the customer experience. In the public sector, teachers and nurses are unhappy about the target-driven, box-ticking methods of the consultants, the accountants and the managers.

These outdated methods of management demoralise the very people who actually do the work. This centralised command and control system is at the heart of many traditional companies, and has been around for years. It was right for its time, but now, in the twenty-first century, it delivers under-performance, disengages people and has a negative impact on the customer experience. There appears to be too much dictating of how things should be done, leaving no room for creativity in either the classroom for children or in the workplace for adults. The key to educating pupils is the connection that the teacher makes with their class.

The key to a creative, forward-thinking, revenue-enhancing company is the connection that the leadership makes with the local management and their teams. If there is no human connection, the environment for delivering customer experiences and learning is not created. Far too many pupils, nurses and employees are not making the most of their potential, as the present system appears to hold them back. It seems that only the strong survive; they are successful despite the system.

I have put my energy into creating solutions and a better way to connect people together positively in their day-to-day activity. From my experience, people have so much to give. In the right environment they are more than willing to add the discretionary effort that makes all the difference. It is not easy changing from the methods that worked in the twentieth century to the ones that are relevant for the twenty-first. When you have been successful doing things one way it is difficult to see a different way. Success leads to complacency and often this can stop the learning process.

So much has changed over the last ten years. Some successful companies have already changed their culture and have designed the company so that is fit for the future. They are approaching this period of our evolution with a more flexible attitude, realising that everything around them is changing. Key to any change is a commitment to engage and involve the people affected. When people are involved in the process they are more likely to be committed to any change decided by the company.

The challenge over the next few years will be to help people change their ways, encouraging them to learn from their own practical experiences.

To assist in this change, I developed the 'Understanding and Learning' process. This was to help people stay engaged in the efforts for change within their companies and fully understand and learn from the actions that they and their companies take. 'Understanding and Learning' has helped to create a team atmosphere in which employees take responsibility and continually look for ways to improve services and to place the customer at the centre of their activities. Not only does it help teams resolve their own problems, but it acts as a catalyst for cross-functional activity, breaking down silos and designing standard approaches for progressing together.

The 'Understanding and Learning' process is about ensuring that people feel there is purpose and meaning to what they are doing. It is also about involving the right people from across the company so that they can contribute their ideas. It gives people the responsibility to make decisions in their own work fields, and makes the connection between the customer experience, the internal targets and the daily activities. It stimulates employees to work together, learn from each other, enjoy what is going on around them and continually improve.

It is successful as it is a continuous process; it is natural and is closely related to the practical actions and experience that people face daily. 'The Understanding and Learning Process' quickly engages people, and helps to bring about company change and improved performance. Most importantly it allows every single person in the company the freedom to contribute their ideas.

Are you creating an environment where creativity, facilitation, motivation and leadership are shared and often done by players in teams?

With this book, leaders will have the opportunity to understand the importance of clear, inspirational leadership when creating and delivering change. Leaders and managers will identify the ineffectiveness of their present company design and the focus on standards and measures. When quality leadership, digital-age design and measurement are provided, companies can accelerate their progress.

Our customers have realised many of the following benefits. By taking action you will be able to:

- improve interpersonal and team processes
- enhance your ability to cope with company problems
- connect people to your vision and strategy
- create a collaborative company with high levels of trust
- make effective decisions where everyone generates ideas
- release the potential of people in your company
- bring Action-Learning into the day-to-day life of your teams
- integrate creativity into the day-to-day activities
- make the emotional connection with customers
- design your company for the challenges ahead
- change the responsibilities of managers and leaders
- improve understanding and remove destructive conflict
- build individual and team learning into the day-to-day work
- create a team that challenges itself to keep on learning

- create the environment where people choose to share knowledge within and across teams
- resolve interdepartmental conflict
- reduce costs and delays

'Understanding and Learning' is a source of competitive advantage when there is little to differentiate the product or service from the competition. In digital-age companies, more people are happy in their work. When people are happy in their work, there tends to be more creativity and customers normally receive improved service. Companies that focus on improving the internal experience for their employees appear to benefit. Happy customers return and buy more and don't even think of leaving. Shareholders are happy too. In a 2012 study by People Metrics, when comparing the 2008 most engaged customers to the 2010 data, they found that a five-point increase in employee engagement correlated with a 56% cumulative share price appreciation.

This book will give you some ideas to help change yourself, your team and your company. Applying the thinking in this book will change your company. Traditional companies need to stop dehumanising the work experience for their people and give management teams and their employees the freedom to bring their own personalities into their day-to-day work. When this is encouraged across the company, I have found that companies can reduce costs, boost morale, increase revenue and customer satisfaction.

Keeping the human factor alive in the digital age is the challenge for all companies. In an environment of continuous change and complexity, companies require creativity and initiative and so there is a need to rely more on people and less on automation. Collaborative teams contributing and improving together will become the key differentiator in high-performing companies. Social networks inside and outside companies are open, transparent and creative. The combination of knowledge shared freely and relationships that are built on trust and understanding make the difference and will continue to do so. The business model of the past needs to change not incrementally, but fundamentally. The new digital-age business model needs to embrace change and become quick and easy.

I hope that this book gives you a few ideas on how you can improve productivity, reduce the costs to serve customers, connect with your teams and increase customer loyalty. Have fun implementing the 'Understanding and Learning' process. It is the next differentiator, the next step for digital- and traditional-age companies who want to deliver an ever-improving internal and external experience that matches their values by taking action and doing things differently.

Digital now touches every part of an organisation, internally and externally. It's where a lot of your customers are now and where a lot of your team players want to be. How we create, deliver and capture the value of the contribution of teams is my passion. The social age has already disrupted so many industries and companies for the benefit of consumers. The companies that will be successful in the future are the ones that make the customer and people experience easy and quick. They will put their people and customers at the centre of their strategy.

The future will be exciting for the leaders who grasp the opportunity. Senior executives need to remove some of the controls that slow progress. Give intelligent people the opportunity to do their best work. With clear purpose, human beings in teams can achieve more than they can alone.

Right now what the business world needs are companies that can adapt, are capable of continuous innovation and can recover quickly from failures and move on. The 'Understanding and Learning' process will help your teams to contribute, take on the challenge of the digital age and the social media revolution ahead of us. Have fun!

Richard Brimble, April 2012

Executive
Overview

The book starts with an insight into the future challenges for companies within a digital-age society. The need to build lasting emotional connections with customers is explored and we are introduced to the remaining differentiator – 'The Understanding and Learning process'.

I take a historical look into how modern day customer service has its routes within manufacturing. Service companies' use of standards to manage performance is shown to be very similar to those implemented within Taylorism. The impact of such approaches is also introduced. I talk about Action-Learning and how it does not appear to be consistently applied in day-to-day company life.

Chapter 2 explains the ten company attributes I consider essential to the running of companies. How they are applied can determine the characteristics and behaviour within the company. We learn the organisation attributes leaders and managers are responsible for. We also learn the attributes I consider the responsibility of everyone. Brand and knowledge management is explored and targets are discussed. The chapter also introduces the pivotal thinking preferences – traditional and digital. These are the key concepts throughout the book.

Chapter 3 explains the first of the ten company attributes – **control**. This is shown to be a leadership responsibility. There are sections on budget and fiddling the operational figures and we are introduced to the difference between compliance and commitment. The need to have a clear purpose is provided as an alternative to some traditional methods.

Chapter 4 is about the second leadership attribute – **design**. This section challenges traditional structures – particularly how they create internal inefficiencies, delay customers, reduce trust, reduce creativity and devalue the work that people do. A more fluid alternative is provided. Design replaces structure and the key focus is on designing the company around the customer, driving out failures and with good leadership, minimising company politics.

Chapter 5 looks at the third leadership attribute of **decision-making**. The importance of listening is explored along with the need to take considered risks. The need to build decision-making into the daily activity is also discussed. I explain the need to create the environment where people feel able to, and choose to make, decisions, through reducing fear. The impact of working in companies where risks cannot be taken is shared, to highlight the need for change.

Chapter 6 looks at the final leadership attribute – **reward**. An interesting critique of incentives opens the chapter with a particular stress on how work is devalued and how we can lose sight of the purpose, through using too much incentive. An alternative approach is again provided highlighting the need to focus attention on purpose, team contribution and improvement. Teams are rewarded based on everyone working together to achieve a common goal. The benefits of this approach –

improvement, creativity, commitment, feedback and learning are also discussed.

Chapter 7 looks at the first of three management attributes - **people development.** This section particularly focuses on the need for companies to move away from traditional approaches to people development. Training courses are discussed at length. Additionally there is a critique of standardised people development initiatives such as National Vocational Qualifications and Investors in People. An alternative approach is provided that focuses on the need to build learning and development into daily activity. It is argued that such learning initiatives add greater value, reduce training costs and are more sustainable.

Chapter 8 explores the second management attribute - **quality.** This section focuses on the need to build quality into the daily activity. It is suggested that too much time is spent checking that people are doing their jobs rather than creating interesting roles and then trusting people to contribute effectively. The need to work within and across teams is covered as an alternative to politics and working in silos. The concepts of responsibility and challenge are discussed to indicate how individuals can support the change process.

Chapter 9 discusses the final management attribute - **knowledge.** This section focuses on the need to create the environment in companies where people choose to share their tacit knowledge. The value of creating engaging internal experiences really encourages people to be creative and become involved in improving things. This increases the visibility of things not going well and things going well. Traditional reporting is challenged as being labour-intensive and adding minimal value to the purpose. Everyone listening and learning from players in teams, and promoting continual learning, are heralded as alternatives.

Chapter 10 looks at the first attribute I consider vital for everyone to play their part - **motivation.** This section further stresses the need for everyone to truly understand how his or her role fits in with the overall company purpose. The importance of individuals contributing and taking responsibility for their own motivation is discussed and there are some practical tools to enable people to control emotions and behaviour. Additionally, the value of creating an environment where people are involved in those decisions that affect them is cited as a major contributory factor in stimulating people to become more motivated.

Chapter 11 looks at **measurement**. This section challenges traditional measurement and its de-motivational impact on customer-facing staff. The concept of measuring, to improve the experience of customers, is provided as an alternative. Traditional metrics are explored and the need to offer additional products for customers, based on their requirements, is discussed. The impact and pitfalls of using measures just because they are scientific or simple to use are highlighted.

Chapter 12 looks at the final company attribute – the **customer**. This section highlights the need to make lasting connections with customers to improve customer experiences and increase customer loyalty. It challenges scripting customer interactions and highlights the need to create interesting roles where front-line people are encouraged to become involved in improving things. Finally this section looks at the need to create a customer culture where customers are liked.

Chapter 13 identifies why understanding and learning is so important and will help your thinking in a digital capacity to prepare you and your teams for the digital and social challenges that are quickly approaching.

Chapter 14 looks at the key behaviours that are essential in truly great teams.

Chapter 15 outlines the measurable benefits of thinking in a digital-age way and gives you a fifteen-point checklist that can be used as you set about implementing the thinking into your everyday work and life.

Background

For all the talk about the customer and how important people are, my experience and research suggest that many traditional companies are struggling to make the changes required to bring about improved and sustainable customer and people experiences.

During the late 1990s there was considerable focus by companies on the customer experience with extensive Customer Relationship Management (CRM) programmes. These were often driven by the latest information technology developments and were not always successful.

Many value-driven and behaviour-change initiatives were launched, focusing on ensuring that all employees demonstrated behaviour that was aligned to the values. These initiatives, normally held in the training room away from the actual work, were one-off events. Did they change the culture of the company? I spoke to some motivated people and even they were cynical about the longer-term impact of such programmes.

Future challenges

The next competitive battleground will not just be about satisfying customers and delivering the experience. It will be about creating an internal environment where everyone has opportunities and can choose to contribute more to company success.

In the early part of this century, some companies truly connected with their customers, such as O2 and First Direct in the UK, and zappos.com in the USA. These companies understood that competitive sustainable advantage is gained by emotionally connecting all of their teams to the company strategy through ongoing involvement.

Are all the players in your company involved and contributing their best?

This differentiating factor gives all team players the freedom as individuals to make decisions in favour of customers, making the emotional connection with the customer with a complete understanding of the commercial realities.

With this understanding, truly remarkable performance can be achieved. Companies make money, reduce costs and satisfy more customers. In these ground-breaking companies, players choose to respond with enthusiasm and commitment when contribution is required. The business results speak for themselves.

In the digital age, more and more companies are putting customers in control, making it quick and easy to transact. Good examples would be giffgaff, easyJet, and of course eBay and PayPal. Their processes are focused on customer requirements and the customers feel involved with the company. Social media will increasingly put consumers in control of a company's brand and reputation. How quickly companies predict or recover from an incident will be essential to building a competitive reputation.

Fully engaged, open collaborative teams who have full understanding will be essential in the future.

Competitive threats

New competitors are also making their mark and moving in on established companies with increasing vigour and determination. With the onset of mobile internet and new engagement channels, companies have needed to focus on implementing customer-focused systems and processes to improve the customer experience. The banking system is changing with the introduction of the Barclays Pingit system that allows users of smart phones to make payments using their mobile phone numbers.

In some industries customers have been choosing to do the transaction themselves for years. For example, six years ago, amazon.co.uk knew my book and music preferences due to my previous purchases and often recommended new titles whenever I logged on to their site. I could sell and buy items on eBay.co.uk. I could purchase tickets to fly cheaply to Europe through a number of sources. I could compare prices on sites specifically dedicated to that purpose.

These days this can be done on my mobile and on the move with little interaction. I can barcode in shops to check the best prices. When I decide to make a purchase I can quickly find feedback from my 'virtual friends'. We now appear to trust the opinions of people we do not even know when making purchasing decisions. We certainly trust them more that the companies we are purchasing from.

If there is a failure that requires a contact, technology can now segment our best customers, directing them to the right team and the right engagement channel, helping to deliver a truly differentiated service.

Customer transactions

With technology in place, it has been possible to deliver improved transactions for the customer based on their long-term value to the business. Customers can now choose the engagement channel that suits them – in the hand, in the home and in the community. With the right technology, the engagement with the customer is less stressful. The technology is focused on them and their needs. In many cases, the customer wants to do the transaction themselves these days.

I have never spoken to amazon.co.uk. I have not needed to. I believe that their customer service is excellent. The new technological advances, with transactions in the hands of the customers, mean that I may not speak to my supplier for months. This means that when customers do contact companies, the companies need to concentrate on the interaction with the customer. Companies need to focus on the customer's personal circumstances, treating each one uniquely and ensuring that they do not make mistakes, satisfying them first time.

When customers choose to talk to us, we need to understand them. We need to give them a remarkable experience. Some of this customer understanding is gained by giving the Customer Advisor assists during the contact. These assists can show customer lifetime value, previous purchases, and can even recommend potential solutions. This certainly helps the advisor deliver an improved interaction.

However, the managers I have worked with believe that truly remarkable experiences can only be created with people who are engaged and interested. Motivated people want to create experiences that match the brand values and the customer circumstances.

Basics of customer service

Many products are very similar in price and content. Many companies are scientifically implementing customer segmentation strategies these days using the same technology. Increasingly, there is little opportunity to differentiate. In the mobile business, companies are even sharing the costs of updating and improving their networks. However, this is just a network. These days, customers expect a good connection when using a mobile phone. Companies have to get the basics right with no errors and with quality. It's just the price of entry. It has to be quick and easy. You must have the basics to be in the game. If you are a large company, you will not survive without it. In addition, you must know about your customers and their unique needs.

However, it's different if you are small. The local shopkeepers never needed technology – they just took time to understand their customers. The successful corner shop takes time to understand the customer's changing personal circumstances, makes the emotional connection with their customer, and modifies the behaviour to suit. They probably didn't receive any training - they just liked people! So how happy are your customers? How do you know? How involved are your team players? I believe that it is this deep understanding of each individual customer that develops the longer-term relationship.

The importance of making the emotional connection

How the customer feels needs to be measured on an ongoing basis by the people that are closest to the work. At the same time, they should be identifying what improvements could be made to improve the customer experience and provision of feedback.

It is this powerful combination of technology, process and people improvement, combined with emotional connection with customers, which leads to sustainable improvement and increased profits. Everyone is involved, feels valued and chooses to contribute. Customers enjoy the experience and choose to come back for more. Do your customers return for more? If they do, is it inertia or are they truly committed?

To deliver the external customer experience, it is vital that players in teams are coached in a way that helps them respond with enthusiasm and commitment. The experience of team players right across the company needs to be the focus, so that customers feel the company's advertised values through the communication with the customer-facing teams. It is far too easy these days for companies and managers to confuse commitment with compliance.

My experience suggests that far too many employees come in, do the job, and go home - with opportunities to understand the customer and sell more products being missed.

The importance of being happy in your work

If you are not happy yourself it is difficult to respond with enthusiasm when engaging with internal and external customers.

> *When I was 5 years old, my mother always told me that happiness was the key to life. When I went to school, they asked me what I wanted to be when I grew up. I wrote down 'happy'. They told me I didn't understand the assignment, and I told them they didn't understand life.*
>
> **John Lennon**

When you are not happy in your work, then company-sponsored smile training doesn't make you feel any better!

How happy are you in your day-to-day work?

Millions have been spent on external behaviour training courses in the last ten years, normally away from the workplace. I spoke with thousands of employees, across different industries and companies, and asked these questions:

- Has the training been of any real value?
- Has the training been sustainable?
- Can the impact be measured?
- Is the learning built into the day-to-day work?

Some thought it had been helpful, but many thought it had not changed the way the company worked or how they did business with their customers. The keynote speech at a company conference may stimulate some people on the day it is given, but many have told me that the learning (if there is any) is not actually applied in the workplace. A comprehensive study in 2005 from Rutgers University, New Jersey, USA estimated that between $5.6 billion and $16.8 billion is wasted annually on ineffective training programmes that are focused on so-called soft skills. Award-winning directors have told me that training alone is not the answer. However, behavioural training does have value, yet often it is applied at the wrong time.

Learning by doing

Many companies have focused on marketing and customer relations to differentiate their business, with mixed success. Marketing can deliver a message through any medium to encourage customers to contact the company; however, these days marketing messages are often not believed. Consumers check the internet and within seconds are debating their next move on forums with strangers who are having the same questions. Independently from the marketing, consumers are deciding for themselves their next move.

Getting it right internally will continue to be the challenge for many digital- and traditional-age companies. From a very young age, human beings learn by doing new things. They learn to walk and run, ride a bike and later on to drive a car. In business life, the more interviews you attend the better you can become at them. The more people repeat an experience the greater chance there is that they will improve. It is important to recognise that learning by doing is not about repetition; however, practice can lead to improvement.

Where was your greatest learning experience?

I have asked this question of hundreds of executives. Over 80% explained that it wasn't at school, at university, or in a training course. Where they learned the most was in a real life situation. My observations from business situations is that people appear to learn more effectively by applying the learning from training courses in their day-to-day work. People have told me that training courses, management textbooks, gurus or industry experts may provide stimulus to change but they do not deliver the change. People at the sharp end have told me that they learn by doing. They take the knowledge gained in the training room and use it in the day-to-day work, if they are allowed to.

How do you keep the training alive after the trainer has left your company?

Whilst some individuals are continually learning and benefiting themselves, the power of the team is often not fully realised in many companies. There is still a preoccupation with politics and interdepartmental conflict. The larger the company, the less teamwork there appears to be. Whilst some learning is shared between individuals on an ad hoc basis (such as learning new software skills), it appears only to benefit the few. What happens when no one knows the answer? Creating the environment where people can be open about their (lack of) knowledge, feel free to ask questions without ridicule, feel free to question when there is doubt, and feel free to admit failure and mistakes, is not easy to do; but for the brave it can be enriching. Companies need their staff to learn quicker within their teams and across their hierarchy. Teams need to be more open with one another about their team and individual performance. Building learning into the day-to-day work is vital to the development of companies, teams and individuals. This is what is missing within many traditional companies today. However, it is not missing in the digital world at home. Through Facebook and Twitter, collaboration and openness is easily applied in our personal life. Everything is changing. Traditional-age thinkers need to wake up and get into the world of uncertainty and action learning.

The remaining differentiator

Whilst nearly all processes have now been defined and continually improved, there is still one process that has not been defined in many companies. It is the process that improves the internal communication and makes the most of people's potential and brings out their inherent creativity. I call it the 'Understanding and Learning' process. In one company the Chief Executive described it as the last remaining unique selling point of the company. The 'Understanding and Learning' process helps teams resolve their problems. It engages everyone and brings the differentiating factor to companies and teams. The customers tell me that it has made a unique contribution to their business helping them to increase their profits, become more customer-centric, and improve their internal culture.

Without the 'Understanding and Learning' process the contribution that people can make to the success of the company is restricted and limited. When implemented, there are plenty of opportunities to bring about substantial improvements in shareholder value, people and customer satisfaction. In addition, it encourages self-reliance, develops people and helps companies change the way they behave. However to sustain the progress, it does require a change of thinking and that is difficult for everyone.

In a changing environment, where there is ambiguity, uncertainty and confusion, there is now a real need to take action and learn. The early adopters (Dell, BTCare) have understood social media. The companies that waited are now playing catch-up. The time for action and learning is now here. There are some problems that have no known solution. In a changing digital-age world the answers do not come from one individual but from collaborative teams who fully trust one another. Teams working together will find the answers if they are given the freedom to explore the solutions enabling them to take decisions and to learn.

Do you remember when people were concerned that computers would put us all out of work? In fact, what happened was that computers just made the tedious work easier. Some enlightened companies created new and interesting roles that tapped into the potential of people, helping them bring creativity to the situations when it matters most - when engaging customers and solving company problems.

The challenge for all companies in the digital age is to keep the human factor alive, increase productivity, and release the talents that people naturally have. The 'Understanding and Learning process' does just that.

So why is the 'Understanding and Learning process' so important, right now?

There continues to be conflict between teams and individuals in many companies, often due to egos and ineffective team structures. There must be a better way to resolve differences and disagreements. There is a real need to understand people and situations and learn from them. It's only when people step back from their own point of view, suspend judgment, ask questions and really listen to others that real learning takes place. However, this is easier said than done – try it at home in your own family!

We appear to live in a debate-driven world. There has to be a right and a wrong. Someone has to win and someone has to lose. Why? We need to keep the debate alive whilst ensuring that we do not destroy relationships and the trust: without both - people have nothing! Real debate brings about creativity; however, it also requires a change of thinking from everyone.

What is needed is real, meaningful dialogue, where trust and relationships are built into the process. Managers in companies seem too busy these days to stop and take time to listen to one another, build relationships, and make the emotional connection with people.

Do you sit and communicate with your own family?

The TV and digital-age activities can easily take over our lives; computer games leave children in their bedroom all evening and the internet can tie you up for hours. You can watch TV and be involved in worldwide or local debates, communicating with millions through social media. Some people are enjoying this. Are they still talking? Is the relationship as strong? Interestingly enough, a recent happiness survey highlighted that the people of Nigeria were the happiest in the world. It is clear that in a materialistic world having everything does not make you any happier. The 'Understanding and Learning process', integrated into the way you work and live, keeps the human factor alive during these turbulent and changing times both at home and in the digital-age company.

Understanding the history

Many front-line people I have spoken to across Europe feel that managers are still paid to think, whilst employees are paid to do. What companies need is thinking implementers; people who implement and also think about ways to do it better. These people review their work daily and look for ways to improve things tomorrow. Do your teams review their achievements daily?

Are your frontline colleagues thinking implementers?

As computers and mobile technology increasingly make life simpler, then there will be a need for a more intelligent and well trained workforce. In the next twenty years there will be even more new jobs created, replacing the jobs that are now not needed. In fact, they are not even jobs; some companies call them roles now! I agree; for me, a job is digging the garden, cutting the grass – something I have to do! It is hard work that requires little cerebral thought.

These changes will need an 'Understanding and Learning process' built into every single company to help team players through the journey.

In 1776 Adam Smith published *An Inquiry into the Nature and Causes of the Wealth of Nations*. This book looks at the nature and causes of national economic development. Central to the thought process is that greater productivity can be delivered by manufacturing. He explained that leaps of productivity could be attributed to company and technology. He visited a pin factory and noted that teams of people, with each person becoming a specialist in his own area, could produce more pins per day than one man alone. This approach underpinned many of the thoughts and implementation during the Industrial Revolution (1750-1870). It was clearly a huge leap for productivity.

> *In 1978, I was in the printing industry and it was clear that there were specialists. I was one of them. I could only contribute in my area of specialisation. The productivity slowed whilst I waited for the next specialist to arrive. Even worse, I knew what needed to be done but I couldn't do it, as it was not my job! I complained but there was not an environment that listened to my improvements. I was only 18. What did I know! For a quiet life I did my job. I became totally frustrated. I decided to move into marketing and eventually customer relations. It will be different there, I thought.*

The impact on customer service

The service industry has become obsessed with a focus on selling products and achieving standards. The standards are often internally focused and are not aligned to any customer requirements.

Have you ever asked McDonald's to remove the gherkins from a Big Mac?

Try it sometime – it creates the maximum fuss. The staff look at you as if you are a real problem, not a customer. It appears that many companies are still very much product-focused.

Today, in some contact centres, there are still specialists handling certain types of calls, as this appears efficient. Doing the same thing repeatedly, meeting the set standards, in some ways appears efficient. However, the people doing the work can become frustrated with the repetition, leading to them becoming less emotionally attached to their work. It just becomes a job that needs doing. There is less emotion shown to customers. This leads to mistakes and increasing levels of customer dissatisfaction. Eventually many people decide to do something else.

Understanding Taylorism

Frederick Winslow Taylor is often called the Father of Modern Management. He believed that management is the collaboration of people and machines to create value. He pioneered the Scientific Management approach with his book *Shop Management* in 1903. He took time to observe men at work. If they worked hard and finished their work early, they would not have any work to do. No work meant they didn't receive any pay, so they worked slower. He identified that this made the workers inefficient. In addition, he believed that management failed to organise work and failed to provide the right incentives.

Taylor's solution involved defining the work standard and fitting wages to this standard. Management should specify the targets and pay the workers for delivering the tasks or goals.

The main elements of this theory were:

- Management is a true science – there is one right way for work to be performed.
- Selection of workers is a science – management role was to determine which employee was most suited to the job and hire accordingly.

- Management's job was to engineer a job so that it could be done efficiently and train the worker on specifically how the job needs to be done.
- Managers are not responsible for the execution of work but they are responsible for how the work is done.

This approach was right for its time and brought increased productivity. The workers didn't need to think at all. Allocating tasks and measuring to the standard brought early benefits and the approach was copied across the world. One of the criticisms of this approach is that it did not ask the worker how to design the work. Employers didn't need to ask the worker's opinion. The work was typically simple repetitive tasks that did not need people to think. All they needed to do was work. That is what workers did. Managers did the thinking and the employees did the work.

Are the measures of success the right measures?

Taylorism brought significant benefits to the economies of many countries. It was the cornerstone of the manufacturing boom during the early part of the twentieth century. It was so successful that we haven't really been able to let it go, particularly in some service industries.

The impact of standards

During the late twentieth century there were many initiatives to drive out this thinking. Many managers, from the private sector and the public services, explained that they had been involved in quality circles, continuous improvement initiatives, quality standard initiatives, quality departments and various checking procedures.

Some managers have spent hours away from the business looking at government-sponsored initiatives such as ISO 9000 accreditation.

> In one company, directors took a whole day out to review their business against this standard. I was invited along to review. Outside consultants were brought in to facilitate the day (they were the experts) and to help the managers understand the process. The directors self-assessed themselves against the standard and each director put forward their ideas on how they could improve things.
>
> The Managing Director was supposed to come but he didn't make it. He had another meeting to attend. Wasn't he lucky!
>
> The day added no value at all. Many of the directors looked forward to the break so that they could make telephone calls. I overheard sales being made and problems being solved. More value was being added during the breaks than in the actual meeting!

Many of these initiatives have sought to involve more people in improving work. Often they are implemented away from the actual work. Things have not really changed because many companies haven't really changed their thinking. This thought process was transferred into the service business and created increased costs and dissatisfied customers. When you serve customers they really don't like standards. Different customers accept different standards. What is right for one customer will be wrong for another. These days the customer defines the standard. Standards follow process and everything is OK as long as customers do not ask questions outside of the advisors' responsibility. Many contact centres and some retail outlets are managed using a measurement model that was alright for its time but is now out of date.

Years ago in manufacturing we had supervisors checking the quality of shoes, adding lots of cost and very little value. Can you imagine how dreadfully soul-destroying that checking job was? Eventually, managers were brought in to manage the supervisors, adding extra cost and bringing communication challenges to the company. Some years later factories closed down and everyone lost their jobs.

Action-Learning in the '50s and '60s

It is not easy being a pioneer. People do not always agree with you. You are different. Your ideas are not always accepted. You can easily lose focus. However, some just keep going. Reg Revans, the inspired management thinker, pioneered Action-Learning as a practical tool for human development and problem solving.

During my research into the subject of Action-Learning I came across the Revans Centre for Action-Learning at the University of Salford, set up by Professor David Botham during the mid-1990s. This centre has helped me understand more about the concept of Action-Learning. The term Action-Learning emphasises learning by doing. Action-Learning combines learnt information with the ability to question how that knowledge can be applied to individual situations. Action-Learning is a framework which highlights that programmed knowledge combined with an environment where you can ask insightful questions, leads to a more creative solution. It is not just learning from experience but creating the conditions where teams can challenge one another in a trusting environment to find the best way forward.

Reg Revans realised that people learnt more when they did things and learnt more when they could be open about their lack of knowledge. Reg Revans died in 2003. In a changing political, economic and technical world, I think that action learning is now here to stay.

Six Sigma in Customer Service

In the last few years there have been a number of efforts to bring manufacturing methods into the service world. One such method is Six Sigma. Experts in Six Sigma will explain that this has delivered success to their service company.

Teams of experts set about designing business processes identifying how predictable a process is, and if it is predictable then it must be measurable. Apparently, the more predictable and measurable a process, the better it is.

Six Sigma has been put forward as a way to improve
service. Thousands of pounds have been spent on
training the experts. It works if you are building a car
or making a product, but does it work in service? In
many cases where processes are broken, it has
improved the transaction. It has helped to make the process easy
for customers. However, if you have an excellent world-beating
process (measurable and predictable) does it ensure good service?
My research and experience suggests that some people are bored
out of their minds at the repetition.

During the course of my work I travel extensively around Europe,
visiting many airports in many countries. I am regularly put through
a business process. The process is standardised across the world. It
is measurable and it is predictable, but do customers receive good
service? What is the service like from the ground staff? What would
make it better? How happy are the employees? Can they take
decisions in unfamiliar situations? How emotionally connected are
the people and the customers? Six Sigma works when the process is
simple and straightforward. When the situation is complex or
ambiguous (as often it is in front of customers) then ingenuity and
thought are often required. Is the interaction with customers
measurable and predictable?

Without spending thousands on customer surveys, teams have
helped me to predict what customers want. People have told me
that what customers want is a quality product that is relevant to
their needs, and when it goes wrong, they want employees who are
free to take decisions without delays or having to pass those
decisions on. When the situation is unfamiliar, customers want
customer-facing teams to take responsibility and help them.
Companies with excellent products and empowered people have a
high level of customer loyalty.

The best companies give people the freedom to satisfy their
customers. Is it too much to ask? From my experience, where
people have freedom and control of their work and are involved in
improvement they are more motivated. Customers feel the
difference.

What works in manufacturing does not always work in service. Giving people the freedom to satisfy customers (who are not predictable) affects the measurability and the predictability of the process. Keeping existing customers happy is vital in every industry now and many successful companies have decided to give their teams the freedom to satisfy customers without the hindrance of inappropriate targets that often drive the wrong behaviour.

Costly customer service

In 2006, a survey produced by Dimension Data revealed that the number of calls where the customer was mutually satisfied stood at just 70%. Not enough customers are receiving experiences that they are happy with. It seems that many customer-facing people are following standards that do not continually improve the quality of the interaction or the transaction. Maybe managers are measuring the wrong things, leading to increased costs for their company. I have seen supervisors using tick sheets to ensure that during calls the customer advisors use:

- the customer's name three times
- buzz words aligned to the company values
- set-phrases when managing the customer

All these measurements involve checking to a standard, defined by the managers and not the customer. In these contact centres, the customer advisors do not need to think about the customer. They just need to hit their internal targets and use the correct script.

> *In one company, I witnessed customer advisors not saying 'Happy Christmas' to customers. I was keen to know why. Apparently, the management had not changed the script to accommodate Christmas greetings. Some customer advisors decided to use their own common sense, building emotionally connected relationships with customers. They sensibly amended their language to suit the individual customers. Whilst the customers were happy the supervisors were not. Customer advisors were not following the script! The supervisors could not agree how to measure situations*

> *where different words were being used by the customer advisors. The supervisors had a standard and it was linked to the bonus system. Any changes had to be agreed between supervisors and this often took four to five hours of meeting time. They called these levelling meetings. Supervisors travelled from all parts of the country to attend these meetings. They were having a great time, enjoying their overnight stays at top hotels. It was expensive and it was not improving customer service.*
>
> *I attended one of these meetings and at no time did anyone talk about how the customer felt, and the levelling was actually bringing the quality down. It was complete madness. The supervisors were adding very little real value. The calls just kept on coming!*

I have witnessed customer advisors who have done everything correctly, following the set standards, but the customer is still unhappy. When supervisors do the checking they do not even see it from the customers' point of view. They are too busy preparing the information for the eventual feedback session with the employee! In these companies people soon become ill.

A recent survey by the insurance group AXA pointed out that UK business is losing 12.2 billion pounds annually due to staff absence. Nearly 14% of the reason for this absence is due to people pretending to be sick when they are not - costing UK business 1.7 billion. You can see why, in some contact centres, turnover is high and sickness has to be managed. If the job is painful or boring, intelligent people will do something else. These days young people bring cognitive thought into their companies – we would be wise to use it or lose it!

In another contact centre, they were committed to selling additional products to customers. They wanted to move from a cost centre to a profit centre. Of course, this makes sense. Everyone was trained and set off to meet their targets. Unfortunately, management had not planned the impact of this activity. Eventually customers were complaining that they were waiting too long to be answered. Management did some analysis. They identified that on Tuesdays and Thursdays the teams were less busy. The customer advisors were told to only sell to customers on Tuesdays and Thursdays. Even when customers had a requirement the customer advisors could only sell on these days. During the contact the customer advisors had to remember what day it was before they sold anything to a customer! This was a solution that did not take into consideration the impact on the customers or the people in the teams.

The role of management in the future is to design work and measurement around the needs of customers and ensure that it is interesting and meaningful for the team players in their teams.

Measuring the capabilities

There are occasions when teams achieve their targets but the management have no idea what the teams did to achieve them.

> *I listened to the retail sales senior manager becoming very excited by the increase in sales in his chain of shops on a particular day. He had absolutely no idea what caused the improvement. He set about asking his teams why.*
>
> *He found out it was the weather! It had been particularly hot for a few weeks. On the day in question, it was cooler. Apparently, this brought more customers to the shops, giving the teams a greater chance to close the sale.*

At the operational level the key is to measure what capabilities you are improving. For example, in contact centres, 90% of the reasons for customer hold-time are due to circumstances outside of the customer advisor role, such as systems not working or certain people not being available. Surprisingly, some companies are still measuring and targeting their operational teams and managers on hitting this target. They believe that it is a people problem. Sometimes it is. But more often, it is not. In most cases, 95% of underperformance in organisations has to do with the way of working. It just seems easy to blame people.

In teams managed by traditional thinkers, individuals have told me that they are using their ingenuity to scam the system. I have seen senior managers manipulating reports to show improved figures to higher management. Really, the customers are getting a raw deal. Companies need to engage their people so that they are using their ingenuity to solve problems for customers and create value for the company. The challenge is to build trust into the process and measure the right things so that we can continually improve. In a world where the customer is calling the shots and has many competitors to choose from, there is a need to think differently, if we are to create remarkable experiences.

Traditional-age thinking has had its day. The best are now practising digital-age thinking and are seeing the benefits. For example, the profit at Apple in the period October to December 2011 hit $1 billion a week.

We need to change the way that people think about their work. This is perhaps the greatest challenge facing traditional companies today.

Summary

Within companies there are various types of people from different backgrounds and nationalities, all with experience and history to help them make sense of the world around them. In the recent past this experience was useful, as it helped all of us take the time to consider and take the correct action when satisfying customers.

These days people have told me that they want more from work than just doing the job. Increasingly, what worked a few years ago is no longer relevant as there are new challenges facing everyone. People are becoming more educated and are making their own choices as to their next career move. Talented people will not sit about and allow the local management to affect them with managerial practices and traditional thinking that is not fit for today's purpose.

People really do want to contribute to company success and want their opinion heard. If people are not listened to, they don't feel valued. Holding on to your most talented people will be vital, as companies compete not just in their own country but also in the global context.

Traditional or Digital Age

Traditional thinking drives the behaviour of many of our management teams and underpins many of the solutions that companies implement. Traditional thinking creates confusion, communication difficulties and unnecessary company politics, increasing costs and upsetting customers.

In conversations I have seen that this confusion and lack of understanding restricts the contributions that people can make. It creates fear, pressure and stress when delivering the customer experience. The impact on customers can be delay and frustration. The customers often receive an experience that they would not recommend to others.

The ten company attributes

Over the last few years, through extensive practical research, I have identified ten company attributes that control and determine the longer-term success of teams and companies. How you think drives your behaviour and the solutions you design for the company. The closer these ten individual attributes are to the leaders, the less involved people feel - leading to less commitment, less productivity and increased internal conflict. Conversely, the closer that all of these ten company attributes are to the people that serve customers, the greater the opportunity to save money and deliver experiences that customers will want to return for.

These key company attributes can be grouped together so that they relate to leaders, managers, coaches and everyone in teams. In award-winning companies, leaders, managers and coaches are increasingly responsible for each of the company attributes below.

THE TEN COMPANY ATTRIBUTES

Leaders	Managers/Coaches	Everyone
Control	Quality	Measurement
Design	Knowledge	Motivation
Decision-making	People Development	Customer
Reward		

Contribution of Traditional Thinkers

Generally, in companies, the traditional thinkers want to be involved in many of these attributes. They can't stop themselves. They believe that they are responsible for all of the above. They actively involve themselves in everything. I have seen many of them unnecessarily waste time by measuring the wrong things and wanting to determine what people do and how they do it. Traditional-management thinkers spend hours discussing and agreeing the way forward on a number of company projects but unfortunately this normally doesn't involve the people it affects – the people doing the job! These people often do not attend the meetings.

I have witnessed traditional thinkers:

- Blaming managers for the present performance when their own leadership does not allow open challenge or questioning.

- Having two-day workshops on improving the customer experience but not including anyone who talks to customers.
- Designing new ways of working without including anyone who might have to do the job.
- Holding workshops on how to improve motivation without asking the people who have a problem with motivation.
- Pontificating about company politics instead of solving customer problems.
- Having weekly meetings to discuss the numbers, none of which relate to capability improvement or the customer.
- Sitting around in meetings discussing and justifying the numbers on Excel spreadsheets instead of improving things.

Of course, there are a lot more examples where time is wasted within companies. Traditional thinking can bring short-term results but is rarely sustainable. Eventually, often months or years later, this approach costs money for shareholders. The banking crisis of 2008 was replete with examples where directors made decisions that at the time no one was prepared to question.

There was clearly fear in some of the high-profile companies. These companies had an internal culture where no one had the confidence to challenge the decisions being taken. In companies with traditional thinking it is better to keep quiet and contribute with compliance and little real commitment. Of course, this approach ensures that the best people just leave!

Do you know who your best people are?

People talking with customers become so internally focused that they only deliver an OK service to customers. The problem is that traditional thinkers focus on the targets and not improvement at the individual and the team level.

Contribution of digital thinkers

The digital thinkers just see it differently. They are always looking to ensure that an environment is created where everyone takes responsibility for their own development, motivation and measurement. Managers spend their time ensuring that teams have the tools to do the job well and are trained to meet the emerging needs. They spend their time in the work teams, asking questions. Not any old questions but questions related to making things better! The teams are encouraged to put forward ideas and challenge the direction of the business.

What one thing could I do to make your role better?

The leaders have a clear understanding of the capability gaps within their teams. The best leaders and managers take action, and spend time talking to their teams to update them on the progress that is being made to resolve those issues that affect their work.

They just keep on communicating to build the understanding, sometimes in meetings, but more often face-to-face. They don't hide in offices having meetings all day. They visit their teams doing the day-to-day activity.

They focus on people development, process and system improvement to improve quality because they know that these capability improvements will predict and sustain team performance. These days it is the contribution of people and the choices they make that creates the value in companies.

What do you need to satisfy your customers?

Digital thinkers are always looking to measure to improve themselves and the team so that they hit their targets. The approach saves money for shareholders. People with deep purpose and understanding enthusiastically choose to make contributions towards the team success. Not because they have to - they actually want to!

It is much easier to satisfy and develop sustainable customer relationships when you understand the direction, feel valued, involved and committed to improvement.

The unsettling impact on the leaders of companies

The constant change of the last few years has been unsettling for everyone, but for leaders it has been particularly challenging. Leaders have needed to make decisions and judgments quickly, often with insufficient data. Sometimes they have been correct and sometimes they have been wrong.

> *I attended a company meeting where the Director responsible for customer satisfaction talked at length about emotion and the need to be customer-centric. It sounded impressive and the management team seemed up for the challenge. I thought I would investigate and go where the rubber hits the road - where the customer touches the company. I had the opportunity to visit the contact centre and a branch.*
>
> *There was not a lot of customer empathy and very little emotion in front of the customer. The contact centre customer advisor was taking calls and the branches were offering Visa cards to everyone who came in. Apparently, it was 'Visa Week' and the product manager needed to hit his targets. It was a large branch and one of the staff told me that a customer had been offered the Visa card three times.*
>
> *The customer had made a big mistake - she had come into the branch three times!*

Clearly, there was a disconnection between the customer relations director, the marketing team, and the sales force, and the resulting impact on the customer was not good.

The competitive threats

There is competition in nearly every industry. In the aviation, financial services and telecommunications sectors new entrants have put pressure on the established companies to improve. The competition crosses international borders and now there are competitive threats from all around the world. Mobile apps have enabled people to find the best price at the touch of a button.

Price has been a major differentiating factor and will continue to be as new entrants drive the cost down. However, concentrating on price is not sustainable nor is quality of product as people expect quality these days as a minimum. Creating innovative products like the Kindle and the iPhone has helped Amazon and Apple lead the world in innovation. Over 50% of all books bought on Amazon now are digitally downloaded to an e-reader. We have not seen an information change as great as this since Johan Gutenberg invented the printing press in the fifteenth century. Exciting times for the brave leaders.

The best companies are differentiating themselves on their product design, brand and the quality of their customer service. They are focusing on making the customer service easy and bringing their brand alive in front of customers, in the retail outlets, online or through traditional contact channels.

The internal experience is as important as the external experience. There is little point spending money creating a brand, if, when customers touch your business, they do not feel the message.

In some companies, players in teams can often recite the vision and brand values but see little evidence that the values are being built into the actual work or in the way that they are managed locally. They want to feel involved and supported by their local management team but most of all they want the basics to do the job well. They want systems that work, processes that make their job easier and the ability to take decisions in front of customers.

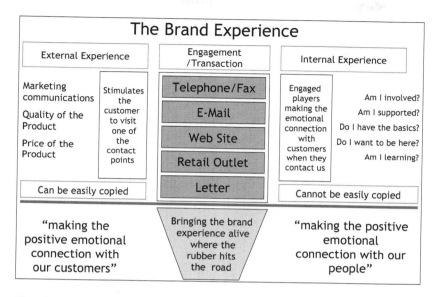

The future will be about giving people a deep purpose to believe in, focusing on the customer and designing roles to meet their needs. To do this successfully companies will need to look at how they manage internally so that what the Chief Executive says is mirrored throughout the company.

The leader who connects and communicates

The leaders have a clear role to play here to create the environment that brings their visions, passions and missions alive, where it matters most, in front of customers! The best leaders are taking time out to understand the day-to-day feedback without impacting on the need to take the strategic decisions. They are realising that strategy these days needs to be integrated into the day-to-day work! The inspiring leaders show passion and help people to love what they do.

Do your directors actually know what is going on in teams or only what they are told?

There is a real need to improve the internal communication within some companies. Many managing directors have told me that communication and inter-departmental conflict wastes time and causes much frustration for people within their company. The top-down cascade approach, where questions are asked at the end of communication events, isn't really working. The participants are not really listening and more often than not the cascade does not focus on the day-to-day problems. The participants are normally managers with little involvement of the customer-facing teams doing the work; the teams are too busy to attend meetings! Annual management communication events need to involve people more. It shouldn't just be a top-down communication - but it often is. The whole structure of team meetings needs to change. There is often little time to ask questions as the participants are not really listened to. If you want people to understand you, you need to listen to them first!

The best leaders make the human connection with people when they meet them. They create internal communication processes that give them information to develop the business. They engage people and inspire people naturally. They develop a group of managers that really understand the capability gaps in the company (the issues between teams) and rigorously set about improving them on a daily basis.

It's no longer enough for leaders to rely on the management to pass information around the business. The best companies create environments that naturally facilitate teams working together and help them communicate, and help everyone contribute to meet the needs of customers. In the best companies, the management can discuss the company issues without looking to blame someone. The worst are blaming and the best are learning.

Is there a culture of blame in your business?

Leaders and managers need to ask questions so that understanding and learning can prosper. The digital-age leaders tap into the company grapevine and use information to improve things. In companies, smokers often know what is going wrong. I was told by one customer advisor that there are more ideas and opinions shared in a smoking room than in some of the meetings. In traditional-thinking companies, very little sustainable action occurs once all the cigarettes have been extinguished.

In the best teams these days, the conditions are being created where leadership, facilitation, coaching and motivation are the responsibility of more than just the managers and the leaders. Depending on what is being discussed, different roles at different times can take the lead. The best teams openly discuss their achievements and their failures. They don't look to blame others. They take action on the system that caused the problem in the first place. Often the way the company is designed leads to inefficiency and problems.

> *I was in one company where the manager responsible for customer service met all the new employees in their training and explained that the most important people in the business were the customers and the second most important people were the people who spoke to customers. This wasn't just delivered in training to make them feel good. It was built into the day-to-day activities. If a meeting needed to be held to talk about customers then the customer-facing teams were involved. The management team knew exactly what their role was. They were there to solve the problems for the people who served customers. Everyone knew their role. The team won many quality awards and everyone enjoyed themselves.*

I have seen customer-facing employees lead, coach and motivate people around them. I have seen that it makes a real difference to the team and their performance. I have seen it save millions and improve customer retention. You see the teams get teamwork. They understand it. Teamwork starts to break down when you need to check with your director before doing something.

Ensuring that leaders are communicating consistently whilst taking people through change is vital. Leaders need to over-communicate the direction and the plans, ensuring that individuals can see the links with their day-to-day job. It is not possible to inspire your people if you sit behind a desk or attend meetings all day. Management through walking around is a style that has been there for years, but in some companies there doesn't appear to be enough of it.

The four company attributes for leaders

The challenge over the last few years for leaders of teams has been focused in the four company attributes below. Depending on their underlying management philosophy, each leader will think differently about each of these attributes.

What kind of leader are you: digital, traditional or a bit of both?

Control
- Traditional thinkers relate control to the budget or their target. Everything is in control and everything is in budget – *Pity the customers are leaving, but at least I hit my budget or target.* They think - *How many?*
- Digital-age thinkers are aware of and manage the budget but focus daily on their purpose, continually improving their output and the capability (people, process and technology) of their teams/companies. They think – *What and why?*

Design
- Traditional-age thinkers create functions and hierarchy within their company without thinking how this affects the customers. They focus on the

internal, and change the structure of the team regularly, but the change rarely works.

- Digital thinkers are always looking at how the design of the company affects customers and how it helps individuals to contribute to team achievement. They design their team or company around the customers. They focus on the external and not just the internal. They don't just talk about it; they change it.

Reward

- Traditional-age thinkers spend far too much time on creating elaborate reward systems that reward individuals; however, the reward is often not fair and it is de-motivating to many members of the team.

- Digital-age thinkers focus on team rewards, creating a real purpose for their teams and ensuring that everyone is rewarded fairly if the team hits its targets or achievements.

Decision Making

- The traditional-age thinker ensures that major decisions are not made by employees close to the customer. The best people sit at the back. Decisions are not integrated with the work. Major decisions are taken by others, often in a back office department and this leads to delays for customers and increased cost to the company.

- The digital thinker continually looks at bringing decision-making close to the customer so that they can make decisions themselves often in the palm of their hand with no delays. In customer service teams they sit the best people at the front. They trust their teams. When things are uncertain players are encouraged to use common sense and make a decision. The team led by a digital thinker will satisfy many more customers than the one led by a traditional thinker.

These four key company attributes will need to be addressed strategically by leaders in the next few years. Tough decisions have been taken by leaders in many industries since the stock market crash in the late twentieth century and the more recent financial crisis. It has not been easy and leaders will continue to have challenges to build and develop the profitability of their companies on the back of uncertainty and ambiguity.

The challenge is to release the potential of our people whilst maintaining the control to manage the business profitably. The successful companies will transform themselves and their businesses. If they do not, they will no longer be in business. Many of the top companies in the world today were not even thought of twenty years ago!

Where will your company be in twenty years' time? Where will you be?

The three company attributes for managers

The best managers of the most motivated teams in your company will be continually thinking in a digital way; very few traditional thinkers manage to fully connect all their teams. Why? The answer is normally how they think about the following three attributes.

People Development
- Traditional-age thinkers see the value of training but make the mistake of separating it from the work. They organise motivational games, behaviour training programmes and many activities that appear to avoid solving the actual problems in the day-to-day activity.

- The digital thinker also values training but focuses on ensuring that learning is built into the day-to-day work. They don't just rely on training courses. They believe and know that many people learn much more from doing things than they do on the training course.

Quality

- Traditional thinkers ensure that they have plenty of checks in place to ensure that people are delivering quality. In a manufacturing environment, this would normally be at the end of the line. If something goes wrong the traditional thinker looks to blame someone for not doing something right.

- The digital thinker creates the environment where quality is built into the day-to-day work by engaging everyone in ensuring that they continually improve their work. They focus on being customer-centric and continually improving the technology and the processes. When something goes wrong they change the processes and share learning with everyone so everyone learns.

Knowledge

- The traditional thinker ensures that everyone has the knowledge to do the job. They send many emails. They send many reports. They send lots of analysis. They create teams with lots of knowledge. They are busy in meetings. In some cases, so much information is sent that the workers do not have time to read it. They are overwhelmed with explicit knowledge. Much of this can be written down.

- The digital thinker ensures that people are not just given information but that they understand it. They don't always send emails as it is not always the best way to share understanding. Sometimes you learn a lot by talking with people. These days, people do not need to know everything; they just need to know where the information is. They create the environment where tacit knowledge (the knowledge in your head that only comes out in conversation and dialogue) is easily shared with little fear but lots of comfort.

Managers of the future must focus on the aforementioned company attributes to build success in their teams or companies. The key is to ensure that managers and coaches are aware of the company targets but focus on a daily basis to continually improve the capability of their people, processes and systems. Whilst digital thinkers do this naturally, the traditional thinkers are busily blaming people for the situation that they are in!

Creating the environment where players motivate one another, measure themselves, share their knowledge and agree their contribution to team achievements is the key. This is made possible when managers consistently communicate to improve understanding and create the environment where learning is built into the work. The customers benefit, you save money and customers buy more products!

Operational managers need to focus on consistently improving the capabilities that they presently have. Some of these will be easy and some will be more difficult. The focus is on continually improving the people, the processes and the systems of work. It is the only way to bring about sustainable change. Operational managers, who focus on measuring for continual improvement and building understanding, often over-achieve their targets. They create the environment where players motivate one another, measure themselves and agree their contribution to team achievements. This environment requires less checking and removes the non-value work that many managers are involved in today. Traditional thinkers are looking for stretching targets (often set by themselves). With the above approach the digital thinkers achieve ground-breaking goals, as individuals choose to contribute in an environment of continuous improvement or innovation.

The three company attributes for all team players

To deliver remarkable customer experiences, all team players (every role in the company) need to take responsibility for their personal motivation and how they measure their own achievements. We all make choices in our day-to-day interactions with internal and external customers and this can have an effect on our workplace or with the customer relationship.

When the employees are given freedom in unfamiliar situations to do what is right for the customer, everyone benefits. The behaviour they demonstrate is linked to how they think about the attributes below.

Measurement
- Traditional-age thinkers only think about hitting the target. The target of the senior manager or the directorate becomes the only way forward for traditional thinkers. As long as they hit their numbers they are happy. Traditional thinkers often do not know what they did to achieve their target.

- Digital thinkers also think about the target but add in additional measures to ensure that they are continually improving and learning at the company, on the team and individual levels. The digital thinker has a very good understanding of what brought about the improvement.

Motivation
- Traditional-age thinkers believe that managers alone should motivate. They believe that people cannot really be trusted and you need to manage them tightly. They devise incentive schemes and lots of external motivation instead of solving the problems that teams are having. People don't feel involved. They lose that vital spark.

- Digital-age thinkers are often experts at motivating others and set about creating an environment where the managers lead people to have a real purpose and continually improve their work. They create an environment where people take responsibility and motivate themselves and others to achieve success for themselves and their teams. People feel involved. They love their work.

Customer

- Traditional-age thinkers are very internally focused and spend the majority of their day either talking to customers because they are unhappy or avoiding customers and their problems. Their meetings do not often talk about customers.

- Digital-age thinkers have a passion for customers and everything they do is to improve the experience for the external customers. Whilst they improve things for external customers this has a positive impact on the customer-facing people who do the activity.

How great teams move forward

If players believe that you do not have to like customers and they should only be concerned about hitting targets and not making improvements, then they and the customers will be unhappy. In companies where I have seen happy people, they have happy customers and the employees like the customers. In some award-winning companies they even talk about love!

For me the most important thing in my life is love. I think you have to be in love with your family, with your job, with the people who work for you. If you are not in love with your wife you have to divorce. If you are not in love with your kids you are not a human being so you have to kill yourself. If you are not in love with your job you must change (or improve) your job.

Ex-Chelsea manager José Mourinho, from the documentary *Being José Mourinho*

Happy players are not waiting for managers to motivate them; they take responsibility to measure and improve themselves. On a daily basis, they keep on improving and they are always looking to make it easy for customers.

Do you love your job?

Creating this environment is not easy, but for the brave it brings remarkable success and releases the potential of everyone within the team and the company.

Digital-age thinking is not just about the people aspects; it's about the way that everyone in the company thinks about their work, how they improve it and the contribution that they can make. It is also about ensuring that people have the capabilities to do the job they are paid to do. Managers have a key role to play here. In the digital-age company players begin, over time, to assume responsibility for many of the ten company attributes above quite naturally, with many obvious benefits.

Do your colleagues challenge and improve their own behaviour?

With the 'Understanding and Learning process', the daily activities are continually challenged by everyone. Through sharing experiences in a structured way individuals and teams see a better way of delivering sustainable results. It is the actual experience that often gives people the opportunity to think about changing their behaviour.

An 'Understanding and Learning' environment is trusting, team-based and customer-focused. Teams understand and learn together. I have seen improved individual commitment and sustained improvements to shareholder value, customer satisfaction and team loyalty. Everything is focused on the customer and the development of people. The team deliver emotionally connected experiences within the team and with customers. The improved results speak for themselves. Key to successful implementation is thinking differently about:

- What is measured to meet the needs of customers?
- How are these measures built into the day-to-day activities?
- How do players challenge and improve their own behaviour?
- How do players provide feedback to improve processes?
- How do players provide feedback to improve their colleagues?

Targets and how they are used

The challenge will continue to be identification of the correct measures to drive improvement and company success. Often the start points are the measures that the strategy and planning teams have used to determine the budget and the future direction of the company. Managers call these 'targets'. Of course, targets are important and the senior managers need to be aware of them. The problem lies in the way that targets are used within the company. I will highlight examples of how this has affected the customers throughout this book. Planning measures should never be used to drive day-to-day measurement. Of course, it depends on how you think.

The best leaders measure what matters to customers and what their people need to deliver those experiences. They want the customer to return for more, and to be happy doing so.

What and how are you measuring?

The measures used at each company level will be different. They are different as each role has different responsibilities due to its position in the company. Successful operational measures lead to continual improvement and the outcomes often exceed the planning and strategy plans. In addition, successful teams implement experimental learning and integrate this approach within their teams on a daily basis. These teams take action and set aside time to review what happened at the team and individual levels.

- What would you want to repeat?
- What would you do differently next time?
- What went well? What didn't go well?

It is the continual use of these types of questions that changes the way that teams work as they create actions and learning from their implementation. When these types of questions are facilitated in teams it encourages creativity and innovation from everyone.

Summary

Creating the right conditions for improved contribution is essential for all companies. This is a leadership and managerial responsibility. The right conditions encourage collaboration to release the potential of human beings, allowing them to bring creativity and innovation to their activities. It gives them the opportunity to develop and choose to make the most of their untapped potential.

Many processes and systems can now be easily copied. In fact, with worldwide benchmarking, it is possible to copy ideas from others and share best practice. The traditional thinkers are always looking at other companies for good ideas. However, they cannot steal the thinking that created the solutions in the first place. Whilst traditional-age thinkers are stealing ideas, the digital-age thinkers are off creating new ways to solve tomorrow's problems. Meanwhile, the traditional thinker is busy holding meetings discussing what happened yesterday.

Can your present approach be replicated easily by your competitors?

The differentiating factor in companies is the contribution that teams and cross-functional teams make together. Teams that think differently about the ten key attributes can create a competitive edge that is sustainable. Other companies find this very difficult to replicate. With the right leadership teams do not let one another down. Whilst others are copying, truly differentiated companies are creating something else.

With these ten thinking attributes understood and with digital- age thinking in place, customers receive ever-improving products and services and employees are connected to your company with enthusiasm. This thinking eventually drives the behaviour of all roles within the company.

The focus for leaders

Understanding control

People at the top become driven by the stats, not relationships with staff and customers. Senior managers sit in their control bunker, assuming you achieve quality by control rather than building it in.

Kate Corfield, It's your call, effective call centre management

The key is to make certain that controls are in place to ensure success for the company. At the senior level these financial, operational, customer and shareholder controls are essential to protect the well-being of the company. In any business, the budget is important. Leaders and managers must be aware of and manage the budget; however, on a daily basis, all employees must focus on creating value for customers and developing a stronger relationship with them, encouraging sales and customer recommendations. Clearly, managers and leaders need to focus on delivering against the budget. However, using some of these operational measures can lead to low productivity and inferior performance, especially in front of customers.

Here is an example of an internal rule that resulted in a customer having to wait. The management team had put a rule in place but no one thought about the impact on the customer.

> *I was in a hotel in Den Haag, in the Netherlands, and I needed a ticket for the tram. Whilst I was checking out I asked for one. I was checking out early as I had an early morning flight to Paris and I was in a bit of a hurry.*
>
> *Unfortunately, the overnight reception guy couldn't give me the ticket as they were stored in the safe and this was not opened until 7am. This didn't seem very customer-focused so I asked why they were in the safe and not in Reception. He told me that they had had some internal problems in the past where tram tickets had been stolen and to protect themselves, they had locked them up!*
>
> *Fifteen minutes later, a manager turned up, opened the safe, and gave me a ticket. Everything was in control and inside budget, but I was running even later and I wasn't satisfied. No one seemed to notice as I ran for my tram!*

Controlling your budget

The time-consuming budget process within companies encourages managers to do very interesting things. Some managers have told me that they buy training that they don't really need. They invest in solutions that they don't need for six months. They have to spend the money. If they do not, there is a real worry that they will lose it next year.

> *In one large company in the UK managers were not allowed to recruit full-time employees until after the end of the financial year. They could employ more expensive temps or interim managers as these were not on the payroll. Apparently, there was a target related to how many full-time roles were in the company. This was only scrutinised at the end of every financial year. If they hit this target the company were seen as more efficient.*

I was told that many consultants or training providers tactically telephone companies near the end of the financial year because they know that there might be some spare money about. How often, near the end of the year, do you hear managers spending their budget so that they do not lose it next year?

Of course the budget is important - it's a question of balance. There needs to be an increasing focus on creating a purpose that engages individuals.

The leader's role is to ensure that the managers are creating the conditions where everyone is continually measuring and improving the people, systems and process capabilities. It is the only way to sustain and continually improve things.

The effect of too many rules and procedures

Whatever sector you work in, procedures and rules remain commonplace within companies. They are often translated by operational management as being essential to the efficient running of the company. This may be the case but people have told me that they play a major part in devaluing work and disengaging players.

> *When I was a student I worked as a checkout operator for a supermarket. We were all targeted on the accuracy of our cash register at the end of our shift. There was never any mention of customer satisfaction. At the end of my shift I would follow the cash-office supervisor into the office and watch nervously as she 'cashed-up'. On one occasion my till was five pounds under. I was given a first verbal warning!*
>
> *My till had never been wrong in the previous three years of working there, yet the 'one cap fits all' rule was applied. I felt terrible. I was hurt and felt let down.*
>
> *In the evening I received a call from the supervisor to tell me not to worry and that the five pounds had been located within the float, and my verbal warning would be erased from my record. By then the damage had already been done.*

This is a classic example of rules and procedures getting in the way of common sense. Did I make the mistake on purpose? Were they implying I had stolen the money?

The only outcome of handling situations in the above way is to create disconnected players. These players feel more pressure and anxiety, which really hinders future performance. Additionally, trust breaks down and 'us and them' relationships develop. Not all rules and procedures are detrimental to companies. However, it is important to ensure that there are not too many and they allow creativity and do not instil a fear culture. Mistakes are a vital element of learning and improvement. Human beings will always make mistakes, so why not use them in a positive way? Rules all too often hold people back.

One company conducted quarterly employee engagement surveys to ascertain the teams/departments that are most connected to their work, colleagues and company. For two years running the night-shift teams came out on top. This would appear strange to many. Why would people having to work unsociable hours be more connected than others? I asked this question of some of the key players in these teams and they highlighted that the day shift is so much more intense. They said that there is much more management about and you always have to keep your head down.

They also intimated that in the evening and throughout the night everyone pulls together. They stated that the managers are supportive and there is the opportunity to have fun, make extra decisions for customers and relax because of fewer rules. They were also more productive. When there are too many rules and procedure enforcers, it appears that some people just do the bare minimum. The culture is a fearful one and commitment is replaced with compliance.

Do your existing rules and procedures stop you satisfying your customers?

The alternative is firstly to look at all existing rules and procedures and ascertain their value. Do they devalue work? Do they create a fear culture? Do they disconnect players? Do they improve things?

Fiddling the figures

The problems in operational teams start when the budget figures are used to measure and drive performance improvements on a daily basis within all roles.

> *To meet punctuality targets, train drivers have been known to drive past passengers waiting on the platform!*
>
> *A bus driver asked all his customers to get off the bus and wait for the next one whilst he drove quickly to the bus station.*

Answering the telephone quickly is a vital customer process measure in contact centres. Research reminds us that it is a key driver of customer satisfaction. Of course, we need to measure it. However, for sustainable results we need to identify more than how quickly the phone is answered. I was told by many that we measure this because it is the easy thing to measure.

> *I was in one company where the customer advisors were tapping in codes to determine what each customer contact was about. There were over two hundred codes. This is when I start to worry.*
>
> *I visited the contact centre. I wanted to see the activities for myself. The advisors were not really focused on keying in the codes. There were just too many of them. The codes being keyed in often had no relation at all to the actual call. I listened in to calls and identified the top calls were:*
>
> *"I called yesterday..."*
> *"I was speaking to someone a few moments ago..."*
> *"Hello, I've just been cut off..."*

These were all categorised as billing-related calls. They probably were but this measure was not controlling anything and certainly didn't help this contact centre become efficient.

When was the last time you listened in to customer contact?

Many of the customers were ringing for the second or third time. They were all failure calls (calls into the centre that should have been handled the first time). The managers knew nothing about this as they were too busy designing Excel charts to show the number of calls their teams were taking. The managers were creating additional codes to assist their analysis; however, they would have learnt a lot by listening in to the actual calls themselves.

When teams measure the wrong things, players use their ingenuity to scam the system to hit their targets. Companies that achieve award-winning results identify measures that drive continuous improvement so that the teams can over-achieve. In the digital age, managers ask questions about the work and think. The most important question to ask these days is *why*.

Why do customers ring?

When organisations measure the wrong things it upsets players and customers and increases costs, whilst giving the illusion of being in control.

To make a significant change in performance and improve stakeholder results, award-winning teams focus on measuring what matters to customers at the point of contact and identifying areas of improvement, leading to a better customer experience.

They see things through the eyes of the customer.

> *I was talking to a Senior Partner in a large criminal solicitors practice a few days ago. She talks with criminals on a regular basis. It is clear that things are not working if you see it from the criminals' point of view. Some of the criminals want to be reformed – however, the system just keeps locking them up!*
>
> *If the actual purpose of prisons is to reform people, the system appears to be failing. Once a criminal ends up in prison it is clear that many face a life of crime.*

If the main purpose of police is to prevent crime, then why is the best job not in crime prevention, rather than working in the Criminal Investigation Department? If you work in the C.I.D. you receive more respect from your colleagues. Prisons and the police are examples of where control is used to bring about change. Controls and measurement are important but only when it is linked to purpose and continual improvement.

Three questions to solve problems and organise yourself

Three questions help everyone get through their day-to-day activities. They are very natural and everyone uses them subconsciously, but they are not regularly asked in companies. They should be. They are:

- What do I/we want to do?
- What do I/we need to do it?
- How do I/we do it?

The three questions work because it is how we think on a daily basis. Whether you are a child on the way to school, going on holiday, making a fruit cake or satisfying a customer today – the three questions work, but only when they become part of your daily thoughts.

Most people agree to do something (What do I want to do?) and set off to do it (How do I do it?). They jump straight into the how, without thinking about what they need to be able to do it. When this happens, there will be delays.

Delays such as:

- Arriving at school without your daily diary because it was left at home.
- Arriving at the airport without your passport because it was left at home.
- Waiting for someone to buy some fruit, halfway through making a fruit cake.
- Not being able to satisfy a customer now because of a rule or lack of information.

In all the above cases, the key question that needed to be asked was, *What do I need to do it?* If this question had been asked before all the above activities started, then there would not be so many delays and frustrations. When teams ask these questions, the results can be very powerful.

> *In one company I worked in, the Director responsible for customer service involved the right people at the right time in the decision-making process, based on their ability to influence the implementation. The senior management team agreed the principles of a solution and the team members who were most affected by the change were involved in rolling out the solution. The management team were never involved in the 'how'. It wasn't their role. It wasn't their responsibility. Their role was to provide direction and leadership and agree the requirements of any solution. The managers encouraged dialogue between teams and helped to facilitate the best way forward within the implementation teams. People felt connected. Their opinion was valued.*

In some companies, the customer-facing teams always know what they need to satisfy customers but for some reason the decision-making of the company does not appear to let them have it. There is a need to involve the relevant roles when improving things in companies.

> *I was in one company a few months ago to review the operations as part of the judging panel for a national customer service awards. The teams had worked hard on the behavioural aspects of culture change. When I asked the field-based engineers what had made the difference they didn't mention the culture change sessions. The biggest improvement they saw was the provision of handhelds that didn't lose data or fail. They loved the GPS capability as it helped them to find locations quicker so that they could do their job better.*

Often managers meet to discuss a problem but the people who need to solve it are not in the room. When trying to solve problems it is essential to have the right people in the room and ask some key questions before you start. Traditional-age companies spend hours in meetings discussing things that the participants cannot resolve. They talk about inefficiencies but the meeting itself is inefficient. These questions are useful as they will save you time.

- Who understands the problem?
- Are they here?
- Can the participants make the final decision?
- Do they have the power to change things?
- Is everyone emotionally committed to wanting to solve the problem?

If any of these are not answered positively then I can predict that there will need to be another meeting where the participants discuss the same things again and again and again.

How much time is wasted in your meetings discussing things that you or your team cannot resolve?

There is a better approach to ensure that everyone is engaged in the decision-making. For example, as a leadership team you may make a decision to put in place a process where the customer-facing people make the emotional connection with customers. The digital-age thinkers would approach this by asking the above questions. Once you have decided that making the emotional connection is _what you want to do_, you agree the concept/principles/requirements with the management team and they will find out _what is needed to do it_. It may involve spending some money, agreeing the key stages of the new process or systems to support the process, and together you might need to agree the budget. However, once this has been agreed, it does make sense to involve the customer-facing people who actually serve customers so that they can determine _how to do it_. In this case, involving the customer-facing people would be essential so that they can emotionally commit to this new way of working. There are some great strategies; they often fail due to the wrong people being involved at the wrong time, perhaps entering the process too late. In the above example, the traditional-age thinkers would not involve enough of the customer-facing staff and of course, the implementation would not go as well. Whilst the traditional-age thinkers would be holding an inquest into who got it wrong, the digital-age thinkers would be moving on to the next improvement activity and predicting the future.

The challenge is to involve the right roles at the right time, take action and build learning into the work. In too many companies, the manager always wants to determine how to do things. This approach takes away the creativity of people who actually do the job. They become disconnected and the managers ask why. The answer is simple: Get out of the way and let people do the job and then measure the customer reaction and the team engagement. You will be surprised.

Involving all roles so that creativity and innovation can emerge

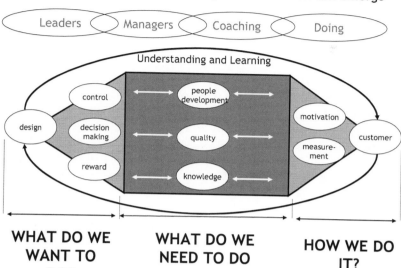

WHAT DO WE WANT TO DO?

WHAT DO WE NEED TO DO IT?

HOW WE DO IT?

The importance of an inspiring purpose

Having an inspiring purpose is vital. In education, social welfare and the National Health Service people have a clear and potentially inspiring purpose - the chance to change people's lives for the better. An inspiring purpose tied with a competitive threat can bring remarkable results.

> *A few years ago Britain's favourite carrier, British Airways, was flying aeroplanes across the Atlantic - they were in the transportation business. Richard Branson took them on and proudly announced that Virgin Airlines "were in the entertainment business at 25,000 feet."*
>
> *The experience was just different for everyone. One was transporting people the other was entertaining people. The customers felt the difference.*

When the purpose is clear, when people understand, many people have told me that they enthusiastically get out of bed in the morning. They are not late for work and when they arrive they contribute and deliver excellent results. With excellent leadership and clear measures of performance, it is amazing what can be achieved within teams.

Directors and senior management need to focus on providing motivational leadership and measures that are understood and agreed by everyone. Leadership and the measurement of success are vital with any effort for change. Once these two are correct the managers in companies need to focus on ensuring that the people who are satisfying customers have all the capabilities to do the job.

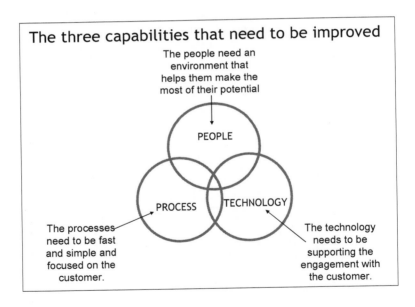

The three capabilities that need to be improved

The people need an environment that helps them make the most of their potential

PEOPLE

PROCESS   TECHNOLOGY

The processes need to be fast and simple and focused on the customer.

The technology needs to be supporting the engagement with the customer.

How many marks out of ten would you give your people, process and technology capabilities in your company?

When people in teams have the tools to do the job they are ready to be inspired.

Stephen Covey, the inspirational international consultant, talked at length in his best-selling book, *The Seven Habits of Highly Effective People*, about the importance of things and people. He pointed out that you manage things and you lead people.

Whilst some people will still need managing, the challenge is to lead people and give them a purpose that they believe in. When teams have purpose, you don't need control. You just need guidance!

Do you have a clear purpose and is it understood?

That's where leadership comes in! The best leaders control the people, process and technical capability improvement allowing the team to be remarkable.

Summary

The near-obsession with control within companies is a key strategic area holding them back from delivering benefits for customers. Poor performance is all too often the outcome of companies that strive to exercise control over their teams.

There is minimal trust and this simply leads to people scamming ways around the numerous control mechanisms. People who are not trusted very often become quite rebellious or simply compliant. Both responses have a negative impact on the team and the customers. The most creative, the most energised, just leave.

Budgetary controls are so often used as a driver for customer satisfaction. Yes, we need to continue to answer the phone quickly, but we need to protect people satisfying customers from the budget targets. As soon as the budget targets, such as length of call, length of job or speed of answer become the main purpose of people's roles, there is little focus on what matters to customers. People demonstrate behaviour that will help them hit target at the expense of the real purpose, and the customer calls keep on coming!

The challenge is on to let go of the need to control the budget by using it for targeting people. We need to trust our people and let them be creative. We need to build action and learning into the day-to-day activities of teams. We need to ensure that everyone has a clearly defined purpose and knows what their individual contribution should be. When this is in place, people have no need to scam the system. They are engaged; customers have a great time buying products, telling others about you through social media channels and never think of leaving your company!

Practical actions to understand and learn about control

- Ask yourself whether your company spends too much time focusing on the internal at the expense of the external customer experience.

- Try to build relationships across your business. When satisfying customers it is important that silos are broken down through interdependent teams engaging in dialogue.

- Review current process, policy and procedure. Ask whether they are helping or hindering the people and customer experience. Involve your teams in the improvement process. Are the right people involved?

- Try using the three questions (what, need and how) in a structured way when you have a problem to solve, or need to resolve a situation.

- Why are customers contacting you? Is it failure or value contact?

- How many contacts have been converted to sales?

Understanding
design

Open Leadership argues that a new organizational structure is required to accommodate and benefit from the culture of sharing that social media has fuelled over the last four years. The information flow we all experience daily can no longer be organized into neat org-chart silos, she posits. Instead, it demands a new kind of leadership — one based on letting go of the command-and-control model and embracing openness and relationship building.

Lori Laurent Smith reviewing a conference speech by Charlene Li,
Author of Open Leadership

Designing the company around the customer has been the challenge for companies over the last few years. Customer engagement choices are changing. Some customers still just want the local branch. Some want a truly integrated approach that includes a combination of branch, telephone, text messages, web and social media channels. Designing to meet this emerging need will mean that we need to think differently. Many customers do the transaction themselves now over the internet. They are happy to do that. They feel that they are in control. Every key retail player has an app these days that enables the customer to transact on the move in the palm of their hand. New entrants to the market have been able to design their business, efficiently, to meet the needs of these customers. They were able to move quickly as they have no inbuilt structure to dismantle. Sometimes it is easier to start something new than try to change it!

Problems with traditional structures

The traditional structures were based around departments, with little reference to the customer. In some industry sectors you didn't need to worry about the customer and how they felt at all. In telecommunications and utility companies there was no competition and so service didn't matter. There is competition now and service does matter!

The traditional structure of companies followed on from the belief that the managers were responsible for thinking and the players were responsible for doing. This created cross-functional delays, between departments and people, encouraging behaviour that was not always focused on the customers.

> *In one company, I was brought in to look at what efficiency savings could be made within the business. I always start with the customer and so I went to the contact centre to track the flow of the customer through the business.*
>
> *There were lots of examples of inefficiency. This is one that stood out.*
>
> *This customer had been billed incorrectly. It was obvious. The advisor called over her supervisor to check if it was OK to give the customer a credit note. The supervisor said it was OK and the advisor filled in the credit note book and the supervisor signed it. (This was later used by the supervisor to check the number of credit notes her team had raised. If her team had too many, she was in trouble!) The customer was promised a credit note within the next few weeks. I thought that would be the end of the transaction. My hopes were raised too high. Credit notes were*

> *produced by the finance department and they had to do a second check.*
>
> *So I went to finance, who were in a different building. Unfortunately, finance had a backlog and was running five weeks behind with the credit notes. (These were only added on after the month end as it helped the figures.) There were six people checking credit notes and it was an incredibly uninteresting job. Each credit note was checked for accuracy. Over 99% of credit notes were deemed to be correctly applied and eventually sent to the customer.*

This was so inefficient. This company was designed to be inefficient and had two senior managers responsible for different targets. I had to change it. I changed the design. The credit note team were given new roles satisfying customers and customers no longer had the five-week delay. The solution saved money, and everyone was happy. I only ask three questions: What do customers want? How do we measure it? How do we do it?

The hierarchical template, designed in the last century, will not help companies in the future. Things are moving too quickly. It was a structure that was right for its time.

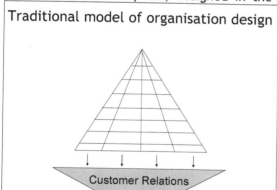

Traditional model of organisation design

Customer Relations

If you really want to start changing your business, look at things from the customer point of view.

In another company, I was with a group of managers who were meeting to discuss ways in which they could improve customers' satisfaction. I thought the best way was to understand the customers. So I asked a simple question.

When was the last time you spoke to a customer?

They explained that they were managers and they didn't speak to customers as it was not their role! I suggested that maybe they might want to include a few people who did speak to customers to understand how we could make improvements. They had a problem with that as the advisors were all busy taking calls from customers and couldn't be released from their phone duties! When work and responsibilities are divided up in this way you always find inefficiencies. Some companies are still designed for the past and not the present. It really is terribly inefficient. It was built to last – like the Eiffel Tower. Unlike the Eiffel Tower, the structure needs to be pulled down!

The above model just causes too many problems in this changing world. The internal dynamics are just too painful. In brainstorming sessions over the last few years, managers have told me that:

- Functions become unfocused on the customer.
- Functions act as power bases from which empires are built.
- There are communication difficulties between functions.
- Senior management are not told everything.
- Measurements are internally/functionally focused.
- Measurements are fudged to meet target.
- Junior managers have lots of meetings to resolve problems.
- Change does not happen quickly enough.
- Key managers do not have the authority to change anything.
- There are silos within each function.
- The egos of directors get in the way of achievement.

There is very little learning from mistakes.

Can you identify the above problems in your company? If you can you need 'The Understanding and Learning Process'.

Managers told me that they produce reports and analysis that add little real sustainable value. When there are lots of managers there are always communication difficulties. Regular reports and tight procedures do not produce the environment where everyone is focused on cost-saving or on satisfied customers.

How much time is your company spending on producing and writing reports?

How many are actually read? Does the information drive improvement?

Understanding creativity and non-value work

Successful companies engage all of their teams in creatively finding the best way forward together. Managers talk to the negative ones and listen to the cynics. They involve everyone. It is no longer sensible or acceptable to leave creativity to the chosen few at the top. Digital-age thinkers engage everyone. This means that all players in our teams will need to change the way that they think.

Can you be confident that each role adds significant value?

Whilst a traditional-age thinking culture may bring short-term results it does not bring sustainable improvement. Players can quickly become disengaged. They become sick and eventually leave, costing the company thousands in recruitment costs and loss of revenue.

> *I visited a company in Europe that was having problems with staff turnover, recruitment and absence. There was little creativity. Their exit interviews highlighted that people were not paid enough. They decided to give everyone an increase in salary. People didn't feel motivated. They put people on a motivation course. They put lots of short-term fixes in place but none of them were working. The new manager started listening to people and started to make changes to improve their work. He started removing the non-value work that people were doing. He set up a feedback process that ensured that he knew what the problems were. He didn't hide in his office or attend meetings all day. He solved people's problems and people started smiling and enjoying their work. They were now adding value and contributing.*

The amount of non-value activity appears to be on the increase!

In contact centres, players become bored doing simple jobs and management time is spent on internal business processes that add little value to the customer experience.

Are you adding value or adding costs?

What do you do all day?

In head office environments, team players can occupy themselves in a number of non-value activities. Much time is spent at the coffee machine and in meetings discussing frustrations with recurring issues. Some managers can spend their whole day in planned meetings, ad hoc meetings and in preparation for those meetings. Some are relevant, and some are not adding value. Often, managers are at their PC moving emails around or sitting in on a conference call. Sometimes too many managers are on conference calls – they all seem to attend. Why?

Designing around the customer requirement

The challenge for customer-centric companies is to design the company so that roles have a real purpose. All thinking needs to be focused on the customer requirements and delivery of team achievements. The processes need to be designed to deliver customer experiences wherever the customer chooses to contact the company. All contribution must be focused on delivery of the customer experience.

What does the customer want from the contact and how long does it take?

> *I was in a company where customer credit notes were only run at the end of the month. Apparently, it was easier for the finance department.*
>
> *On closer inspection, the finance team were targeted on the amount of revenue they were collecting. Credit notes reduced this target. Once the team were aware of the amount of revenue they had collected they made arbitrary decisions to include or not include the credit notes. Of course, they were hitting their target but the customer was receiving a raw deal.*

This process was causing all sorts of customer delay and extra non-value calls into the contact centre. This process was costing the company lots of money and the managers thought they were in control. The problem was created by the structure of the company.

Each senior manager had different targets and did what they needed to do to meet them! Finance met their targets and customer service was struggling. Everything was in control, apart from the customers - who were leaving!

Before the investigation, the customer-service managers didn't know about this. They were too busy hitting service level, asking the teams to fill in tick sheets and holding disciplinary meetings for team players that had been late back from lunch! The customers were leaving and no one knew why. No one was listening to the people who spoke to the customers and it had to change.

The importance of design

The design is the key. The May 2006 edition of 'McKinsey Quarterly' suggested that companies that restructure contact centres can cut their costs by up to 25% and boost revenue by as much as 35%.

> Whenever I visit companies I always ask to see the organisation chart. If it is not available the manager will write it on a piece of paper. As soon as I see the chart I can see inefficiencies. Why? In nearly every case, the customer is never included. If you don't include the customer in the design, then you become internally focused, focusing on the internal politics and not the customer.

Are you designed around the customer requirements?

Funny thing is, the closer you are to the customer, the quicker you understand what needs to be done.

> *In the early 1990s National & Provincial Building Society, in Bradford in the United Kingdom, set about changing their company from a functional hierarchy.*
>
> *Over a four year period, through the charismatic leadership of David O'Brien, they stripped away years of tradition and changed their business. They did it by focusing on the customer and*

designing to meet the demand. They stripped away jobs that didn't add value and created roles that did. Each individual had responsibilities and was free to satisfy their customer.

They focused on changing the thinking of the managers by involving them in changing the actual work that people did. Roles were created that had interest and variety built in and everything was focused on the customer.

N&P were controversial as they did things differently. They used different language internally. They talked about engagement and the people in teams were called players. Players worked in teams as they believed that creativity and ideas came from groups of people contributing together.

They didn't believe that in the future people would work in companies. They believed that in the future computers would do the work - leaving people to do the more creative things. How right they were!

The approach had a positive effect on many people who worked within the company. They were enthusiastically engaged because the design encouraged everyone's contribution. This enthusiasm was passed on to the customers. Many look back with fond memories of their learning experience. It was a good example of how you need to experience something to understand it. People outside the business didn't understand it; however, the players inside it did, and so did the customers.

It was a remarkable success story and is often used in business schools as an example of a successful transformational change programme. The capitalised value of the company quadrupled.

Processes and the roles

In digital-age companies, design is vital due to the changing demands on the roles and the company. At N&P, they changed the role titles to reflect the actual responsibilities. Agents were called customer advisors. On some UK trains the customer-facing employees are still called Revenue Protection Officers. They are only interested in checking tickets. There is little eye contact and little added emotion. Whilst the title is not focused on customers, I guess their purpose is very clear!

Does the role title of your customer-facing people accurately reflect what they do?

I believe that in order to create a truly differentiated and efficient customer-centric environment there are four key processes. All other processes are business processes that just need to be error-free. For example, in any customer contact company the focus would be on four key processes that, when implemented, will lead to sustainable customer-centricity.

The four key processes are:

- **The capacity/capability planning process** to ensure capacity/capability is in place to deliver the service to customers.

- **The customer contact process** to ensure that the customer receives the service that they require and choose your company for more products and services in the future.

- **The improvement process** to ensure that errors and customer dissatisfaction are systemically removed from the experience by involving everyone in feedback and improvement.

- **The understanding and learning process** to ensure that everyone is fully connected and making the most of their potential.

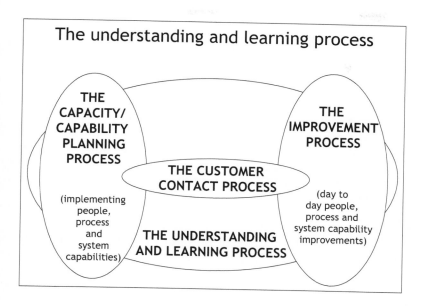

The understanding and learning process

THE CAPACITY/ CAPABILITY PLANNING PROCESS

(implementing people, process and system capabilities)

THE CUSTOMER CONTACT PROCESS

THE UNDERSTANDING AND LEARNING PROCESS

THE IMPROVEMENT PROCESS

(day to day people, process and system capability improvements)

Which processes would you be in? If you are not in one of these processes what role do you do? If you are not doing the actual work with customers (planning things, solving things, satisfying them, etc.) what are you doing to help the ones that are?

All of these processes are focused on improving the customer and team player experience within the company. All roles are focused on contributing in all these processes, whenever there is a need or customer demand. Roles' titles reflect the roles that people do, feedback is built into the process and people are encouraged to challenge and improve the experience for people in the team and with customers. When all the capabilities (people, process and technology) are in place, players in the company are free to make the most of their potential and customers are given a service that meets their needs.

There are some key questions that need to be asked:

- How many players do you have within each of these four processes?
- Is it possible to measure the value that each role offers the customer?
- How many non-customer-facing roles do you actually need?
- What real value do the non-customer-facing roles add?

All these questions will be answered during the move from the hierarchal approach to one that is totally focused on customers. In addition, the design gives everyone the opportunity to make the most of their skills and talents. Integral to the design is an improved internal communication process, called the 'Understanding and Learning process'. This process enables teams to review their successes together and to look at what action they can take to improve upon their achievements. Within this design, when additional contacts come into the centre or department, everyone responds and helps meet the needs of customers. No-one needs to be told – they understand why we are here. All of these processes are focused on improving the customer and player experience within the company. All roles are focused on contributing in all these areas whenever there is a need or customer demands. Everyone feels part of the improvement process.

> *In one company I worked with they had some real problems with improvement and cross-functional working. The customer satisfaction was not good and there needed to be changes to the internal company. As part of the change effort they created teams of improvement advisors. Each team had an improvement advisor. These players were not managers but people who did the work. These players had their normal role but 20% of their role involved working in their own teams to identify and implement improvements. Teams took responsibility to improve things. When they couldn't resolve concerns in their own teams or department, issues were shared with other departments and people were given responsibility to resolve things.*

> *The directors took interest in the cross-functional problems and reviewed the progress on a monthly basis. Cross-functional teams were now changing things. The Manager of the Improvement Process knew exactly what was going on and so did the directors. They implemented, in a systemic way, a companywide understanding and learning process.*

The further away you are from the actual customer experience the more you should ask the following question: Do I add value or do I just add costs?

Do you add value or add costs?

If you don't know the value you add - be careful. Someone may find out one day and you might find yourself out of a job!

Trust in teams

In traditional designs trust has always been a problem. The above design implicitly builds in the trust. There are a number of ways that companies have tried to improve trust in teams. Many involve a behavioural approach, normally away from the work.

> *I was attending a team leadership course at a large country hotel in the UK and during the break I looked outside though an open window. Another company were doing an interesting team-building exercise. The trainer was explaining the importance of trust and was arranging a practical exercise to highlight it.*
>
> *The group stood in a line, with each person looking at the person in front. There were sixteen of them and they were standing about one metre apart from one another. The trainer asked if everyone was ready. The first person fell backwards and was caught by his colleague, and this was quickly followed by others falling backwards until everyone was on the floor.*

> *Most were laughing and wriggling about. The guy at the end was neither wriggling nor laughing. It must have been like waiting for a train to hit him!*
>
> *When they recovered the trainer talked again about trust. He explained that when you fall backwards you have to trust the person behind! Many obviously agreed. He explained that whether we trust someone or not depends on the choices we all make at any moment of time. I felt the exercise was not really necessary to highlight that. I am sure the guy at the end of the line agreed. He explained that his problem was he made a bad choice to be at the end! Everyone laughed again. They seemed to be having a good time. It was probably more fun than their actual jobs.*

The particular design of companies to meet the challenges of the future will be one of the greatest challenges facing existing companies. The combinations of process and systems changes are sometimes difficult. However, when you add people to the equation, then the fun really starts!

The start point is to design the company around customers. Focus everyone's contribution on improving the experience and companies can achieve early, remarkable and sustainable performance.

Summary

Getting rid of functional structures remains a major challenge within traditional companies. With it comes inefficiency and vast amounts of politics and non-value activity that have nothing to do with satisfying customers or supporting those who do.

The hierarchy approach designed years ago is too static and cannot move quickly enough to deal with the emerging needs of customers. The structure creates delays and customer dissatisfaction. The structure needs to come down and be replaced with a design that is focused on individual customers and their needs. Unless this occurs quickly, communication problems will continue within companies and customers will continue to get a raw deal. Competitors will start doing things quicker than you, with quality, and you may be out of business.

The challenge is on to design companies around customers. Everyone needs to have a high degree of clarity about their purpose and they need to know how they contribute. When the design is focused on the customer, companies can cut out a lot of waste.

It is essential to make the design quick and easy for customers and for the people in the company. This new design ensures a much more efficient operation, improves the internal communication, fully engages teams and customers are satisfied more quickly and buy more of your products.

Practical actions to understand and learn about design

- Ask your teams what they consider their role to be. If it doesn't include anything about the customer, then review your culture and role design.

- Ensure that you can articulate what you consider your role to be and how your individual contribution fits into the overall business purpose.

- Review how your company is designed using the thoughts in this chapter. This will strip out unnecessary costs and connect your employees.

- How many people do you have in each of the four processes in this chapter? Are they allocated efficiently?

- Create the environment where there is a flattened hierarchy. Try and see managers and customer advisors as human beings who do different roles, rather than superior versus subordinate.

- Listen to your cynics. Are they right?

- Review your role titles. Do they reflect the responsibilities of the roles?

Understanding decision-making

*Leadership always has the most influence on a company's culture.
It is the leaders who determine how the companies work. They
set the measures. The leader's behaviour, whether they like it or
not, has a powerful influence on the culture.*

Professor John Adair, Exeter University

A key management responsibility is to decide who has responsibility
for making decisions when implementing customer or business
processes or delivering products and services to customers. This
responsibility, and the resulting management decision, has a huge
impact on the motivation and creativity within companies and in
front of customers.

Some companies unintentionally (and some intentionally) separate
decision-making from the people who satisfy customers or do the
activity. Other companies ensure that decision-making is built in
and integrated into the various companies' processes. One is an
enjoyable place to work; the other is not!

When people are not free to make decisions, having to check with
others first or pass things on, it causes frustration and helps to

build a lack of trust within the company. When the delay involves customers then it causes increased costs and potential customer dissatisfaction. In one company I worked in, the delays were costing in excess of €10million.

Amazon has made it easy for their customers. Customers rarely need to contact them through traditional channels. I have purchased items from Amazon and have never needed to ring them. They are successful. They make money and have loyalty from their customers. The service is failure-free and they don't talk to anyone. Amazon is a great example of a digital-age company.

Learning a lot by listening

All companies have challenges holding on to their best customers. In competitive industries, customers make choices to move from one supplier to the next. In some companies, there are problems with customer churn. In addition, there are lots of other problems including staff satisfaction and turnover.

In the best companies, the start point of any change is to listen to the people who do the work, as they often know more about the problems than customers. Conversely, the best way to understand the experience that customers receive is to listen to customers and watch their journey through the company's processes.

> *I was asked to review the performance of a contact centre. The journey for the customer was full of delay and disappointment. Customers were asked to wait during the call and often could not be satisfied without having to ring back.*
>
> *The management had recently decided that the retention team would only work 9-5, Monday to Friday. Any customers who phoned after hours looking for a new telephone or a new deal were very politely asked to ring back on Monday when the retention team would be able to deal with their request.*
>
> *The customer had to wait all weekend!*

I made a note of the telephone numbers. In nearly every case, the customer had visited a competitor's shop on the Saturday and purchased a new phone. When they phoned back on the Monday they were no longer looking for a new phone but phoned to cancel their contract. The management decision to close at the weekend was affecting revenue and increasing costs.

When taking decisions it is vital to see everything from the customer point of view. Listening to the customer and understanding them is vital. When you listen to the customer and see it through their eyes you learn a lot.

Taking considered risks

The very best companies listen to their people, especially the ones who are directly facing the customers. The best Chief Executives and Directors do this regularly - they build it into the way that they work. They listen to their teams and when they do, they learn a lot.

Do you take time out to listen to your people so that they can tell you what needs improving?

Really listen to understand the delays that customers receive due to people not being able to make and take decisions. Listen to understand what customers want now and what they might want in the future.

In our personal lives, taking a decision is often more important than procrastinating over one. We all take considered risks. Sometimes, it's not that important if it goes wrong. Sometimes it is.

Every time drivers overtake, they take a risk. Every time pedestrians cross the road, they take a risk. If you are in Amsterdam, you have to look out for trams, trains, cars, buses and bicycles! Risk is all around us. We learn to cope with ambiguity in our own lives.

Some human beings have learnt to take decisions and face the consequences of their decisions. They take responsibility. When people take responsibility you automatically and naturally take action.

However, it depends on where you sit in the company. The closer you are to the operation or the customer, the sooner the consequences of your decision will be felt - perhaps in hours. Operational management decisions' consequences are not felt for between one and six months. The consequences of strategic decisions taken by directors can sometimes not be felt for between one and five years. The banking crisis of 2008 was a good example of results of decisions taken a few years ago. Some economists have suggested the problem began in the 1980s!

Decisions and consequences

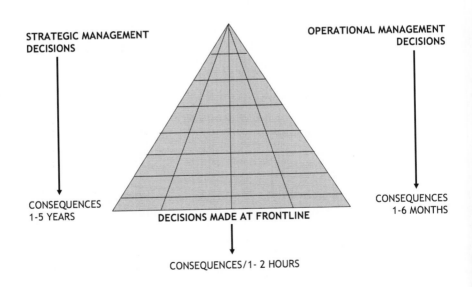

STRATEGIC MANAGEMENT
DECISIONS

OPERATIONAL MANAGEMENT
DECISIONS

CONSEQUENCES
1-5 YEARS

DECISIONS MADE AT FRONTLINE

CONSEQUENCES
1-6 MONTHS

CONSEQUENCES/1- 2 HOURS

People have explained to me that conditions need to be created where people in companies can solve their problems by taking considered risks.

A considered risk is one where you take a short while to consider the outcome of the decision. A considered risk involves judgment. We need people to make judgments. We need them to own the problem, decide what to do, and have the confidence to do it. There is little room these days for indecision – especially in front of customers. Whilst we are deciding they are leaving.

Owning the problem and deciding what to do is often difficult in some companies.

My family and I had a disappointing experience at a leading restaurant chain in the UK.

We had been on holiday and had just returned on a long-haul flight landing at London Heathrow at 7.30pm. We live four hours away from the airport and I planned to drive the family home. We set off, but after about an hour, we were all just too tired and so we checked in to a roadside motel. We needed a bite to eat and we didn't fancy a full meal, just a snack. Next door to the motel there was a restaurant. It was part of the same chain. This is when the fun started!

I explained to the waiter that I was in the motel and wanted to order a few small meals to take back to my family who were waiting in the room. He explained that it was company policy not to provide a take-away service. I asked to speak to the manager and the waiter told me that the manager would not be able to change the decision. Eventually, the manager arrived. He listened and he understood my circumstances. He took a different decision. He decided to take my order. His approach was so different. He checked back with me to see that I was OK. He even gave me a drink on the house. Shortly afterwards the food arrived and I took it to the motel. Two different people - one could make a decision, the other could not.

The impact of fear

People have told me that they want to take decisions. Often the people in front of customers know exactly what to do. But if they are in an environment where there is fear, decisions are delayed.

In companies, nothing slows down decision-making quicker than fear. Fear can be a motivating factor with some. It is often not the fear of the decision that needs to be made but the fear of the reaction if a mistake is made.

- Fear drives out creativity.
- Fear very quickly disengages the best people.
- Fear makes you stop.
- Fear makes you think.
- Fear encourages you to check.
- Fear makes you ask questions.
- Fear encourages people to play it safe.
- Fear causes more stress.
- Fear makes you sick.
- Fear makes people hide mistakes.
- Fear is not sustainable in the long term.

How much fear is there in your company?

The most talented and confident employees are not frightened at all. They just leave and join one of your competitors.

When your best people leave – how are you going to differentiate now?

Decisions and choices

The very best service companies ensure that customer service teams are given the freedom to take and make decisions. But not all companies do!

We all make decisions. At the time we make them, we believe that they were right at the time.

I don't know anyone who deliberately set off to make a wrong decision. I don't know anyone who arrives at work deliberately to make a mistake. A wrong decision is only clear after the event. Of course, in our personal lives we all take risks with decisions we take. Over-stretching yourself with a large mortgage is a decision some take. It is only a wrong decision when you lose your job and still have to repay the mortgage. However, when you make decisions you have to make an assessment of the situation, sometimes with minimal facts, and take a considered risk.

Directors need to take considered risks in many situations and sometimes have to wait for three years to find out they were right. In the early part of this century, many Chief Executives had strategies to cope with the emerging internet technologies. Some Chief Executives succeeded and some did not.

I was halfway through a six-month contract in the Netherlands and was staying in a hotel, in the capital of the Netherlands, Den Haag. I always stayed there.

I was in my room one evening and realised that I would need to leave a day earlier than I had originally planned. It was 8.05 pm. I phoned reception to explain that I would need to leave the day after tomorrow.

The receptionist surprisingly said, "You will be charged for the room as you have phoned after 8pm." Apparently, a decision had been taken that any guests who phone after 8pm would incur the charge. I explained that I was regular guest and would she re-consider. She didn't have the authority as the reservations manager had gone home. This was a hotel and the reservations manager had gone home and so no one could make a decision - I couldn't believe it! I asked her if she could make a special arrangement, taking into account that I was a regular customer.

> "We treat our regular customers in exactly the same way as others", she explained.
>
> There was no way to solve it until the morning. In the morning, the manager arrived, offered many apologies and gave me a free meal in the restaurant for the confusion. The decision was an easy one to make but only the manager could make it! It cost them money and I wasn't really happy. I was a regular customer but didn't feel like it.

We make decisions daily. We decide to be enthusiastic or not. Every single day, everyone makes lots of little decisions that they have to live with.

> As I write this chapter of the book, it is during the Easter holidays and my children have ideas that involve me. They want me to go with their grandparents to Waterstones, the famous bookstore.
>
> I love Waterstones. I love the experience. I love books. I love my children. I have a choice to make. It is now 9.30 and they are leaving at 11.30. They really want me to go. I want to go but I want to finish this chapter as I have a deadline that my publisher has asked me to meet.
>
> The children are using all their sales techniques and they are only ten and eleven years old! They have just popped by and told me that they are going to have fish and chips on the way. They know I love fish and chips. It's all very tempting. I will find a way to do it!

Emotions play a big part in our decision-making process. Taking decisions is very natural for human beings in day-to-day life.

Creating the right conditions

In companies where people are free to take decisions, you will see increased productivity and increased commitment. You also see less stress and less staff turnover. The key for management is to create the conditions where people are free to take decisions where it matters most – in front of customers! In a world where the customer is doing the transactions themselves then delays must be reduced to nil. If there is ever uncertainty in front of customers, it is normally better for the employee to satisfy customers now and ask questions later.

What is the cost to your company of not satisfying the customer now? This is an old question but one that needs to be continually thought about by operational managers so that they can drive efficiency. Take time to measure the cost of not satisfying customers. It can run into thousands of pounds.

Customer circumstances change and so do their requirements - sometimes at short notice.

> *I was in a coffee shop in Prague, capital of the Czech Republic, and I ordered a cappuccino. I looked outside and it was cold and snowing so I changed my mind. I wanted to order an Irish coffee instead. I noticed that the waiter had not given the order to the coffee maker.*
>
> *I called the waiter over to explain my change of plan. He explained that it was not possible to change the order. I asked why and he said it was a management decision. I wanted to investigate this further but I was with my family and decided not to pursue it.*
>
> *It was another example of management making decisions - or was he deciding to be unhelpful? Whatever it was, it was a decision in front of customers. The cappuccino was fine but I left the coffee shop with a nasty taste in my mouth! Needless to say, I didn't go back.*

Frustrations of not being able to take decisions

Inability to implement decisions creates internal delays too! In some companies, people are not clear about the actual requirements when designing new products and solutions and this causes longer lead times. This is very noticeable in marketing departments as everything needs to be signed off by the marketing director and in some cases the managing board.

This leaves some marketing managers and their teams feeling that their contribution is not valued. Far too many managers become involved in the detail of how things are done. They are so involved that their teams (who also have the creativity) slowly switch off. Whilst they are discussing the best way they are not thinking about the future direction of the business. In head office environments, some feel they have to be involved in every decision. This creates even more frustration.

However, some companies do allow people to take decisions. When they do the customer feels the benefits.

A few years ago I purchased a portable satellite navigation system and I often use it in Europe when travelling either on holiday or to see clients. A plastic bracket attaches the system to the windscreen of the car.

On one occasion I forgot to take the plastic bracket off the windscreen of the rental car. I needed a new plastic bracket; I contacted the supplier and the person I spoke with was free to take a decision. She understood and sent out a new bracket immediately, first class. She phoned me a few days later to check that I was happy with it. Excellent service by someone who could make a decision.

Often people in contact centres cannot make a decision in front of customers, as the responsibility for the decision or necessary information is with another department. This becomes obvious when customers ask unfamiliar questions, outside of the advisor's responsibility. Sometimes customers have many different questions that need resolution on one call.

> *I had an intermittent fault with my broadband connection. I decided to phone the customer service number.*
>
> *I listened carefully to the various options and pressed the right buttons and eventually spoke to a lady in Newcastle. She was very helpful and did all she could; however, as the fault was technical, she couldn't help so gave me a new number to ring. I had three different numbers and have spoken to five different people. At the end of the call one of the advisors asked me if there was anything else she could help me with. She couldn't help me with my original problem so it sounded really daft. This was probably part of her script so I guess she had to say it.*

Making decisions to divide the work into simple activities doesn't work in service companies. It builds in additional costs and causes problems with morale and customer satisfaction. In the above case, there was nothing wrong with the people who spoke to me.

However, someone made a decision to design the experience in that way for me.

Depending on what department you speak to, you can receive a different standard of service and behaviour. This becomes apparent when customers forget to pay their bill or credit card.

When the customer ends up in the collection cycle the brand and the CRM programme go out of the window! Separating customer service from collections is a good example of how good customers are treated differently and in some cases badly.

> *I had been on a business assignment abroad for a few weeks and I had forgotten to pay my credit card bill. I have a bank account, a mortgage and house insurance with the company. My lifetime value must be worth thousands. I received a call from the collection part of the bank. She treated me with little respect. I was a non-payer and that meant I received the treatment that was reserved for people who do not pay their bill. I accepted that I was in error and that I would pay the outstanding balance (£47.00). She wanted payment straightaway. I explained that I*

> *would be transferring the sum over to the account via the internet this evening. She persisted to ask me to pay now. I began to get quite annoyed about her attitude and explained the product relationship I had with the bank.*
>
> *She explained that she was not interested in my other products all she wanted was the £47.00. I asked to speak to her manager and I am still waiting. I paid the account off in full that evening. However, I am now switched off from that bank and over the next few months I will transfer my account elsewhere. I am sure she hit her targets that day and maybe I should complain, but to be honest, I am now indifferent. I couldn't care less.*

When you no longer care in a relationship you might not leave today or tomorrow but you make plans, and when you are ready you find another partner – or in this case another bank. They were so product-focused, insurance, credit and mortgages were all handled by a different team. They will have a sophisticated CRM solution costing millions but even today they have no idea!

The importance of trust

Giving people the freedom to satisfy customers with no restrictions saves money in the long term. The key is to give people the tools to do the job and to trust the people to deliver results.

Teams need to trust one another and share their mistakes. It is not easy to do, but in the right environments teams can build in regular reviews on how well (or not) they are doing and challenge themselves to improve.

The best companies appear to trust people to make the right decisions.

> *I was talking to a Director who had turned around the performance of his sales and customer service teams and I asked him what he had done. It seemed so simple. He explained that he ensured that the managers spent their time understanding the*

problems that customers were having and putting in place long-lasting solutions. He wasn't interested in the day-to-day ups and downs of customer service performance. He focused his managers on the long term solutions. It was a painful journey for him and some of his team leaders. His team leaders worked in their teams identifying what was needed by their teams to deliver a better experience. Some team leaders found it difficult as he was asking them to think differently about what their job was about. That was not all that he did.

He also encouraged his customer-facing teams to make decisions in front of customers. He asked them to use common sense. He didn't want the customers to have to wait. He trusted the people in his teams; he trusted the customers and he asked his team to satisfy customers now. When his customer-facing people couldn't satisfy customers they highlighted the problems. The team shared mistakes, looked at better ways to do things and improved individually and collectively. There was a buzz in this sales and service team and it was not generated by incentives or a league table.

With a trusting environment and increased responsibility within our teams, it is possible to strip out layers of cost, improve morale and the customer experience. However, the best companies look at all situations through the eyes of the customer. How does it affect them? Managers need to ask this key question.

How much does it cost the company to not satisfy the customer now?

Making decisions to design the company around customers; giving everyone clear direction and authority to decide brings immense benefits to customers.

Summary

Companies that are differentiating are not separating decision-making from the people who satisfy customers. They are building decision-making and improvement into the work.

If players constantly have to check, the outcome can only be frustration, customer delays and internal inefficiencies. This increases costs and reduces the emotional engagement of players in teams.

People need to be allowed to take considered risks. People are not stupid. They spend their lives making decisions. They buy houses, have children and go on holiday. Maybe then they should be allowed to apply an extra five pounds to a customer account when they deem it appropriate!

We need to reduce fear by creating the conditions whereby players feel confident in making decisions. We need to create a trusting environment. Yes, mistakes will occur. Not all decisions will be the right ones, but this does not mean we need to delay customers.

When decision-making is built in to the work there is creativity and energy. People are engaged and respond positively to the responsibility. They bring their brain into work and it benefits customers. You just have to let them.

Practical actions to understand and learn about decision-making

- Try trusting your teams to make decisions. They will respond with enthusiasm if they are allowed to. Help them when they make mistakes. Definitely don't look for someone to blame.

- When you do not know the answer to a problem – don't panic! Identify the right people who have a genuine and emotional interest in solving the problem. Help everyone understand the problem and create the conditions where together people can agree the best way forward. Give them the power to resolve it.

- Look to implement methods to engage teams to make decisions for customers based on their unique circumstance. Do you have too many rules to prevent any creativity?

- Check that you are being considerate of others when making decisions. Look at things from everyone's perspective.

- Do you listen to your customer-facing teams? Are they cynical or connected?

Understanding reward

It's simpler for managers to tinker with compensation than to change the company's culture. Most merit-pay systems share two attributes: they absorb a vast amount of management time and make everybody unhappy.

Harvard Business Review May/June 1998

Years ago managers agreed - what gets measured gets done! Companies can and do spend days deciding a fair system and then allocating reward to individuals. In some companies, a whole day of management time is allocated just to deciding the reward of people in their teams. Desperate attempts are made to ensure that the decisions taken are scientific. One thing I have been told by many managers is reward takes a lot of management time; it's unfair and de-motivates many.

The impact of incentives

Incentives are used to motivate. In most cases, these approaches motivate individuals to get the reward, devaluing the work along the way, and not assisting the development of the customer relationship. In one automobile company customer orders were delayed so that the sales people could meet their monthly targets.

This happened because if they over-achieved their targets the manager would increase them next month. It was just easier to fiddle the figures. In one contact centre I visited difficult customers were 'accidentally' cut off so that individuals could take more calls and meet their call targets. There was no incentive at all to satisfy customers. The calls had to last no more than three minutes otherwise there would be trouble for the customer advisor whose call-handling time was high.

> *Yesterday evening, I was finishing off the previous chapter and my wife called me. The BBC, the national television provider in the UK, was running a programme on contact centres. I had to see it. It was enlightening for lots of reasons.*
>
> *One company was automatically cutting customers off after 15 minutes - I am not sure that this was to do with reward or not but one thing we can be sure of - the customers were receiving a raw deal. The company probably hit their contact centre standards, but still the customers were leaving.*

Often individuals in companies hit their sales targets, and the monthly figures look good, but the customers don't return to purchase more. It's not really just about selling these days - it's about whether the customers return to purchase a product from you again. In short, will they come back? What experience did you create? Would customers remark about it, positively, on social media sites?

The importance of teamwork

Whilst we all know that teamwork plays a vital part in delivering the customer experience, often the reward is not aligned to team success. This can lead to competition between people, normally to the detriment of the customer. This is very noticeable in an aggressive sales environment. In some retail outlets I have been helped by an assistant and they have escorted me to the cash desk to ensure that the sale is registered against them. There are many examples where the behaviour in front of customers reflects the internal reward process.

> *I was in an estate agent's and the agent took a telephone call from a colleague. Annoyingly, I had to wait whilst she finished the call. The discussion went on for quite a while. Apparently, there were difficulties with one of their clients - the client wanted to purchase a property!*
>
> *However, there were problems, as the agents could not agree who would receive the commission for the sale. The client had seen one particular property twice and now wanted to buy. Each visit to the property was accompanied by a different agent (from the same company) and so this caused commission discussions. At the end of the call, they agreed to satisfy the client and deal with the commission later with their manager! The agent didn't seem to worry that I had been kept waiting!*

Some companies focus on ensuring that reward is based upon the company delivering results. At N&P Building Society, Bradford, United Kingdom, the recognition and reward system was built around a combination of basic pay and a reward system that focused on team play and company performance. The approach encouraged the management team to contribute together to achieve. It was challenging for everyone. The individual reward depended on each player's role and their ability to influence the company performance. It had nothing to do with grade, only delivery of team achievements. They worked across teams to deliver results. Teams agreed if they met achievements or didn't meet achievements. They often over-achieved. They proved that you could achieve more when teams are serious about working together. They had to work as a team. It was not easy. There was no room for politics. There was no room for poor performance. If you did not deliver results, the team told you in regular feedback sessions. When you succeeded, the team let you know.

Does your reward system fit in with your overall performance?

Naturally, people who did not perform either improved or decided to leave the company.

Continually learning transportable skills

Great teams are normally led by great leaders. Leaders that take control and responsibility for their success. Leaders that focus on ensuring that everyone has the tools to do the job well. They focus on identifying what is happening and why it is happening. In addition to providing the capabilities that people need, great coaches create the conditions to enhance the confidence of the people in their teams. They ensure that individuals are learning, adding value and meeting or exceeding their targets. They take time to recognise the little things that their teams do.

Over the last few years it has not just been about doing your job. The key is continually to learn. You have to do that to keep up. We live in a different world now and rewarding people for learning new transportable skills is essential if we are to remain competitive. These are skills that can be used across the company - not just in specific departments. Individuals need to keep questioning themselves and the contribution that they are making.

What have you learnt in the last 12 months?

Successful teams consistently deliver sustainable results. They don't just win once; they win again and again. During the '90s Manchester United proved that with good leadership, players and teamwork it is possible to repeat success. In the UK the mobile phone company Orange consistently won awards for the quality of their service – year after year. Great teams ensure that they can repeat their success.

Team and individual feedback

Really great teams provide feedback to one another on their contribution and their behaviour. It's about creating the environment where it is expected. It's about leading the team and encouraging people to be open and honest to help everyone achieve. It's not as difficult as behaviour psychologists would suggest. However, managers need to work consistently on the environment and ensure that appropriate reward is built into the process. The best companies have built feedback into their activities on a daily basis. It remains one of the differentiating factors that separated the good team from the great. I have seen great coaches in action. Great teams take advantage of the inherent critical nature of human beings and rely on team feedback to strengthen the team. Everybody learns and improves. It's also difficult to copy. In team sports, feedback is the norm and sometimes it isn't enjoyable – sometimes it is. In great teams, they give one another positive and negative feedback and just keep on improving.

I have retired from playing football now and only have memories - mostly good ones. I played in teams that won things. One such memory is the day when I played in the final of the Somerset Cup. We won 3-1 and I scored all three goals. I received lots of feedback that day. I felt great.

We were in the dressing room at the end of the game and the manager talked to us about how we had all played. He wanted us to think about each of the players and at the next training session, he asked us all to share the feedback with our team mates. He had never done this before, but in the moment of our greatest success he took the opportunity to ensure that we learnt from the experience.

We trusted one another and we gave it a go. When everyone did it together, it did not seem so bad. I received feedback about my strengths and my weaknesses. So did everyone else. It developed our team spirit and improved our understanding of one another. We became a much better team and won more football matches. We also built relationships that lasted.

Giving feedback to one another in teams really does make a huge difference. On a daily basis, people give feedback to their families and friends. They do it with sensitivity and they see behaviour changes. The best teams bring this type of feedback into their day-to-day working life. I have seen Directors' teams sharing the positive and the negative thoughts about their contribution; I have seen team leaders and their teams improving one another. It is not just done in training programmes but built into the recognition and reward process. It really is easy – but people have to give it a go. The best don't just do it in the training course - they build it into their work. The more you open up the better everyone becomes at it. Go on, give it a try!

What real difference have you made to your company in the last 12 months?

Companies can do as much benchmarking as they like but they can't copy teams that trust one another to share individual feedback with each other and continually improve. This can be very rewarding for everyone and is a differentiating factor between good teams and great teams.

Making the link with behaviour

Increasingly, companies have realised that rewards need to be focused on displaying the right behaviour. In corporate business, there have been attempts to agree specific behaviour by role. Companies have created specific competencies. They are often linked to the company or brand values.

> *In one company, the Commercial Director used all the wrong behaviours whilst hitting his targets. The company did not attempt to encourage him to change his behaviour. It was explained to me that he was bringing in so much revenue that the company did not want to upset him! His team soon started to mirror his behaviour. The company was bringing in new customers but they were not staying for long.*

> *Interestingly, a behaviours directory was created to outline the behaviours needed within the company. It was used to recruit people. Interviewees were asked to provide examples of situations so that they could be assessed on their competence/behaviour. Once people were appointed, they soon realised that they could use any behaviour as long as they hit their targets. The situation was out of hand and HR could do nothing about it!*

This company also had specific values and behaviours on the wall but no one really took any notice. People in teams felt that they were like wallpaper. They were also agreed by the management team with no input from people in the teams. It was clear that as long as you hit your targets you could use any behaviour you like. Of course, the real behaviour used daily would never be written on a wall. What is your culture really like?

Devaluing the work

To achieve the very best results people need to have a real purpose when doing their work. They need to have passion. Giving people a bonus when they hit their targets has become very popular. It appears to bring a short-term result. However, it depends what you are measuring. The things that actually matter to improve individual performance are often difficult to measure.

Incentive is all around us, at school, at home and in our workplace. Everyone appears to think it works. Does it? What we appear to have is compliance when what we are looking for is commitment. Team players with commitment happily contribute to the planned team achievements.

Are you committed or are you just complying?

We are in danger of treating people no better than we treat dogs. My Labrador will sit for a biscuit. All she is focused on is the biscuit. She will do almost anything for a biscuit. I am sure you can think of your own examples where to deliver a short-term result you have offered an incentive. It just seems easier.

Does it work in the long term? In education, we need to concentrate on the importance of learning and its impact on life choices/chances. In too many schools there are incentives that reward good work with a DVD player or a bowling trip!

As soon as you use incentive you immediately devalue the actual work. When used in customer service it can have a disastrous impact on the customer. This is most obvious in customer contact centres. If you are targeted on length of call time you cut difficult customers off, do not sell any additional solutions and you rush the customer. If you are an engineer dealing with customer problems, you skip past the difficult customers especially if solving the problem may take time. Inappropriate rewards do not encourage the building of relationships between and across company teams. The target for one department is often in direct conflict with another department and causes all sorts of customer dissatisfaction. It is possible to hit all your internal targets and still have unhappy customers.

In the mobile telecoms industry there are continual battles between retaining customers and ensuring that bad debt is reduced or kept to an acceptable figure. Often these teams are in separate departments. As soon as you have separate departments with conflicting measures you will see politics and fractured relationships.

Improvement and creativity

In excessive reward cultures there is very little improvement. People do not look for improvement, and worse, the measurements do not encourage improvement. Look at your own measures. Are they targets or are they helping you measure to improve?
When teams are engaged in improvement they save money and help the company become successful.

Does your reward system stimulate creativity and continual improvement?

Players in teams have told me that when you reward people inappropriately you drive out any creativity and people avoid any risk-taking. They do what they need to do to hit their targets. The larger the incentive the more outrageous the behaviour can become. Banks 2008!

> During my career, I managed one of three contact centres and my targets were all linked to the percentage of calls answered by my team. Everyone was focused on this figure. They would be - it was in everyone's objectives. It was a nightmare; no one was looking at improvement, the customers were getting a raw deal, the advisors were unhappy and the calls just kept on coming. The immediate manager was comparing one contact centre to another and some were not productive enough. Something had to be done. He did what all managers do when there are problems - he called a meeting. We discussed ways that we could improve productivity. I talked about looking at why the calls came in and my colleagues talked about how we could shorten the call length. I talked about giving the advisors more responsibility to satisfy customers and my colleagues talked about disciplining the advisors who were not hitting their targets. I talked about involving people, improving the job design and allowing people to take decisions in favour of customers.
>
> They didn't agree and decided that what people needed was an incentive to work harder. You see, they thought it was a people problem. It clearly was not! They offered an incentive of £50 if the department answered 90% of all calls in 15 seconds. The targets were hit, everyone received their £50 and the customers continued to leave the company. There was nothing about quality and I had lost the battle. Much like the customers, I decided to leave the company, as did many others.

Contribution and commitment

There is a much better way to recognise and reward people for their contribution.

I suggest companies:

- Improve the design of jobs giving people freedom to do it their way.
- Give people a real purpose that means something to them.
- Create roles that give people the freedom to satisfy customers.
- Measure the outcomes, not the way the work is done.
- Encourage/reward teamwork, creativity and continual improvement.
- Pay people a rate that they believe is fair in relation to the market.
- Share company success with everyone.
- Relate the reward to each person's ability to influence the bottom line.

Implementing the above will bring commitment and improvement to the customer experience. As you deliver results ensure that everyone is given a share of the company's success.

Summary

Changing existing reward structures is never easy. However, for the brave the rewards are significant. Reward plays an essential part when going through any change. Often the reward system needs to change to reinforce the changes that are occurring. From my research and experience, if the reward and performance management system doesn't change then things don't change.

Managers spending hours in meetings agreeing a 'fair' and scientific reward system remains rife within companies. Scientific methods are used because they are easy to quantify, but they often end up disengaging people and customers, devaluing work and become very expensive. Incentives bring about short-term success. They encourage people to focus on the reward and lose sight of the purpose. This creates behaviour that harms relationships with customers. People quickly become disengaged, as the work is devalued.

There also remains a lack of team reward for teams working towards agreed team achievement. It is replaced by individually derived bonus schemes that bring about a silo mentality, diminishing team learning and the team dynamic. People need to be rewarded for learning new transportable skills. These skills are vital in fast-moving sectors. We need to encourage people to be constantly challenging themselves to improve – not just to benefit the company but to benefit themselves. This needs to be on a team and individual level and feedback within and across teams needs to be built in to the daily work. For this to be successful, people need real clarity around their purpose and their responsibilities. The 'bonus for hitting targets' approach is outdated and short-term.The reality is that engaged teams drive innovation and save money, while traditional reward systems tend to just drive out creativity, shared learning and risk-taking. This is often to the detriment of the overall purpose of satisfying customers.

We need to encourage: fair pay, the creation of interesting and stimulating roles with real purpose, freedom to satisfy customers, creativity and continual improvement.

Practical actions to understand and learn about reward

- Review your current reward system and decide whether it is fair and rewards the behaviours you are looking for.

- Is the reward system aligned to the company values? Consider making your reward system more team-focused, building in team feedback to improve performance.

- Review your approach to managing performance. Do you spend too much time with HR doing disciplinary? What value is it adding?

- Set up an annual awards evening based upon the company's values or behaviours. Involve everyone (not just the managers) in deciding the recipients of the award. It doesn't cost much.

- Set up biannual meetings where everyone gives feedback to one another about team and individual performance. It works and changes behaviour.

- Ask yourself whether your reward system recognises the behaviours that equate to customer satisfaction. Are your best people reaping the greatest rewards?

- Does your performance measurement system need to be changed to fit the new approach?

- Agree what you need to achieve as a team. Ask individual players what their contribution could be to the team achievement. Review the contribution of people in regular performance meetings.

- Ask individuals to review their own performance and share the outcome with their colleagues.

The focus for managers

Understanding people development

The focus (has to be) on the processes of learning. It is creating a safe environment where children don't feel afraid to make mistakes. They talk and feed off each other, building ideas and solving problems cohesively. The child who doesn't know the answer knows he can ask someone else in the group who does understand. The child who gets it straight away is still challenged by explaining the solution to his peers.
Rachel Edmonson, Teacher, Old Oaks School, London

Over the last few years there has been a proliferation of behaviour change programmes delivered within companies. Unfortunately, not all of them have brought longer-term behaviour change. For example, costly motivational team-building events bring the team together in the short term, but employees have told me that it does not bring sustainable results.

Many of these are delivered away from the workplace. Building Lego bridges, rafting across a river and shooting paint at one another have all been tried. They do have a place in developing teams; however, they are often deployed at the wrong time.

The future approach to people development and cost-effective interventions lies in building learning activities into the day-to-day work, whilst focusing on improving the activities that people do. The best teams will challenge and assess themselves, learn together and continually develop their skills without the need for many of the traditional training courses.

Whilst training is a vital part of team development, many people are now realising that most of their significant learning experiences have occurred in their day-to-day work.

The challenge is to create the environment where teams naturally trust one another to choose to share learning.

Integrating learning into the work

I have discussed the need to create learning environments within companies with many directors and HR professionals. It appears that, depending on how they think, learning environment solutions can be very different.

In one company the HR team and operational teams felt that the best way to create a learning environment would be to provide everyone with the opportunity to complete a National Vocational Qualification (NVQ). The uptake was very favourable. The problem was that when players started to undertake the NVQ the general feedback was that they were monotonous, historical and labour-intensive. The course required constant collation of evidence to prove that performance was adequate and measured against a clearly defined standard.

Players have told me that they did not learn anything useful. Did they create a learning culture within the team? It seems that they just served to reinforce a standardised, structured and restrictive approach, only serving to increase paperwork and stifle creativity.

In another company they set up an internal intranet to provide everyone with the opportunity to feed back 'ideas' to improve things. The ideas are generally held within a centralised database and the *'suggestions team'* wade through the list of ideas and provide feedback via e-mail to the individual. If the idea is considered viable, it may be implemented. The individual in question may receive a cash prize. The purpose appears to be more of an incentive system whereby players are almost bribed to generate ideas. This is not too dissimilar to a mother offering a child a Mars Bar if he *'tidied his room'*.

The reality of some suggestion schemes is that very few people actually see the value and therefore rarely participate. If they do it is not uncommon for them to be quickly disillusioned because the suggestions team have a budget and therefore have limited scope to reward too many for fear of spending too much! Secondly, the improvement is too far away from the customer and in the above case was handled within the HR function. Finally, any improvement takes that long to implement (once it has been passed from pillar to post to determine the *viability* of the idea), may no longer be valid and the individuals doing the work very rarely feel or see the improvement.

Both the above initiatives provide very little opportunity for quick feedback, learning and therefore improvement. They stifle creativity and do little to engage players in choosing to contribute their implicit or tacit knowledge. In addition, teams have told me that the most creative ideas often come from them working and discussing things together, not just from a few individuals.

> At BT Mobile in the late 1990s, the customer service team, once described as 'one of the top five motivated teams in the world', won many industry awards for their creative and enthusiastic approach to engaging people. The management team set up a process that encouraged people to openly share their views. People creatively worked together to come up with better ways

> of working. When there was a problem they didn't look for someone to blame – they encouraged openness and learnt individually and collectively.
>
> Their feedback process didn't involve any incentive. They spent time working on solving the problem and because everyone felt involved, the eventual solution had the buy-in and commitment that is so necessary when making changes.

The challenge is for companies to recognise that human beings have a great deal of passion for their work and the company when they are trusted (or allowed) to think!

How much passion do you have for your work?

The best companies acknowledge the value of creating a learning environment and regularly communicate the importance of learning and improving. Managers create the environment where people feel able, and therefore want, to be creative. Subsequently and almost naturally, the players happily contribute tacit knowledge because they recognise the importance of their role to the company's success and feel privileged to play their part. It is not rocket science if the thinking is right.

Some human resource professionals and operational managers really do believe that the initiatives they implement are for the good of the company and the people. Despite these best intentions however, the problem is that that way of thinking is outdated and therefore the solution often does not serve to meet the purpose. Players need to feel involved and supported, while roles need to evolve to include improvement activity.

People development is critical to success

> During my time as a manager I have come across performance development plans (PDP), which are in theory, a good idea, but it depends how they are applied practically. My senior manager

> *used to talk regularly about people development and 'walked the talk' by religiously conducting monthly one-to-ones with my colleagues and me. In our one-to-one, we would always start by reviewing achievements and progress against my targets. The bulk of the meeting, however, involved reviewing my Team Managers' PDPs. The PDP was a series of questions I had to ask the Team Managers. I would write their responses. I then had to give them an increased target to achieve ready for review at the next meeting. They would sign the form and I would file it away in their individual PDP file. They all had different coloured files!*

The problem was that this approach did nothing in terms of development. It was formal, boring and labour-intensive. It appeared that the act of conducting, reporting and filing became more important than the actual outcome.

In other words, no one was learning and actually only developed their filing skills!

How often do you see 'identifying feedback or improvements' written into role descriptions?

This highlights that how you think plays such a fundamental part in how you behave. Their intentions were fine, but the solution was one that added minimal value. Not one of the questions on the PDP even mentioned the customer or their behaviour.

The PDP forms were very internally focused and no one learnt anything.

> *After about three months of not using the form, my manager did a spot check on all our PDP files and was horrified to learn that I wasn't using it, even though my results were better than anyone else's! Ingrained thinking really can hold you back.*

Creating the environment for learning

When teams think in a digital-age way, the solution is very natural and other solutions seem ridiculous. It therefore follows that people with traditional thinking see the PDP approach as being the perfect solution and think any alternative is crazy and almost 'maverick'. Traditional-age thinkers need a form, otherwise they believe that employees will take advantage.

The reality was that as they were trusted to be creative, there was no need for anyone to sign anything. If they didn't do something well we would both know and we would use it as an opportunity for dialogue. We still had regular one-to-one contact, but my role as a manager was to create the environment where people learnt as they worked.

Listening and talking to people reaps massive benefits. Alternatively, traditional thinking serves as a justification for managers to sit behind their desks for most of the month and then do their people development once a month in a formal setting with a form, a file and a signature. Digital-age thinking creates the environment where everyone is consistently challenging their own and others' behaviour as they do their work and on a daily basis. The manager is visible and asking questions to stimulate thinking and can be approached at any time and one-to-ones are an open, two-way dialogue between two adults with opinions. They just have different (and interdependent) roles.

Using standards to develop people

This near-obsession with applying a formal solution to people development is epitomised by the Investors in People (IIP) standard. Still a highly regarded process and highly acclaimed award, many companies are striving to attain the standard to send a message of the commitment to people development. It should be applauded that an attempt is being made to develop people. All too often it appears to be driven by a company striving for status and recognition. The standard is incredibly stretching and the award is not given lightly. Numerous initiatives are put in place to prove that the standard is being achieved. IIP assessors test this and the award is given or not.

This use of standards is limiting in terms of people development. Most initiatives (one-off activities that are not really built into the day-to-day work) are management driven and rarely involve other roles. They are therefore implemented with minimal commitment. Even where the standard is implemented, people have told me that they are not developing as quickly as they would like.

Training needs analysis

People development can of course exist in other guises. Some training managers and consultants spend a lot of time conducting lengthy training and business needs analysis. The purpose is to ascertain the people capability gaps that can be filled by various people-development interventions (usually training courses).

The approach involves speaking to or interviewing a cross-section of people across a variety of roles. They will then produce a report and present their findings, along with recommendations to the senior management team. This is part of a budget-requesting process, where the training professionals effectively 'sell' the requirement for training interventions. If they do this well, then budget is allocated.

The problem is twofold.

Firstly, the training professionals usually sit away from the operational areas and do not have a detailed enough understanding of the day-to-day activity. Secondly, decisions have often been made prior to the internal analysis.

> *One consultant I came across pulled together a list of courses he wanted to run for the client the following year. He had assumed the cost. He then laid out the plan of action very neatly to fit in with his and the company's people strategy. He then conducted the analysis. On questioning the approach, he said, "We just need to look as if we are doing things in the right way."*

Despite the fact people development is something that is consistently talked about within companies and has a great deal of money spent on it, the various solutions appear to do very little to develop people.

The required solution is less complex, but more difficult to implement. So, many of the above methods are *'tried and tested'* and therefore *must* be the way to do things. The problem is that they do little to meet the overall purpose. A customer advisor once said to me that *"They do a lot for people development here, most of it is just to keep us sweet."* It was true. A lot was done at that company, but people saw through it. They saw through it because they did not *feel* they were being developed.

The challenge is on to make people development a part of the daily activity. Build it into roles and encourage managers to create the environment where people can learn through experience. Managers need to get out of the way and trust more. They need to acknowledge that people want to do a good job and stretch themselves to get better. Why not let them?

To illustrate the importance of building training into the activity I have included Kirkpatrick's four levels of training evaluation. The quotations in the model were given to me by people in teams who had experienced the Understanding and Learning approach.

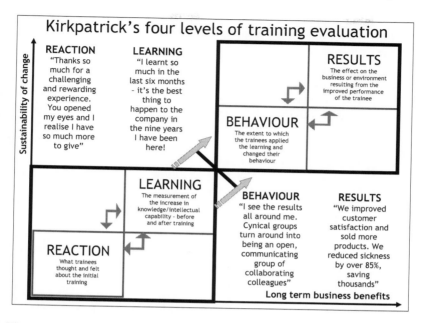

The shortcoming of so much training is that it only ever achieves the first two levels. Subsequently, this means that the benefits tend only to be short-term. People will often enjoy the experience and learn more about themselves, but does the company benefit?

The problems for companies occur due to the fact that learning is rarely applied on the required level to bring about sustained behaviour change. Consequently, the result falls short of the desired outcome. In other words, companies rarely see a financial return on investment.

The impact of separate training courses

Training courses can be fun. They can be an opportunity to take a step back from the hustle and bustle of everyday working life and to reflect with like-minded colleagues. They can be an opportunity to learn something. They can be an opportunity to have a rant and get things off your chest. They can provide an opportunity to get feedback and some coaching from someone who can help. They can also be an opportunity to have a good skive, sleep off the hangover, spend loads of budget and waste your time.

> *One company I worked with had a training budget of two million pounds for the year. They identified that behaviour was a problem among the middle manager group and customer service representatives, and subsequently brought in an outside consultancy to design and deliver a training course to improve things. The course was incredibly enjoyable and was the talk of the business. It cost £500,000.*
>
> *Two years later the behaviour problem was still there. What did the company do? They brought in the consultancy again to repeat the training. It cost a further £500,000!*
>
> *An obvious pattern was emerging. When we pointed out our thoughts on this spending, no one seemed too concerned as they explained that it 'wasn't their budget'.*

The reality is that separate training courses or management conferences are fun and add some immediate value – often a burst of enthusiasm. People will often return to the business full of praise for the trainer and desperate to try their new skills and apply their learning.

The problem is that they are not sustainable. They are not sustainable because the fundamental reason behind the poor behaviour is not being addressed. One example is of a young manager who attended a course entitled 'Influence and Persuasion Skills'. It was delivered by an outside consultancy and a section of the course focused on non-capitulating and standing up for yourself when you were not being listened to. Keen to use his new skills, he tried them out in his next one-to-one with his manager. His manager promptly said, "I've been on that course already, so I know what you are doing - just do what I'm asking you to do - we are too busy for fluffy training course games."

Often traditional-age managers see training as separate from the real work.

Aligning people development to the company capability

Far too many individual development plans are agreed but never implemented. Individuals agree their development plan in isolation with little understanding of what training is available or if there is budget for the training.

Far too often there is no real effort to understand the capability that needs to be in place for individuals to perform their roles well. What companies/teams need to do is to understand and document the key skills that the team or teams need, to perform their purpose. Once this is documented each player in the team should ascertain what skills they have against the 'capability' list (None/Some/Full). This 'capability chart' doesn't need to be complicated, can be as detailed as is necessary and should be updated regularly. It can be done on an Excel chart if necessary. Once this capability chart has been produced the team will have a good understanding of who has the skills and who does not. This capability chart can be used in one-to-one discussions and for creating individual development plans. It can be used in the team to understand overall capability.

The capability chart - Where are we now?

capability/individuals	RS	RA	BA	GF	NS	HT	HA	HE	Total by product
Capability A	1	3	3	2	4	2	5	3	23/40
Capability B	1	2	5	1	4	4	3	4	24/40
Capability C	3	5	5	2	5	1	5	0	26/40
Capability D	4	2	4	2	0	0	4	2	18/40
Capability E	5	5	1	4	3	3	4	0	25/40
Capability F	1	0	0	0	2	0	3	0	6/40
Total by individual	15/30	17/30	18/30	11/30	18/30	10/30	24/30	9/30	

0 = No capability   3 = Some capability   5 = Full capability

Team leaders need to own this chart and continually update it as learning takes place. With an accurate team capability chart, one-to-ones are focused on what really matters – improving the capability of teams and the individuals in it. With this approach people actually create a development plan that can be implemented. Many skills can be learned 'on the job' whilst people do the work.

In the above example, it is possible to see who has the capability and what products were well understood by each member of the sales team. Digital-age thinkers take time to understand the capability gaps in their teams and ensure that training is put in place to close the gaps. They make the link between the training and the improved performance.

Exercising individual choice

This indicates an all too common problem. You can spend as much money as you want on behaviour courses, but ultimately the choice lies with the individual. All courses do is provide people with an alternative insight, which they can choose to utilise or ignore. However, even when people choose to use the insight, if the methods do not fit in with the true culture of the company, they will fall by the wayside very quickly. A manager conceded, *"It is safer to keep my head down."*

The reality is that some companies have a thoroughly ingrained traditional-thinking culture and it is this that requires attention. No amount of soft-skills training will change the underlying culture. Traditional-age thinkers nearly always believe that if a group of individuals are not performing then it is their behaviour that needs addressing. Sometimes it is a behaviour problem but from my experience it is normally a company culture problem that needs addressing. One manager told me, *"It's just easier to run a course than to solve the real problems."*

Imagine this scenario...

A customer service contact centre advisor really wants to do well in her role. She is a very dedicated and thorough worker with good values and a desire to help customers. She wants to ensure that customers feel very happy after they have spoken to her.

Meanwhile she is told that she has to spend no longer than 240 seconds on every call and must follow a script to the letter. She has to say the customer's name three times on every call. She must ask before she goes to the toilet and must not put her coat on the back of the chair in case senior managers visit. People are not always the problem!

This individual does exist and explained this to me in a coaching session. She was identified to me as the 'problem' and it was my job to change her behaviour. Managers had already sent her for extra training and given her an action plan. As she talked incredibly passionately about customers and the fact she wasn't able to help them properly, it was obvious to me that no amount of training or coaching would change her behaviour. She thought in a digital-age manner and could not understand how what she was being 'forced' to do was the right thing.

The problem here was not the customer advisor, but the culture and internal methods of measurement and delivering customer satisfaction. Managers had implemented solutions that were easily measured and able to be controlled, while at the same time stamping on creativity that would ultimately help the business to achieve. It is therefore not enough to develop a people strategy, which is predominantly made up of dated training and coaching methods. People rarely learn too much and the skills learnt in the courses are often not sustainable as they are not built into the company's way of doing things. This results in added costs, disgruntled individuals and teams who either leave or obediently stay and do the bare minimum with their heads down.

Do your coaching methods inspire people?

It is not to say that training courses never have their place. They can be incredibly insightful and a great stimulus to learning and growing as an individual. They are just not sustainable unless they are part of a wider cultural shift, where everybody is focused on challenging themselves and others to continually improve. In order for this to happen there really is a need to challenge existing thinking.

Digital-age thinking is not a soft option, but one that can encourage short- and long-term success. People are supported, involved and are learning. Managers ensure that everyone has the basic tools to do their jobs with no delays and everyone is learning. They ask players: what do you need to do the job better? They don't just listen, they take action. They don't sit about discussing what could be done; they work across the business to solve problems and make life easier for their teams. When leaders solve problems teams have less to complain about and customers feel the benefits. All this learning needs to take place within the daily activity and not in a 'swanky' hotel with a free three-course lunch!

Stopping to review success and disappointments

Companies are constantly reviewing and measuring performance. All kinds of solutions are deployed to ascertain how well they are doing. Generally these are historical numerical figures which are measured against the pre-determined budget targets. They often offer no measures to help understand the work and so do not always help improvement. Secondly, culture surveys are prevalent and often used as a measure of success and disappointments.

The main problem with both of the above methods is that they are measured away from the customer, do not involve the players, and the results are rarely communicated quickly enough. If they are shared it is often so late that the data is no longer valid. Conversely any resulting improvement activity is always in the hands of the managers who put plans in place and implement new initiatives to make changes. People have told me that they have had enough of initiatives.

The fact that key people are not involved obviously reduces their commitment. Also, managers who think in a traditional-age way often believe that if performance is not good enough then tighter controls are needed. The reality is of course that the opposite (trust) would be of much more benefit to the company.

The connection of players in teams

These days staff satisfaction surveys don't always measure the right things and are often expensive. Working with some of the UK's top managers and coaches, I developed a connection survey called 'Connect'. Connect measures the five most significant elements of employee connection. It has helped me understand more about the levels of disconnection in companies that have completed the survey. I have also been able to make the link between employee satisfaction and customer satisfaction and retention. Over ten years ago the Harvard Business Review highlighted that a 5% increase in people satisfaction increased customer satisfaction by 1.3% and increased sales by 0.5%.

What would a 0.5% increase in sales mean to you?

In the example an average Connection Result of 65% in the connect survey would suggest a customer satisfaction result of between 70 and 79%. In this team, employee turnover would be in the region of 13 to 20%.

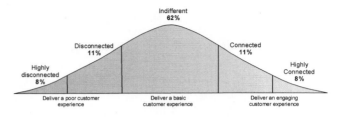

Organisation Performance	Disaster	Trouble	Disappointing	Pleasing	Fantastic
Market Share	Precipitous Decline	Significant Decline	Modest Decline	Significant Increase	Dramatic Increase
Connection Result	**0-20%**	**21-50%**	**51-70%**	**71-85%**	**85%+**
Customer Satisfaction	0-59%	60-69%	70-79%	80-89%	90%+
Customer Retention	0-24%	24-59%	60-75%	76-87%	88%+
Employee Absence	12%+	5-11%	3-4%	2-3%	1-2%
Employee Turnover	50%+	21-49%	13-20%	8-13%	6-8%

My main motivation for creating the survey was due to the fact there seemed to be a severe shortage of surveys that produced real-time textual analysis. I was forever seeing lots of questionnaires and surveys that were too complex, too long and did not enable immediate improvement because the results took so long to produce. Any subsequent improvement would therefore be historical and might no longer be relevant.

Connect is different because there are only twenty questions and results are made available to companies overnight. Yes, overnight! Additionally, the comprehensive analysis is made available to the company but is broken down in terms of individual departments and teams.

The individual manager in effect gets a personalised action plan based on the results derived from their teams' responses. Many companies have actually built this into their own performance management system as a way of measuring and improving performance. During the research I found out there were three main types of employees in companies: disconnected, connected, and indifferent.

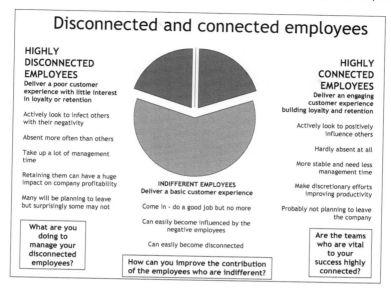

Disconnected and connected employees

HIGHLY DISCONNECTED EMPLOYEES
Deliver a poor customer experience with little interest in loyalty or retention

Actively look to infect others with their negativity

Absent more often than others

Take up a lot of management time

Retaining them can have a huge impact on company profitability

Many will be planning to leave but surprisingly some may not

What are you doing to manage your disconnected employees?

INDIFFERENT EMPLOYEES
Deliver a basic customer experience

Come in - do a good job but no more

Can easily become influenced by the negative employees

Can easily become disconnected

How can you improve the contribution of the employees who are indifferent?

HIGHLY CONNECTED EMPLOYEES
Deliver an engaging customer experience building loyalty and retention

Actively look to positively influence others

Hardly absent at all

More stable and need less management time

Make discretionary efforts improving productivity

Probably not planning to leave the company

Are the teams who are vital to your success highly connected?

'Connect' overcomes many shortfalls of other surveys in that the results are immediate and they can be followed up quickly. They are simple to communicate and people recognise their value.

Team meetings and away days

Team meetings are also used as a method to review success and disappointments. In reality and from experience, many team meetings tend to involve the manager sitting at the front going through the agenda. This approach is happening in thousands of companies across the world. The manager dominates the meeting and there is little opportunity to reflect and be creative. They tend to involve a focus on the negative and historical reviews of the previous meeting. All in all they can be labour-intensive and add minimal value and are often just an excuse to be away from the actual work. Often they are not motivational.

> *In one company I worked with, at the start of the year the senior manager would 'budget in' quarterly manager 'away-days'. These involved going to a nearby hotel and spending the day reviewing success and disappointments. There were lots of*

> breaking into groups and brainstorming ideas. The whole day was documented, formulated into a plan of activity and communicated via e-mail to the managers who attended.

Did they change things for the better?

Many have said no. They only served to separate the managers from the teams. The team sat in the office working hard, dealing with customers, while the managers were eating biscuits and drinking coffee!

Do your company away-days and team meetings add value?

This is a classic mistake made by management teams. The fact that time is planned in for this periodically implies to everyone that it is not something we do unless we are in the hotel! It separates what should be a daily and constant activity away from the work and away from everyone other than the managers.

The majority of time spent within companies is so hectic that managers all too often spend their day crisis-managing. How often have you been hauled into a meeting to address the present crisis?

- How much time is spent in team meetings in your company?
- What percentage of time is spent on discussing problems?
- How much time is spent on actually resolving things?
- How much time is spent reviewing the actions from previous meetings?

The solution is much simpler. In the digital-age companies, managers spend time planning and less time reacting to events. Team leaders and coaches spend time looking for improvements and people satisfy the customers and when they can't they tell someone about it who does something to resolve it. Now everyone is involved. Improvements are constant because everyone is collectively and individually reviewing. Collaboration is a key value.

The challenge is on to create the environment where all teams are regularly thinking about their own and others' performance and are allowed and want to share experiences with others, so that we all learn quickly.

It is essential that this is built into everyone's role and that success and disappointments are visible so others can learn. This requires a lot of trust and a willingness of some to let go. They need to facilitate their team's creativity and avoid wanting to control everything they do and know.

The challenge is to release the potential of people and help encourage them to communicate their opinions and ideas.

- Do your teams maximise their potential?
- Do they respect you?
- Are they committed or compliant?
- Do they just come to work do their job and go home?

Personal review of performance

In learning sessions, over the last ten years I asked over 10,000 people, *How often do you sit back at work and think about your performance and what you could do to improve?*

It appears that most people do the above infrequently at work, because they have too many tasks to do and so do not have time. Secondly, traditional-age thinkers consider that it is not their responsibility to review their *own* performance. Due to the fact that they are so ingrained in a traditional way of thinking and working, many actually believe it is their managers' responsibility to review them in their performance review meetings!

They also believe that it is the managers' job to motivate.

> *I learnt to juggle five years ago while on a corporate training conference. We were all given some balls and the facilitator passed on some generic instruction. The person who learnt the fastest was told they would receive £200 in vouchers. All those who could already juggle had to sit out. Everyone frantically picked up their balls and started. When we naturally dropped them, we immediately picked them up again and tried again...and again...and again. There was lots of swearing and raucous laughter. Very few of us were making any progress.*
>
> *One guy near to me had a different approach. He stood quietly. He would then try and juggle the balls. Rather than picking them up immediately, he would stop again, think and then pick them up. He did this for the next 10 minutes and each time he tried something slightly differently. As he did this he was making progress. He won the vouchers.*
>
> *He won because he took the time to think about his experiences and concentrated on improving every single time. I knew the man and he was often considered 'slow' by others he worked with.*
>
> *The reality was that he was totally focused on challenging his own behaviour to improve his performance. He was one of the best coaches I have ever come across.*

The value of reflection

It is a very natural thing to do for human beings to reflect on their performance. If you think about it, most people do it regularly although they may not be open about it. For example, golfers are incredibly self-critical of their performance and whatever standard they are, they constantly think of new things to do to rectify and improve their game.

Similarly, we are constantly striving to be better people, thinking about human interaction and appearance, how we are perceived and how we could have behaved differently. Likewise parents will often try a new approach of discipline or praise and reflect upon the success. If it worked they will build upon it. If not, they will modify or change. It happens all the time.

Do you take the time to reflect on your behaviour at home and at work?

Therefore would it not be a good thing to create the environment at work wherein everyone is constantly reviewing his or her own performance and using this as the basis to *internally* motivate?

When we identify these ourselves we are likely to make a huge commitment to keep improving. We don't need to wait for others to do this for us. By constantly reviewing our own performance we will improve much more quickly than attending a training course.

We as human beings fundamentally know ourselves better than anyone else. We are the only ones who are privy to our innermost thoughts.

Anne Frank put it perfectly in her diary.

She wrote:

> *How good everyone would be if, at the end of each day they reviewed their own behaviour...weigh up the rights and wrongs... they would automatically try to do better at the start of each day and after a while, would certainly accomplish a great deal.*

In a working environment the words of Anne Frank remain incredibly powerful.

When we make a conscious effort to maximise the capacity of our brains and coach ourselves to reflect on our actions we certainly can 'accomplish a great deal'.

> *In one company, one manager I knew did this very well. So committed he was to improving that he developed and used a personal diary. After attending a meeting or conducting a feedback session he would spend five minutes jotting down some points he did very well and would use again. He also listed some things he did not do so well and made a note of what he could do differently. This enabled him to learn a lot. He had to be honest with himself.*
>
> *Sometimes this is very painful as, in order to review effectively, we have to relive some experiences that did not go very well at all. In reality it is much easier to forget and push them to the back of the brain. The problem with this of course is that we don't learn as much.*

It is definitely worth trying. The choice is yours!

Can you imagine that if you wrote down the things you do within your role and then regularly reviewed them, in terms of things that have not gone well and gone well, how much better you would become?

You would come up with specific learning and actions and you would be learning every day rather than waiting for the next course or performance review meeting with your manager.

- How well did I conduct that one-to-one?
- How well did I facilitate that team meeting?
- How well did I deliver that presentation?
- How well did I serve that customer?
- How well did I greet the customer?
- How well did I build a rapport with the customer?
- How well did I make the sale?
- How well did I contribute today?

You can simply change the questions to reflect your own personal circumstances. Be your own toughest boss.

You then simply need to ask yourselves two questions:

- What has not gone well that I need to improve?
- What has gone well that I can learn from?

This can be a mental or written process, although it is important that you set aside some time to acknowledge the action you need to take (based on the not-gone-well list) and the specific learning (based on the gone-well list).

Of course, if you have the right environment this can be done at the individual, team and activity levels. It can also be done in your personal life.

Summary

Training will remain a vital part of people development. However, it is becoming increasingly apparent that most learning takes place within the daily activity. The best companies apply the lessons from the training course. People have explained that they learn through experience. They understand what is working for them and what isn't.

Companies need to start recognising the value of creating an integrated learning environment. The unerring reliance on HR professionals to develop people implies that people are unable to develop themselves. The traditional approach is too formalised and reliant upon standards to manage performance. It also happens too far away from the customer and daily challenges, which dilutes the intended impact. Great teams are developing trusting environments where people are able to realise their full potential. When the internal culture allows, people, from my experience, contribute a great deal.

Try incorporating the following two questions into everything you do (one-to-ones, team meetings, feedback sessions, performance management, appraisals).

- What has not gone well that we need to improve?
- What has gone well that we can all learn from?

The best can see the potential of experiential learning. It is faster and more relevant to what people do. Customers benefit and training costs lessen. People are engaged and therefore contribute more *and* become more loyal.

Practical actions to understand and learn about people development

- Try asking people you know professionally and personally for some feedback.

- Review your current coaching and development strategy. Are your internal/external providers bringing a return on investment? Are they helping you make a sustainable change?

- Write down your weekly achievements and set yourself goals for the following week. Outline areas for development and learning to build on.

- Review the amount and quality of feedback you give to others. It's important to do this to increase engagement levels.

- Review the amount of coaching that exists within your company. If there isn't enough then look to build this into managers' roles so it becomes part of the daily routine.

- Look at your leadership style and consider the pros and cons. Use this as the basis to build on your strengths and develop your weaker areas.

- Listen to every bit of feedback you receive, whether at work or in everyday life. It was always said for a reason and therefore should not be dismissed. Use feedback as an opportunity to learn and improve.

- Set up your own personal learning diary to identify how you can make improvements.

- Contact Understanding and Learning to discuss a roll-out of a connect survey at your company.

Understanding quality

What I love about the lads is that if there's somebody messing things up or turning the atmosphere sour, the players sort it out themselves; I don't have to bother about it. If people are not pulling their weight, they'll get dug out by the rest of the team because they're not going to have their lives, and their families, jeopardised. That's what a good squad should be about.

Peter Taylor, Manager of Leicester City

How people feel makes a big difference to the quality of their work. In the eighties and nineties it used to be the management of quality; however, increasingly, it is now about the quality of management that is differentiating the best companies. Are we creating the right conditions for our team players to contribute?

Is it management of quality or quality of management?

In many contact centres, coaches can contribute hours listening in to telephone conversations and assessing the quality of calls against the standard and comparing the results between teams and sites. In some large contact centres, whole teams are dedicated to this activity in an attempt to achieve objectivity and consistency. This approach ensures that the weekly report to management shows good figures for their teams on an ever increasing scale. All this activity adds much cost and little value to the customer, hardly any real improvement to the process or systems, but the numbers look good.

In the future, measuring the transaction and the interaction will be vital to differentiate customer care, but the key is to measure the right things. How the management team use these measures to drive performance will increasingly become essential. Creating the environment where teams take responsibility, are learning from one another, challenging poor performance and where the coach works within the team is the way forward. The best build quality into the work, reducing costs and building enthusiasm into their teams.

Motivated players and their impact on quality

Every company wants its people to be motivated. They are more likely to be enthusiastic, more helpful to customers, more productive, sell more and are less likely to pretend to be ill. It is not surprising, therefore, that there has been an influx of training interventions within companies to hit this issue head on.

Have you ever been on a 'Motivation' training course or conference and left feeling less motivated than before you went? In series one of the BBC's classic comedy 'The Office', this was outlined in an incredibly humorous way. The writers Ricky Gervais and Stephen Merchant tackled this. In one episode they showed David Brent (Gervais' character) as a motivational training 'guru'. His technique was to try and motivate people by using lots of energy, buzz words and Tina Turner's 'Simply the Best'. The more he said the less engaged everyone became.

> *I was once delivering some training in a conference auditorium and in the room next to us, all I could here was chanting, cheering, shouting and laughter. When I looked on the door it became apparent the course was entitled 'Motivation Skills'. We broke for coffee at the same time and these very upbeat trainers began marshalling the troops into a long line to form a human train. One of the trainers then said, "Right guys...before coffee let's all hold onto the person in front of you and sing 'The Loco-Motion' as loud as you can through the conference centre grounds...then we can have coffee...Come on!"*

This is a classic type of what I would call 'RAH RAH RAH' training. Did it motivate people? It motivated some, but not enough.

There are always a couple of extroverts who loved the idea of singing 'The Loco-Motion', but the majority looked horrified. In fact, on their return I overheard one of them say *'I need a brandy, not a coffee'*.

The consensus was that people were embarrassed and uncomfortable and that it was a very childish approach. It is incredibly naïve that people signing off money for such courses think that you will receive a return on investment.

Has the recent training course given you the return on investment that you were expecting?

Has it changed anything?

Choosing to contribute

Can you be motivated by anyone else? I have asked this question to a lot of people and the vast majority believe that others can motivate you. With this in mind, consider this...Without force, can anyone motivate you to do something that you don't want to do? Most people answer 'NO' to this question. The reality is, of course, that others can stimulate you to motivate yourself. They can't make you sell more or to be more enthusiastic. You do that. You choose to contribute enthusiastically, or not. This has an impact on the quality of your activity.

In everyday life, motivation for things is very often on our minds. We say things like, *I need to eat more healthfully, stop smoking, go to the gym* and *decorate the bedroom*. It often causes us a lot of inner guilt and it is sometimes very difficult. The reality is that we only ever achieve these things when we find the inner motivation to do so.

My wife once said after watching BBC television's 'Changing Rooms', *"Right...that has inspired me to get the bathroom decorated."* Her words were very true. The programme had given her some inspiration, but the choice to actually carry out the act of decorating would be found within her inner motivation.

Human beings who are always very positive, energetic and enthusiastic are a rare commodity. People like Sir Alex Ferguson (the Manchester United football club manager) and Sir Steve Redgrave (the former Great Britain Olympic rower) are amazing characters. They consistently demonstrate a kind of inner motivation that is incredibly inspirational to others. They keep going when the chips are down and do not accept second best. This motivation to achieve must come from within. You cannot coach that!

Do you have the drive to deliver the very best results?

In companies there are many outside influences that challenge your internal motivation. These include relationships with colleagues and managers, negative colleagues, boring jobs, too many rules and a lack of support and involvement. Therefore the choice for companies is two-fold. They can challenge the motivation problem, using motivation training courses, or they can address the deeper cause of motivation issues.

Traditional-age thinkers deploy the former method. They often believe that people are the problem and that they need motivating! Conversely, digital-age thinkers believe that motivation must come from within the human being and that companies have a responsibility to create interesting roles, a collaborative and supportive management team and more trust. If this is achieved the likely scenario is that people will be able to choose to be motivated with much greater ease. They will contribute enthusiastically and achieve a great deal more. Meanwhile, the traditional-age thinker will be busily arranging dress-down Fridays and fancy dress days. Have you ever sat on a bus in a Mickey Mouse costume? At the end of the day the best costume wins a prize!

> *I was in one company where the managers were in a two-hour meeting to organise a series of monthly motivation events. They were brainstorming potential ideas to create some fun in the team. There was going to be an all-white day to coincide with Wimbledon. The players in the team would dress in all white. On another day players in the team would dress up in red for Valentine's Day. The whole activity was adding no value whatsoever. All the advisors on the phone wanted was for the managers to be solving their problems, not brainstorming motivation ideas.*

Delivering customer experiences

Unless we care our thinking can never change. The measures, the reward, the control, etc. will reflect an uncaring experience for customers. Do customer advisors care enough to deliver quality in front of customers?

> *A consultant colleague of mine was asked to review how customer-centric their company was. To determine this he conducted a full internal audit of the customer service operation. He found that the managers said that it was a very customer-focused company to work for. However, he also learnt that the Customer Advisors never mentioned customers. He asked them what they considered their job to be. The generic answer was that they were there to 'take calls and hit internal targets'.*

Lots of Senior Management communication and corporate literature talks about the company's vision, mission and values. They always include the customer somewhere, yet when you get to 'where the rubber hits the road' – the people who talk to customers - I often see and feel a huge disconnection between these words and the reality.

The fact is that these words mean very little to people who work for the company unless they feel evidence right through the hierarchy. If there is a gap, some people lose interest and become disheartened whilst others become cynical. People have told me that they often *'go to work, do their job and go home'*.

Quality and job descriptions

When reading job (role) descriptions, middle management roles always include the customer in them.

> *As a young manager, I was given the opportunity to 'lead, motivate and manage a group of Team Managers to deliver the highest quality of customer service, to build loyalty and support the company in generating increased revenue'. That was the general flavour, and as a people- and customer-focused character I was thrilled at being given this opportunity.*
>
> *After doing the role for three months disillusion set in. There was very little need for inspiring, leading and motivating and more for controlling, managing and checking work. There was even less time for delivering the 'highest quality of customer*

> *service'. Quality was in the job description but was not part of the daily activity.*
>
> *I was too busy printing and distributing 'stats' and disciplining people for spending too much time at the toilet! The only real customer experience coaching I was asked to do was to ensure everyone adhered to the customer script. In other words, I needed to ensure everyone said the same things at the same time to every customer! Our target was 98%. We regularly achieved this target.*

However an external company who surveyed the customers' perceptions and experiences provided a very different insight. They found that the customers were nearer the 50% mark in terms of their satisfaction.

Senior Management was horrified. They cascaded their disappointment through the channels and the operational managers were the main targets. As a result, the managers had options. They could tighten controls or they could review their whole approach to satisfying and measuring customer satisfaction. Many opted for the former traditional-age approach. This involved extra coaching and forceful communication that everyone had to be more customer-focused. However, without getting to the root cause, the problem continued!

Taking a leap of faith and delivering quality

The solution is a review of the approach to the running of the operation. Half-measures and token gestures are not enough. Positive change requires a leap of faith and real action. Customers are getting a raw deal and customer advisors are disinterested because they are just taking calls and saying the same thing to every customer.

There is rarely any attempt to make the emotional connection and those who attempt to do so are branded as problems. Extra coaching will fail because the actual customer service delivery process doesn't change. Even if it does change, it is replaced by another solution that has been designed by the same people with the same thinking. These changes are normally made by people who do not talk to customers.

Are you ready to change things?

Roles (not job descriptions) need to change to include reference to the customers' experiences. People need to be recruited who 'like' customers. Leaders need to continue talking about customer experiences. Any company can deliver basic customer service but the complete customer experience is the combination of customer service and all the other teams within the company working together to resolve organisation failures. In the best companies everyone takes responsibility to improve the internal processes to benefit the customer experience. Managers need to implement solutions that actually focus on quality and reflect the importance of customers. Customer experience can never be absent from the agenda. It needs to be discussed in every one-to-one and team meeting. Everyone needs to focus on quality, individually and collectively.

Likewise, traditional budget targets need to be kept away from people satisfying customers. They can confuse the issue and focus people on the wrong measures. People doing the work simply need to view their role as satisfying customers and feeding back improvements when customer satisfaction is delayed or not possible. In addition, they must challenge themselves to improve. Managers can continue to measure the numbers but they become an outcome rather than the 'driver'. This approach builds quality into the end result for customers.

In order for this to work effectively we need to start trusting people and giving them the quality processes and systems to do the job. To make a quality cake the ingredients need to be of the highest quality. It is hard to make a fruit cake when you do not have any fruit. No amount of coaching will help the end result. Showing me a better way to mix the ingredients does not motivate me when the main problem is that I do not have any fruit! We need to focus on consistent and sustainable capability improvement.

> It's all about omelettes and eggs. No eggs, no omelette. It depends on the quality of the eggs.
>
> In the supermarket, you have eggs class one, class two, class three. Some are more expensive than others and some give you better omelettes. So when the class one eggs are in Waitrose and you cannot go there you have a problem.
>
> **José Mourinho, Chelsea manager the day before he lost his job**

We all converse with people very effectively at home without the need of a script, so why is one necessary at work? It is patronising to human beings and leaves customers with a feeling of indifference. We need to measure the right things in the right places and create the environment where people are seen as doing different roles rather than senior verses subordinate.

Feeling valued by others

We all need some recognition from others from time to time. A thumbs-up, pat on the back or a verbal compliment about how we look can do wonders for our short-term confidence and self-esteem. Even showing interest in your team's day-to-day activity can show people that you value them.

Similarly, people never fail to acknowledge how it feels to be told they are doing a great job by a colleague, manager or customer. The problem is that this recognition we crave is very often a rarity in companies. It is very often something you only get in a formal setting. It needs to be built into the company's way of working. It should not be over-used but delivered consistently when deserved.

Managers should constantly be looking for behaviour and achievements that deserve some credit. Traditional-age thinkers are all too often searching for the negative and miss countless opportunities to value contribution. When they do give praise it is very often for something *major* and for something that detracts from purpose.

> In one company, field-based employees were measured on how many jobs they did in a day. One team member completed far more than anyone else in a six-month period. Senior managers came to visit him and in one month he won the prestigious employee of the month award. He was given some vouchers for his efforts and placed on the management fast-tracking programme.
>
> On speaking to his colleagues in a review meeting, I made reference to his efforts. They looked disgruntled. When I explored why, I was made aware that he was not completing jobs, and rushing customer contact. Because the planning systems were not very sophisticated, managers had no way of knowing.

This is a classic example of how measuring the wrong things can set us up for devaluing the majority in favour of a few individuals cheating the system.

Feedback still carries some stigma. Hard-nosed experienced managers often refer to it as 'soft and fluffy'. It is considered of secondary importance. *'We are here to make money and do our jobs'* is the kind of comment frequently heard. Digital-age thinkers, on the other hand, recognise the sustainable benefits of creating the environment where people feel valued. The company makes money; the customers are happy and people in teams do more than their job. They acknowledge that building this into everyone's role increases morale, productivity and customer satisfaction, while at the same time reducing costs.

How often do you give positive feedback to others?

In order for people in teams to feel valued the best leaders make sure that they are listened to, involved, supported and get regular feedback and recognition. These do not need to be manager-led initiatives, but part of everyday life. They make it feel natural and consistent, rather than something that is separate and only done in a formal setting.

Continuously improving the capabilities of teams

One of the best Team Managers I ever came across would just make himself visible. He didn't spend all day sitting at his desk checking quality; he would be among his teams. He would sit next to them while they were on a call to a customer and take a blank piece of paper to jot some points down. At the end of the call he would say something brief, precise and positive. Additionally, he would always be listening to his team's customer interactions as he walked by. If he heard something good, he would give them thumbs-up to acknowledge them. He would then write it on a team communication board for everyone to see and learn. He was a digital-age thinker who truly created the environment where team players were valued. His team didn't pretend to be ill. They didn't cheat the system. They didn't fob customers off. They felt valued and they came to work.

I would call the above manager a 'capability manager'. They constantly work towards improving capabilities (people, processes, technology) by ensuring players have what they need in order to perform their role. For example, if they use a computer then it is essential that the response time is to a high standard. Additionally, if there are barriers in the way to satisfying customers, the capability manager works towards removing them. Quality is ongoing and never stops for these managers.

If you are not doing the actual activity, what are you doing to help the people who are?

Some managers do not focus on helping their teams. They spend more time enforcing rules and standards and do not look at ongoing improvement. The best managers are never too busy to look for improvement. They make sure that it is part of everyone's daily activities. They set off looking to solve problems so that the team and the customer benefit.

In one company, a capability manager I knew worked tirelessly to support the insurance department. Claims were on the increase, and demand to contact the insurance team meant front-line customer advisors had to wait in a queue before speaking to them.

As a consequence hold times and average handling time increased.

The traditional-age thinker would have endless meetings to agree a plan of action to improve the 'metrics'. The digital-age capability manager worked with the department to share/shift resources, explore at the front-end why claims were increasing and make changes to the overall process (using the knowledge of the front-line and insurance advisors).

Working across departments to deliver quality results

Senior and middle management can spend a whole day, week or month on fine-tuning their political 'spin' techniques. Self-preservation, one-upmanship and glory hunting remain paramount in companies, with many managers having an unerring appetite for gaining 'brownie points', usually at the expense of someone else. Are you playing games at work?

'Watching your back' syndrome is commonly accepted within many companies. People will cover tracks, keep records of events and try and trip people up, to self-preserve and defeat the opposition. The problem is that this so-called opposition is generally someone who works within or outside your department. All too often the lack of trusting relationships is holding companies back. Even when departments are interdependent they operate in silos. There may seem to be five companies within one company.

Sales and service departments provide one of the most obvious examples. In one company I implemented a change programme in both areas and the amount of animosity that existed was like nothing I had seen before. This was not visibly between the management teams, but between the sales and service advisors.

They blamed the other for 'all evils' and could not acknowledge the other in any other way than as a 'problem'. The people in both departments were great people. They had just been allowed to latch on to the 'us and them' scenario. The main problem was that although the roles obviously overlapped, no one had ever tried to understand the other. The sales teams were measured on sales conversion rate. The customer service teams were measured on customer satisfaction. If both teams didn't hit their targets they were placed on action plans. They were pulling in different directions.

It was only when there was willingness to understand and acknowledge each other's difficulties was there a sign of improvement. Taking time to understand others is the starting point for any conflict resolution, but someone has to start listening first.

Are you working with or against other departments?

The customer had to be placed at the centre of everything and dialogue had to take place regularly to review and improve. The progress was gradual but sustainable. Relationships improved and both departments improved their performance.

Demonstrating individual values

The role of the manager is changing. The values such as trust, respect and understanding do need to be lived more consistently. Watching your back all day wastes time. No one dare make a decision or take responsibility and everyone forgets the purpose. The customer almost disappears into a distant memory. Politics clouds people's judgment. It becomes so much fun for some that they pride themselves on improving their 'spin' at the expense of anything else.

Do you partake in internal politics? If so, why?

This silo mentality has not been helped by functional structures within a hierarchy. Specialisation and top-heavy operations result in 'too many chiefs'.

> *I was in one company and one of the employees said, "There is an unhealthy imbalance between the people managing the honey bees and the people making the honey." Unfortunately, the bees making the honey were being stung every day and they didn't like it!*

Working collectively to deliver results

The best recognise the benefits of working together to deliver quality. Leaders design the company around the customer. If the customer is at the heart of everything then, managers' roles and responsibilities will become interdependent. The requirement will never change, but people will contribute in different ways to allow the achievement. In other words sales will find it very difficult to achieve their targets without working *with* service and vice versa.

One advisor worked in sales and service in the same company. He told me, *"The people are the same, the managers are the same; but no one is prepared to listen and talk about how we could co-operate and improve things."*

Do your interdependent teams understand each other?

One way to do this is to involve the teams to measure regularly their interdependent teams or departments. Teams need to agree the common questions. The types of questions would include taking these ideas under consideration:

- Their willingness to take the time to help others
- Having pleasant, friendly and polite team players
- The speed with which requests/actions are followed up
- The ease of contacting the team
- The quality and accuracy of their work
- Their knowledge to offer advice and support to the customer
- Taking ownership of the problem and doing what they agree to do
- Seeing the problem from the customer's point of view
- Their understanding of each individual's overall responsibilities
- Their overall contribution to supporting individuals in their roles

The managers will then have some raw data that they can share with one another. The responses may be emotional, but it requires adult behaviour, lots of dialogue, understanding and compromise. Then and only then can everyone gain a fuller picture of reality. Teams see this happening and change their perception. 'Us and them' is gradually worn away because everyone understands and recognises the benefits of supporting one another.

Challenging to bring about fundamental change

Education theory often refers to the words of Plato and Aristotle to illustrate how human beings learn. Plato believed in 'empty-head' theory that assumed individuals essentially have brains that require filling in order to reach their potential. This 'filling' process requires an external party to pass on knowledge and expertise. It is often referred to as the 'polytechnic' approach. Conversely, Aristotle argued that individuals already have 'full heads' and that the role of another party is to provide people with information that they can then choose what to do with it. This is often referred to as the 'university' approach.

Plato's work is obviously outdated in modern day society, particularly in the Western world. In the UK we live in a democracy, and this environment in which we live is the predominant reason why people feel able to challenge things for change. We have seen evidence of this in terms of gay rights in the UK. Gay couples are now able to be in a civil partnership. People have a voice and if they keep going they can change things. Social media has helped teams, companies and even countries to make fundamental changes to their working practices.

In companies, however, it appears that much of Plato's thinking is 'alive and kicking'. The true cultures of many companies imply that people should 'put up or shut up'. This is never communicated as bluntly as this but managers will still hold forums and send out communications. They encourage 'suggestion schemes', and tell everyone that they are very important. The sad reality is, however, that many people do not *feel* important.

The issue with forums is that they are so formal. I even know of managers who have vetted the questions prior to its commencement. During forums the manager holds the corporate line, using lots of spin and jargon. The attendees sit nervously and speak only when it is their turn. There is no dialogue and if someone dares to show too much emotion or speaks too often, you can feel the annoyance of the senior managers.

The manager usually ends the session by taking actions away that they can or will do something about and everyone goes back to their own jobs. It is another example of 'us and them', where the power and knowledge remain in the hands of a very small minority.

Challenging things to bring change

The solution requires a fundamental shift in thinking. However, implementing some practical shifts can have lasting benefits. The starting point is for some leaders and managers getting off their pedestals and recognising that they just do a different role. This is vital because thinking drives behaviour.

Some people think that men are better drivers than women are. If something happens on the road, some automatically say *'bloody woman'* even without full knowledge as to the gender of the other driver. This is because how you think generates emotion (in this case negativity about women's capability as drivers) that then stimulates actions. The thinking can be incredibly ingrained.

We should be removing barriers and encouraging people to challenge. One manager said that he always surrounds himself with the ones nobody else wants. He says, "*Opinionated people come up with the best ideas. Although it sometimes gets heated - there is a respect and a unity. There is no hidden agenda.*" This manager is a digital-age thinker. He doesn't always have to be right and genuinely wants challenge in his team.

Are you afraid of what you will hear?

Traditional-age thinkers would view this environment as one in which there was disobedience and that the manager needs to regain control.

However, so ingrained is our thinking that many can't afford to disagree. They do this for an easy life or because they really need the work. They have a mortgage to pay and debts to pay off. Therefore it implies that many people have either apathy towards work and/or are living in fear. Both these negative emotions are far from conducive to creating stimulating experiences for people and customers. If you are frightened then it is difficult to smile at customers.

> *I recently heard, through a friend, an example that illustrates very clearly how traditional-age thinkers disapprove of challenge. She told me that the best people manager in her company was very outspoken in team meetings and would often challenge his manager.*
>
> *On one occasion he challenged the fact that he wasn't getting any one-to-one development. After the meeting he was sent an internal memo that he needed to sign and return to his manager. It was a written warning for his attitude!*

In some companies and teams people told me that they were simply not allowed to challenge what senior people say or ask questions to clarify understanding.

Do you encourage your teams to challenge?

Senior managers hold meetings but many do not give people time to ask questions. Encouraging teams to ask a question when they do not understand is an enlightening experience. As a manager you will not always like the questions. You will get some pretty honest feedback at times and you might go through phases of self-doubt. However, human beings do not have 'empty-heads'. They are intelligent and have valid opinions. When teams ask questions it is normally because they are interested and this should be encouraged. Even better, build questions into the day-to-day work so that quality is continually challenged.

Do you encourage your teams to ask questions and raise concerns?

Creating a challenging environment builds trust, team-play, understanding and learning. It must be done with respect for others' feelings and should always support your purpose.

Summary

Checking quality with no learning is a pointless and inefficient approach to running operations.

In their quest for consistency, companies create quasi-scientific standards that provide numbers for analysis. They try and turn something that is inherently emotional – *delivering an engaging customer experience* - into something that is largely transactional.

When standards are created, I generally see robotic workforces who stick rigidly to the rules. There is little room for creativity and people soon lose any sense of enjoyment or pride in their work. In short, people lose motivation. They are not allowed to use their brains!

Delivering quality is essential if companies are to differentiate. This cannot be achieved through a pre-defined standard, which has been created by managers. It needs to be a constant and fluid process where the measures are focused on customers and players/teams set about improving quality by exercising creative solutions.

In order for the above to happen it is essential people are trusted. We cannot continue to allow traditional-age thinkers to control how players behave and interact with customers. They are intelligent human beings. We must encourage them to challenge and we need to provide feedback to let them know we value them.

You never know...customers might even enjoy speaking to a real person, who is motivated and feels valued!

Practical actions to understand and learn about quality

- Ask your teams what could be done to improve the customer experience.

- Ask your teams what they need to deliver improved customer experiences.

- Ask what improvements you have implemented this week.

- Review your contribution regularly and ask yourself what value you are adding.

- Review the amount of time you are spending at your desk. Are you writing too many reports?

- Review how much time you are spending in team meetings.

- How much time are you spending on email? Try talking to people instead.

- Try and challenge behaviour that it is not in line with the changes you are attempting. Consistent behaviour that is not in line with your approach can really hinder the change process.

- Identify who in your teams care enough about solving problems, and find ways to involve them in finding the best way forward. Often they are close to the actual work.

- Implement a key-dependency survey of your cross-functional teams to understand the company problems.

Understanding knowledge

The real key to high performance is combining individual talents through shared understanding and 'hidden' tacit knowledge gained through intense company sociability. Innovation depends on creativity. A key factor in creativity is sociability. Generating and managing tacit knowledge through colleague sociability will be a major challenge.

Professor Richard Scase, University of Kent

These days, there is more and more information/data available for customers, and players in teams learn from a variety of sources. With the internet you can search internationally for the best deal. It is possible to use an iPhone app to search for the best deal in your local community. If you need a product now you can sit in the comfort of your own home or on the move and order it online to collect at the retail outlet of our choice a few hours later. Cars are still cheaper in Europe than they are in the UK. We now live in a world where products and service can be delivered anywhere at cheaper cost.

There is certainly more access to knowledge but often little understanding. Human capital within companies is not just about knowledge. Do team players want to share their knowledge? The social interaction with customers/teams and the emotional connection players choose to make with their work will increasingly be the differentiating factor within award-winning companies. On a daily basis, individuals within teams make the choice to share information and their experiences. Some choose not to!

Creating the environment, where, through dialogue, players can listen and learn from one another and be creative, will be a differentiator. We waste a lot of time in management meetings in debate when we should be developing improved understanding, through dialogue. In a world where everyone is mobile and does not always need face to face contact, it is even more important. The digital-age future will see managers having a few key vital measures that are well understood by everyone, with meetings focused on team purpose, and reports kept to the bare minimum.

Explicit and tacit knowledge

It is well documented that knowledge management owes its inspiration to the work of the philosopher Michael Polanyi and the Japanese organisation learning 'guru' Ikujiro Nonaka. Both of these theorists argued that knowledge has two forms: explicit and tacit. Explicit knowledge is the obvious knowledge found in manuals, documentation and company intranets. Increasingly, this is easy to access and easy to use. In some companies time has been spent documenting this knowledge. This has been useful to ensure that standard information is available to minimise errors. For example, employees can obtain information about a new product at the touch of a button, via the internet - so can the customers! These days, when you need information, you can obtain it fast. These days many of the answers to problems are on the internet and not inside people's heads! Technical people often indicate that some of the answers to their problems could be found on Google, the internet search engine. Forums have been created in many industries where experts, who often have no established relationship with you, can easily and quickly be found, often providing the answer to your problem free. Yes, free! Giffgaff, the O2 driven social media mobile company, and BTCare have their own customers providing service to other customers for free. The knowledge is out there already - we just need to get people collaborating.

Implicit or tacit knowledge is found in the heads of company employees. The employees make daily decisions on whether to share the knowledge or not. Many believe that this is the glue that holds a company together. Every single person has more information in their head than they can write down. Every single person does things and they don't even think about it. Successful companies create the environment where people want to share the knowledge about what they did and why. They learn a lot! Due to the atmosphere and culture within some companies, tacit knowledge is more difficult to access because of the choices that people make.

> *I was in a company where the manager encouraged openness and the sharing of mistakes. The team learnt much during this period. We hit our targets and we developed one another. We were having fun and this helped us be more creative. Some months later the manager changed and the whole atmosphere changed. Within a few weeks no one was sharing anything, we were not having fun and we were not hitting are targets! We had stopped sharing the knowledge.*

During the late 1990s, knowledge management increasingly became a key topic. Often this was left in the hands of the systems people to design systems to be able to capture information. For knowledge management to work successfully, the following three key components need to be built into everything that we do.

Many companies now have systems and technology in place to help teams learn and to measure the capabilities of their people. We have the technology; all we need now is enthusiastic players who have the collaborative environment around them to help them want to contribute.

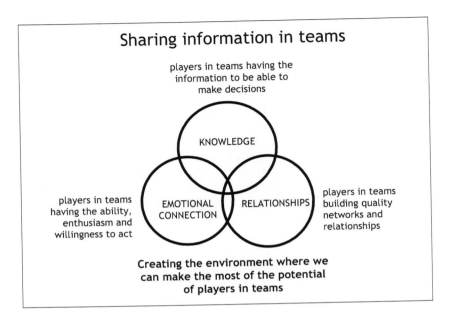

Sharing information in teams

players in teams having the
information to be able to
make decisions

KNOWLEDGE

players in teams
having the ability,
enthusiasm and
willingness to act

EMOTIONAL
CONNECTION

RELATIONSHIPS

players in teams
building quality
networks and
relationships

**Creating the environment where we
can make the most of the potential
of players in teams**

Sharing information in teams

The first component, knowledge, is increasingly causing difficulties for people in teams and companies. Product life cycles and intense competition mean that there are continual changes to the knowledge that people need to develop in order to satisfy their customers.

In some cases, what people knew last year is no longer relevant. We live in times where new challenges are faced almost daily. Everyone has to keep learning and developing their skills. Technology will certainly help to create a knowledge environment but there is still something missing.

For knowledge to be shared, people need to invest in relationships, the second component. Spending time developing relationships with others is vital for trust to prosper. Taking the time to listen and understand is vital too.

Only through developing relationships will we create the conditions where we trust each other to share the knowledge that we have. This knowledge might be a mistake we have made. If you don't trust your colleagues then you are unlikely to share your mistakes openly. The future is uncertain and there will be many errors/mistakes made as we search for the right way. The key is to learn quickly and recover. The more people you know, the better opportunities there are to find the answer when you need help.

The final component is the emotional choice that people make to share their knowledge. On a daily basis we all have choices that decide our future. Players can be happy or sad. Players can choose to be enthusiastic or not.

In the wrong environment people choose to keep knowledge to themselves, in the mistaken belief that this protects them. In fact, this approach protects no one. Creating the environment where people share openly is the challenge for the next few years. Teams that create the right conditions and learn together just learn faster. If you are having fun you tend to stay for more. In these companies players are happier and customers can feel the warmth.

We cannot really carry on just delivering training and hoping that this will resolve our company's learning problems. We need to build the learning into the work and that takes time and trust.

Awareness of issues affecting customers

Many companies spend a lot of money on project resources to scope and implement major system and process improvement initiatives. These are sometimes essential. However, in having this resource it seems that companies miss many, many opportunities to gain access to vast amounts of real-time improvement possibilities.

How many companies truly know how their customers feel?

People who do the activity always have some excellent ideas about things that are not working and how they could be fixed. In other words, they know the problems and creative solutions to fix them. The problem is that some management teams do not truly recognise that people who do the activity are part of the improvement process and thus do not actively seek their implicit or tacit knowledge. As a result people carry on doing their jobs and leave their knowledge where it does not add any real value - in their heads.

Many of the improvements players in teams have shared with me are 'smaller things'. They do not require vast amounts of project resource. They are creative day-to-day things that really can make a big difference to the customer experience. There could be a minor system or call routing change. There could be a tweak to the marketing process or to a specific business process. Whatever the change, they can only be identified by the people closest to the customer.

Have you ever asked your people how customers are feeling?

The reality of doing this is that managers find out more in a thirty-minute chat than you would by analysing five hundred call monitoring forms. The problem with these is that they generally check a pre-defined standard that has been developed by a traditional way of thinking. Consequently managers only ever get some statistical measurement of the wrong things!

One hundred reasons why customers are not happy

In order to maximise the knowledge potential of teams, the best managers create the environment where players in teams can and do want to share knowledge. They build in feedback and improvement into players' roles so they recognise they don't just implement activity. Finally, managers encourage a digital-age way of thinking throughout their company. The leaders encourage managers to move away from just thinking about the process and setting up project groups to solve things. Some managers love projects – especially as it takes them away from the intense management of people. They see this as something that will raise their profile and probably means they don't have to have anything to do with customers for a while.

The challenge is on to build in solutions that actually involve and engage people at the front-line to share their tacit knowledge. The best leaders make it part of their role and not something that happens once a month in a forum. The purpose is to engage teams to think through the eyes of the customers, to enhance their experience. It creates opportunities for people to release their tacit knowledge to increase their engagement and that of customers.

During a contact with a customer many people hear and see things that need improving. Often they are so busy working that improvement is not built into the day-to-day work. When fully connected to their work the employees often know more than marketing about the customer problems and future plans.

One way to engage teams is to use the following method that I designed for a company that was having problems. The headings in bold can be used in any company.

As a customer I want to be able to:	Where are we now?	How does the customer feel?	How does the advisor feel?	Understanding why the contact
Pay my bill	You transfer me to billing	Frustrated by the delay	Anxious about the customer reaction	Give the responsibility to the first person who took the call

Pass this to your team managers and to your teams. Their role is to think in a very customer-focused mindset, by continually asking themselves the above questions. Their role is making a note of anything that occurs against your set processes and to consider how they and the customer feel. The key area is for them to then think of possible solutions to improve things quickly. I have also used this method in teams who are looking to improve the internal customer experience. With this method you can find one hundred improvement ideas very quickly.

When this is implemented well you can quickly engage teams to share their knowledge. They recognise that part of their role is to improve things and they respond because they feel valued. Subsequently, you are constantly improving things, due to the fact the people closest to the customer are telling you how customers feel and what can be done to improve things. Not all ideas will be implemented, of course. Sometimes there will be delays. People accept this if they understand why. The role of the manager is to facilitate the improvement process, maintain the momentum of the activity and feed back the reasons for any potential delays.

Quickly transferring best practice

Much of the above might well be 'best practice'. The challenge is to move this across the company quickly so everyone learns. The best practice will be continually evolving. Yesterday's best practice can easily become old news.

How long does it take to share tacit knowledge with other stores, departments or buildings?

Some information can be shared very quickly. However, the reality is that sometimes it takes ages. Why? It sounds straightforward enough. You may need some kind of a technological solution but not one that costs thousands. It doesn't need to be complex.

- Firstly you need to ensure that the environment is conducive to people wanting to share knowledge.

- Secondly you need to ensure that there is willingness amongst managers to share best practice and not to withhold knowledge. Some use knowledge as an opportunity to strengthen the knowledge/power base of their silo.

- Thirdly you need to implement a simple process.

To support this transition, the following two questions need to be built into everything that we do:

- What has not gone well that we need to improve?
- What has gone well that we can all learn from?

The answers to these questions need to be added to a central database that everyone can have access to. It would be managed by the team yet it would be used as the basis for team and individual discussion. Everyone can see what everyone else is suggesting as being 'best practice'. Some ideas may be discarded, some will be utilised. This ensures a constant sharing of knowledge and creativity. It breaks down silo mentality and replaces it with open learning that engages interdependent teams. Managers need to ensure that ideas are constantly discussed and remain firmly on the agenda to improve things.

> *In one company they were having problems with the way that they worked across teams within their company. I was asked to help them change their internal culture. I encouraged them to ask themselves the questions discussed above. I changed the format of their team meetings. I encouraged teams to solve their problems. It wasn't easy to implement. I asked people to be open with one another. Along the way we developed the process and eventually people were sharing their views with the chief executive using the same format. Cynical people became open and changes began to happen. The process was used throughout the company and their people became connected and enthused about the company and the contribution that they could then make.*

The problem with some companies is that they are too concerned with what their competitors are doing or have done. They often identify this as best practice. In reality, if managers choose to adopt their ideas, then they are duplicating 'old' ideas. They may have worked at that time, but they are now outdated. Maximising the creativity of the people you have is the key and the answer to many problems are already within your company.

Are you replicating competitors' methods?

By creating an environment that engages people to contribute, companies can become differentiated quickly. This is because there is so much creative energy across the company. Imagine the scenario where everyone in your company is always thinking about how they can improve the customer and people experience. Imagine how much people learn. Imagine how much fun you would be having. Imagine how much money you would save.

Reporting and insight for management

This is a key aspect of many managerial roles. It can take time and is very often an historical piece of work that adds minimal value to the purpose.

I spoke to a manager recently. He is a digital-age thinker who is well respected by his teams for his people- and customer-focused approach. We had a discussion about reporting and how much time he spends on report writing and analysis. He was disillusioned by the whole process.

He told me that every morning when he got to work, he would be handed the departmental 'stats' for the previous day. He would see his colleagues studying them and then hold a meeting with their team managers. He said that he would look at them

> *because he felt obliged to, but had no idea what he was supposed to do with them. All he could think was...what had they to do with customers?*

In one of the meetings to discuss the previous day's performance, the manager listed lots of numbers against target. For example, "Average handling time was 350 seconds yesterday. Can you ensure that it is down to 320 seconds today please?" What was amazing in this, was that everyone just nodded and accepted it. There was no attempt to understand why it was 350. No-one asked the front-line what was going on yesterday. Everyone was just told to hit the target, today. In this company I could predict the problems would surface again tomorrow.

Do your reports help improve the customer experience?

This kind of day-to-day reporting is the worst kind. Everyone gets transfixed with hitting the number; there is no attempt to understand. This tunnel-vision approach is the product of traditional-age thinking. Digital-age thinkers believe that this approach is crazy. They just cannot see the value it brings, because it totally disregards the customer and the people satisfying them.

The above scenario could only have resulted in team managers going to their teams and telling them to be quicker on calls. When I investigated further I noticed that there was a link between this target and the company reward. Most of the people just obediently followed the order. Who loses out? The customer is obviously rushed. Problems remain unresolved, which generates further contact from customers. Customers become incredibly disillusioned and teams quickly get fed up as they can take little pride in their work and they are being shouted at by irate customers.

An alternative way of thinking

The digital-age solutions are at completely the opposite end of the spectrum. Managers need to maintain the customer at the heart of everything they do. When you think in a customer way, everything you do on a daily basis will be assessed in your own mind as to the value this is making to improve the customer experience. Before you engage in any kind of task at work, ask yourself whether it will add value. If the answer is no, then it is probably a waste of time.

Traditional-age thinkers love numbers and day-to-day management of them. Their mindset tells them that improving the numbers equates to success. They cannot see another way. Asking questions to challenge your existing thinking is one of the hardest things to do. Everything you have ever believed in is now being challenged. As a consequence of this, many people use their existing thinking to block anything new and justify old ways. This is one of the reasons why change is so difficult.

Letting go of the wrong measurements

When thinking is deeply entrenched people still have a choice to change or not. Likewise, attempting to change managers' thinking from traditional-age to digital-age can be equally as challenging. Imagine that a manager has in a ten-year period had many promotions and has been very 'successful'. They may have been successful using a style that is full of traditional-age thinking. Now imagine trying to change that person's mind and try another way. It is very difficult but it can be done. Mindsets can be changed by allowing people to experience things. Once people have seen a different way of doing things then they can change.

Is your thinking entrenched?

Reporting information for management is one of the most common areas traditional thinkers hate to relinquish. They often desire vast detail. They believe every scrap of knowledge about what is going on and what people are doing is essential. It enables them to cover tracks and prepare for every eventuality.

> *I recall month-end reporting being a very stressful period for all concerned. As an operational manager I would request updates from all the help-desk managers. I would wade through reams and reams of written analysis and pick out the main points and produce a departmental report. I would send it to the Head of Contact Centre, who would receive five in total. She would read them prior to her deadline and send them back with revisions and things to change, modify or improve. I would have to do this as absolute priority and send it back.*

It was a complete waste of time. The initial reports done by the help-desk managers must have taken them ages. In reality, only about 5% of their work was used. Secondly, the stuff I wrote was with very little commitment. It was historical and was not going to improve anything. It was a political piece of work to make our site look better than the others.

Does your reporting measure the customer experience from the customer point of view?

This really had nothing to do with improvement. It wasn't sharing best practice but was made up of an exaggeration of the good stuff and positive spin of the bad stuff to limit damage to our reputation. Everyone hated month-end. There was a tense atmosphere. It was always a major rush and nobody found it remotely engaging. This is another example of understanding and learning needing to be built into the everyday activity.

Listening to team players who do the job

The best leaders take time out to listen to the players who do the job. The former England football Head Coach, Sven Goran Eriksson, received vast amounts of criticism during his tenure in the role. He was accused of lacking passion and commitment, even when he is spotted at nearly every game and many of the players have shown him vast amounts of public support. It seems that most people believe that he is easily persuaded and lacks the strength to make his own decisions. One reason he has received criticism from the national media is that he allegedly consults senior players on team selection and tactics. Is this a bad thing? I think we must also remember that this is the man that picked Wayne Rooney when most pundits and football managers said he wasn't ready.

How often do you talk about the customer in your team meetings or company events?

The challenges of implementing Understanding and Learning

Digital-age implementation requires lots of energy, patience and belief in your teams. People must feel able to contribute. Digital-age thinkers take time to listen and in doing so receive a detailed insight into the real situation. They are in a much better position to make decisions and implement solutions. If they require the support of others they gain their commitment as they were involved in the decision-making process. Even better, the solution is sustainable as people protect solutions that they have created.

The fact is that people who do the job are the experts in their field. They have the knowledge. Digital-age thinking turns traditional methods on their heads. This is because it has a belief that other people can know more. No one individual has all the answers. People who think in this way do not feel vulnerable asking 'subordinates' for help, as they acknowledge people's value to the improvement process. Conversely, traditional thinkers do not acknowledge subordinates could know more. They think that they know best and like to control people's knowledge. Fear is the origin of this.

A mentor once told me that "creating the right environment where people can reach their full potential can result in people getting better than you...If that happens you have done a great job." Many traditional managers recognise this and subsequently promote people who will be compliant, often excluding talent for fear of them outperforming themselves.   Likewise, they don't actively seek knowledge from the people who do the job.   They don't appear to care about what they have to say.   They believe they should do their job and that is it.   Digital-age thinking builds this process into their daily activity.

How would you feel if someone who worked for you became better than you?

Creating a listening environment is easy if you think in a digital-age way.   It just comes naturally because you really do value the contribution people make.   You want them to reach their full potential and you care about them.   You also realise that by listening to them you can improve the customer experience, increase revenue and reduce costs. Teams working collaboratively together learn more, have more fun and in doing so come up with creative ideas that can differentiate their contribution.

> *The board were increasingly disillusioned with the customer experience external reports.   They stated that customers were not enjoying the experience when they called in for help.   This seemed strange to the board as all the reports they were receiving implied a wonderful time was being had by all.   The reality was that the reports being produced by middle/senior management were full of spin.   Also, the customer delivery process and its implementation were riddled with traditional thinking.*
>
> *As a result of their frustration the board turned up in the various contact centres and held informal chats with a cross-section. They were horrified by what they had learnt.   They found out the reality of the situation and as a result implemented regular direct contact with people 'who do the job'.   Another problem ensued, however.   As this process was formalised the traditional middle/senior management ensured that only traditional*

> customer advisors attended. *They were briefed before they went and stuck rigidly to the corporate line.*

No-one said creating digital-age thinking is an easy task!

Ask yourself, do you add value? Do you value the point of view of others?

Do you really listen or are you too busy thinking of your next question?

Promoting continual learning

Great teams and great individuals do not start out life being great. They become great because they are truly committed to a vision and purpose. They have a clear understanding of their role and required contribution. They then are open to the fact that they can get a lot better. They realise they need to keep learning. They love feedback and challenge themselves to improve.

We have seen many examples of this in the sporting arena. A few years ago Sachin Tendulkar, the Indian cricketer, broke the world record for scoring the most hundreds in international cricket. Yes, he had an incredible amount of natural ability, but he was far from the finished article when he entered the world stage at the age of sixteen years old. He and other great performers in their chosen fields have become great because they keep learning. Only when people allow themselves to believe they know it all do they fail. They fail because they have told themselves they do not need to keep learning. They become arrogant and lose desire, commitment and determination.

> *I recently spoke to an old colleague who was becoming incredibly disillusioned with his fellow managers. He said, "They are just settled and safe. They are just doing enough and sat watching their company pensions grow." The problem with this all too common situation is that if their energy levels are low you could*

> *accurately surmise that the teams and overall culture are lacking energy. You can also surmise that no one is learning anything. It is then that going to work becomes more of a boring ritual. There is a lot of monotony, and apathy soon becomes rife.*

Do you have energy and enthusiasm at work?

When you learn new things it gives you a lift. Your mind is being challenged and it can re-energise. We feel a sense of achievement when we acquire new knowledge that can improve our capability and quality of life. Without learning we become stale. Our minds get bored with the same stuff. They require stretching. In order to do this we need to acknowledge that everyone has the right to learn new things at work.

Traditional thinkers often believe that it is behaviour that needs changing and so managers often have more money spent on them. They get the high-profile executive coaching from the expensive consultancy. The problem with this is that it tends to re-affirm to these managers that their behaviour is fine and that they should carry on believing in themselves. However, the real problem is the work and how it is done. Everyone else doing the work knows exactly what the problems are. The problem is that no one asks them. If they do, they want the 'right' answer. If they don't receive the answer they expect then they accuse people of negativity and thus label them accordingly.

Maintaining the momentum of success

Promoting continual learning is an essential ingredient to maintaining momentum. We need to involve everyone in challenging themselves to get better. The environment is obviously the key to this.

Are you stretching yourself and your teams?

Managers need to recognise the contribution that people make. They need to learn that when connected, people will willingly share their knowledge. If not connected, they will keep it to themselves. This is not because they are selfish. It is because they do not feel it is their right to share their knowledge. They feel it is not wanted. If this is the case the company culture will suffer and you will never differentiate.

Leaders play an important part in inspiring and helping their teams share knowledge. The best leaders think about how the organisation is designed so that knowledge is shared and people are given the chance to contribute and make the most of their potential.

Successful businesses are unlocking the creativity and the special talents of everyone, encouraging creativity, helping people find the best way forward together. The best organisations are continually adapting and surviving.

Summary

Some traditional-age managers spend far too much time debating in meetings and reporting information. Many of them allow themselves to become totally immersed in information, whether it is month-end reports or daily statistics, which results in managers detracting from purpose. They lose sight of the customer and the teams who engage them.

In the digital-age world, managers become facilitators of knowledge. They do not need to control all information and knowledge but are intent on creating an understanding environment, where dialogue is paramount and collaboration is encouraged. They are determined to ensure that they listen to players in teams. They are then much more likely to choose to share their knowledge. Subsequently managers have a real-time understanding of the issues affecting customers and commit to sharing best practices quickly so that everyone continually understands and learns.

Practical actions to understand and learn about knowledge

- Consider talking less when holding team meetings. Become a facilitator and listen attentively to your teams in order to understand.

- Review the amount of time you spend debating with colleagues. Try and ensure you focus more on understanding people and situations through dialogue.

- Hold regular meetings with your team. Be visible and encourage teams to contribute ideas.

- When you stop for a break during a meeting, training, or presentation encourage the team to commit to making it back on time. For example, one way is to address the group and state, "Who thinks they can be back in 10 minutes?" The result is that everyone will say that they can. Once you have a team commitment, attendees are much more likely to take personal responsibility to be on time, as they will not want to let other players down. This can also be used when running teams – and it works.

- Ask yourself how quickly knowledge is transferred. Look to implement solutions that share learning across teams quickly.

- Take time out to reflect on your progress. During your day-to-day activities, build in team and individual reviews of progress. At the end of projects review what has gone well and not gone well.

- Do you listen to understand your colleagues?

- Are your people contributing to share their knowledge particularly when something goes wrong?

The focus for all roles in teams

Understanding motivation

Top executives are beginning to realise that no matter how good their technology needs to be in the 21st century, it is the quality of their people that matters the most. Keeping the right person in a company depends on a company's ability to capture the hearts and minds of its employees.

Susan MacDonald, The Times, May 25, 2000

There is increasing evidence that self-motivation (choosing to react/respond either positively or negatively) is the sustainable factor within companies. People are realising that they have a choice of how to respond to opportunities to contribute. Incentive schemes that devalue the work are a thing of the past. Whilst many in the western world are contributing – are they happy in their work? It is now time to move from compliance to sustainable commitment.

When an environment is created where players take responsibility for their feelings and contribution, it is possible to slash costs dramatically, increase revenue and improve customer satisfaction. In the best teams managers become facilitators. The team will naturally take the responsibility of leadership, coaching, motivation and assessment. Successful implementation sees the team challenge out inferior performance and bring with it superb opportunities for personal development.

Clearly, having leaders who can create this environment is essential and will be the challenge for companies as we develop the company capability.

Clear view of the company purpose

Having a clear view of the company purpose is a prerequisite for every company. How can we achieve anything in business if you do not know what you are trying to achieve? Everyone should know this; otherwise they cannot possibly understand how they fit in and contribute to the overall purpose.

Can you articulate the exact purpose of your company?

Ask your teams what they believe it to be. I can guarantee a hugely varied response that may shock! If the company purpose is unclear then there will be a high degree of fragmentation within the company. People will be driving in different directions and have a lack of clarity.

In everyday life, everything we do successfully must have a purpose. Whether it is cleaning the house, preparing a meal, watching TV or having a glass of wine, there is always a reason. If there wasn't we wouldn't do it. We would also very easily be able to tell someone what that is. Similarly, football managers have only one purpose. Everyone knows what it is. It is to win football matches. If they are not doing that he and his players are responsible. As the manager he can tinker with tactics and the system. He can change the team, change training methods and improve morale. Even though he tries all different methods the purpose has never changed.

It is important to point out that many creative solutions can be implemented. However, they must never detract from the overall purpose. They must be totally aligned. In companies, players need to know what the purpose is. This is predominantly the responsibility of regular and consistent communication from the leader. The same messages need to be transmitted over and over again, in different formats, until everyone knows what they are.

The very best leaders keep this simple and never detract. Even when the chips are down they continue to believe in what the company is about. Managers need to articulate the purpose so the message remains on the agenda. They need to engage in activities that only support the purpose. If something does not relate to purpose the team should not be doing it.

Do you get involved in tasks that do not add value?

The reality is that there is so often a huge disconnection between the company purpose and the daily activities that people perform. There is a lack of alignment, which leaves the strategic teams tearing their hair out. One of the problems is that traditional-age thinkers want to utilise old methods whereby people are controlled. If this is the case, people will never truly commit to the overall purpose. They will just recognise it is corporate language that is totally detached from reality.

Understanding the contribution

Once everyone understands the overall company purpose, people need to fully understand their role in achieving it. Roles need to be written that are closely aligned.

Are your team roles aligned with the overall strategy?

When roles are clearly aligned, then people will become much more committed and choose to contribute with enthusiasm. They do this because they clearly recognise the importance of their role in the overall success of the company. It increases individual responsibility and clarity. People know what their purpose is and they take pride in it. Without that, people feel confused and just engage in tasks with no purpose. They soon become bored. This is the breeding ground for negativity and cynicism.

This method is simpler than it often appears within companies. Lengthy strategic documents and too many people involved confuse the overall purpose. It leaves managers within the middle sector of the company with a very difficult task.

They first have to decipher the real messages through all the waffle and then attempt to make some links. As a result the links are generally vague which means the people actually doing the work are left with a confused purpose.

Often measures are just handed down from the directorate and managers use these as targets. These measures are easily measured and controlled. They can often detract from the overall purpose. The role of the leader is pivotal. He or she needs to be very clear in his/her mind what they really want to achieve. Remember the football manager's purpose.

Is your individual purpose clear?

The more simply it is communicated, the more easily people can connect to it and then understand their own individual contribution. The football players know the overall purpose. They also know that what they must contribute individually to enable it to be achieved. They must work hard, be open to learning, stick together, internalise systems and their role in them, stick to the plan and keep going even when things are not quite working out. There will be other things of course, but this highlights how a simplified purpose enables clarity surrounding individual contribution. If people do not contribute to the required standard this is easily identifiable by the manager, by the other players and by the individual himself. This enables greater transparency of the problems and means they can be quickly improved.

Enjoying the work

How many people truly love their job? From our own research it is clear that many do not. It is strange that many people stay within companies and in roles that they do not enjoy. Why?

It appears that many people generally crave security. It is an in-built need that varies in scale depending on the individual and their circumstance. Some people fear change and would stay in a role they do not enjoy rather than take 'a leap of faith'. To change the situation requires courage and people will often curb their desire by justifying that the 'grass isn't always greener on the other side'. Are you stuck in a rut? We spend so much time at work. It surely makes sense to make the most of it. It is not always as easy as that.

Human beings do have choices. It is too easy to say, 'Well, at least it is close to home', or 'I live for my weekends'. They are the soft option. They are protecting you from taking a leap of faith and doing something you want to do. The possibilities are endless. You could re-train in a different specialist area. You could transfer your skills elsewhere. Alternatively you could stay working where you are and take responsibility for making it more interesting. You could challenge things you are unhappy about. You could make your daily task more challenging and stretch yourself to optimise your performance.

How would you like to be remembered?

It remains the responsibility of every individual to generate their own motivation and to work with others to create an enjoyable environment.

> *In one company that I visited, the management team were really pleased as they had moved on many negative people. However, they did not change the way the company ran and so more people were becoming negative. They gave these people training on how they had a right to choose how they felt. They encouraged them to take responsibility. Oh dear, things were not improving and the customers were continuing to receive poor service!*
>
> *The management team met to find out why the negative people had not been identified last time! It is not always a people problem. What the managers should have been doing is spending time identifying what was making people unhappy. Of course, it was the work.*

It is too easy to blame everyone else for how you are feeling. People cannot make you feel de-motivated. They become an external influence that can be very powerful, but they do not actually de-motivate you. You have the choice to be de-motivated or to respond to any given external stimuli with enthusiasm. This is very much a key differentiating factor in companies.

What do you need in life to make you happy?

The best sales people I have ever met never cease to amaze me. They are so driven. They seize any potential opportunity to close a deal. They love the buzz and crave more and more. Yes, they get knocks. In fact they get more knocks than successes, yet they maintain their positive outlook and move on. They don't sulk or blame the customer for not buying. They have great belief and fall back on previous successes to keep them going. They don't need managers shouting at them. They do it because they enjoy it.

If you do not enjoy your job, why don't you work out why – and then do something about it. When you have done this - look at your choices. You can sulk and complain that it's not fair. Or, you can start taking responsibility for your own state of mind, energy levels and enjoyment. The latter is the harder option. It may take a while and you might have some tough times along the way. It is your choice!

Being involved in decisions

Many just accept that managers make decisions. We might not like them or even understand them but we accept that this is just the way it has always been.

Some managers are missing a trick here. In their many attempts to motivate their teams they are missing an understanding of one essential ingredient. Motivation is very much internally generated.

It is not external. In other words, there is no point in spending the money and wasting time sending teams on expensive motivation training to motivate them. Likewise, shouting "Come on, guys" every five minutes won't work either. This is because 'motivational' training and coaching do nothing if the recipient doesn't want to be motivated. Cynics in training courses do not believe anything will change. They wait to see what happens.

Do you let things affect your mood and behaviour?

We decide if we are going to be energetic, enthusiastic, happy, determined. Likewise, we decide if we are going to be miserable or sulky. No one else can make us if we don't want him or her to. For example, you will decide whether to take action when reading this book. You might read it and do nothing or you might take action.

However, it is the managers who predominantly create the environment. They create the emotional tone of the culture. If the culture is one where fear and control are rife, then the result is that most people are likely to be lacking motivation. Conversely, if the environment is trusting, supportive and involving, it is likely people will respond with enthusiasm. Asking the team their opinion and taking action can be very motivating.

The digital approach does not ensure motivation exists within the company, but it does play a major influencing role in a positive way. The choice does remain with the individual. One major influencing factor to people's motivation levels is the degree to which they are involved in changes that truly affect them. People crave a sense of control. They dislike decisions being made for them.

Some young children are exactly the same. They want to be independent. They want to be listened to. If they feel that this is not happening they let their parents know. The problem in companies is that most people do not show their frustration. If they do it tends to be within small groups of like-minded colleagues. This only serves to fuel negativity.

Similarly, people at work have a right to be consulted. They know their role better than anyone else and obviously will have a point of view when changes are imminent. If they are involved they may well come up with a better solution. As they were involved they will also be more committed to the change. They may still not like it but they will understand it and they will deal with it.

This approach breaks down the 'us and them' mentality. Everyone is working together and there is much more understanding. People feel that they are being treated as adults and will appreciate the empowerment. Subsequently it is likely that they will respond with enthusiasm. The frustrating thing is that this is not a difficult thing to do.

Can you imagine your teams being internally motivated just by

encouraging their contribution to decisions?

You would need to make team meetings an interactive dialogue process and move away from 'the manager monologue'. You need one-to-ones to be a two-way process.

Firstly, however, you may need to change the way you think. If you consider yourself to be superior or more important than others, then it will follow naturally in your behaviour that you do not involve other people or really listen. You probably don't value that others should have a view. You believe they should work and you should manage.

If you let them make some decisions, then you might consider yourself as being 'soft' and lacking strength. If this is the case you think in a traditional way. You will continue to try and motivate externally. You are only succeeding in patronising your teams, and you will never create a truly motivational environment.

Tools and methods to make the change stick

Directors have told me that the problem with so much training is that it rarely provides a return on investment. People in teams have told me that it can be enjoyable and help them to learn more about themselves. Nevertheless, all too often the subject matter is not relevant to the day-to-day activities that people do and is very rarely built into the work.

The Kirkpatrick model provides an illustration of the shortcomings associated with conventional training courses. It shows that there are four stages of evaluation. Some have suggested to me that many courses only ever achieve stage one and stage two.

Does training actually change the way that people work?

It remains remarkable that so many training companies (that only bring benefits in terms of stages one and two) are so regularly employed by companies to 'develop and motivate' people. They are 'expensive and they are nice to have'.

Training & Understanding & Learning

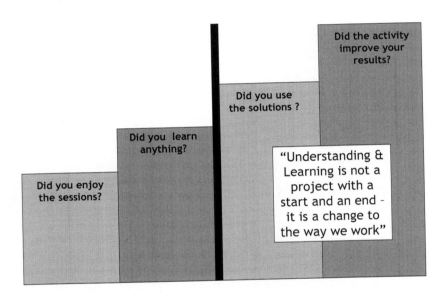

Did you enjoy the sessions?

Did you learn anything?

Did you use the solutions ?

Did the activity improve your results?

"Understanding & Learning is not a project with a start and an end – it is a change to the way we work"

The fact that HR often design material or recruit external suppliers may be an origin of the problem. This is not a slur on people who work in HR, but the fact that HR practice has not appeared to move on for such a long time. Various professional qualifications such as the Certificate in Training Practice (CTP) remain quite rigid and focus on enabling people who undertake the qualification to reach an approved standard. The problem is that the standard was developed years ago.

I once delivered a session to a group of operational managers. I received excellent feedback from most people except from the training manager who attended. He was very unhappy about my

> *delivery. I sometimes use an informal style whereby I stay seated. I also have my own opinions and share them.*
>
> *I do occasionally unwittingly hold a pen while talking and at times write on flip charts using a red pen. The training manager gave me lots of feedback about all that. Red pen is apparently aggressive, holding a pen is distracting and facilitators should invite other people's opinions and I should not share my own. I should be standing up (but not stand in front of visual aids).*

Much of what he said may be true. However, so ingrained was his thinking about standards that he could not let himself partake in the crux of the experience. The others were totally engaged and liked the alternative style.

Companies need to stop worrying about employing trainers who follow the rules. The best companies are employing trainers who can engage others from operational and supporting roles, as this will be essential for the future. Let us not become too obsessed with rules, and allow some creativity to flow. The real challenge is to build theory and new practice into the work.

In order for change to bring a return on investment, it must be linked to the roles people do and change the actual work. Then and only then, can the change really stick. Solutions and ways of working become natural when they are performed every day.

Does your training stick or do you need to repeat it again?

We have all lacked some motivation from time to time. The frequency of this can, however, be harmful to both our state of mind and how productive we are as human beings. Some people seem to revel in their lack of motivation. They seem to be forever moping about being negative about everything. Of course, none of it will be their fault. Their role in life seems like a very sorry existence. They often try to influence others to be just like them.

It is frequently too easy to lack motivation. It is the product of fear and laziness and is a sign of weakness. It implies that external factors can run people's lives and that we are not in control of our actions and behaviour. It is true that some external factors play a pivotal role in determining our motivation levels. Tragedy and serious emotional difficulties will affect the vast majority and reduce their motivation. This section is not going to cover such elements, but rather the everyday external factors that people often let ruin their day.

Coping with feedback

We live in uncertain times and change can be worrying for some people. When people receive feedback they respond in predictable ways. When you receive new information the natural and initial reaction may be one of <u>shock</u>. You may consequently allow your mind to quickly <u>deny</u> the validity of the feedback. You may tell yourself that the people providing the feedback do not understand and their less informed opinion can be discounted. We all follow the process below.

The stages of change
Immobilisation and time

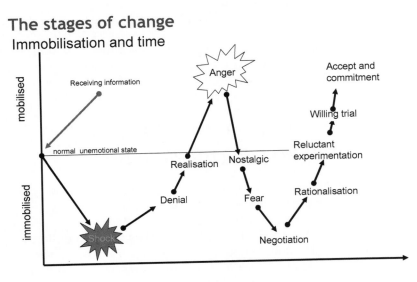

You may start to feel some agitation and while your breathing quickens your emotions leave the pit of your stomach and move towards your chest making breathing more difficult. As the flow of oxygen to your brain is restricted your ability to be rational diminishes and the most common emotion of anger can riddle your body. This can lead you to be vocal about the content of the feedback. You may outwardly or inwardly be shouting, *This feedback is rubbish! How dare they? Who do they think they are? They are useless anyway!*

When the <u>anger</u> naturally subsides (although this can take some time) you can allow yourself to focus on nostalgia (historical events) to justify your capability. This is quite a natural reaction to preserve your self-esteem. You then may slip into a state of <u>self-doubt</u> and fear the consequences of the feedback.

Then, you may well gather your thoughts and reflect, allowing your mind to <u>negotiate</u> and be open to read the feedback in a less emotive state. This paves the way for rational interpretation of the information as your breathing and heart rate regulate. This allows you to be <u>open to dialogue</u> with individuals or teams and to be willing to experiment. Although there will be a degree of reluctance on both parts, you will now start to see the purpose of the process and how *both* parties can benefit. This will lead to <u>acceptance and commitment.</u>

This whole mental and emotional process can be an extremely quick one. The starting point, to ensure it does not prolong to the point of making relationships worse not better, is to ensure you recall the purpose of the activity you are involved in. This is about <u>improving things for yourself and the other party</u> in a sustained way. Letting yourself to be negatively affected for too long will hinder the process and do more harm than good. Everyone has to take responsibility to remain *adult* about the feedback, and to remember that <u>all feedback is given with the best of intentions</u>. Try to focus on the intention rather than the behaviour and recognise that no one has set out to emotionally hurt anybody else.

When using the above approach, I suggest you give yourself enough chance to go through the various stages of change. Ensure you have reached the point where you are in a rational state and willing to experiment and <u>open up dialogue</u>. This method can be used in work and in your personal life.

Controlling your emotions, actions and behaviour

Have you ever woken up in the morning and immediately decided that you were going to have a bad day? You might have a slight cold or have to do something that you weren't looking forward to at work. Try and recall how you felt at that time. Try to imagine what you must have looked like. The reality is that you probably felt tired and perhaps a little anxious. You would probably have looked rather miserable. Your shoulders would be slumped forward and your movements would be slow. You would then perhaps allow yourself to feel sorry for yourself to counter these feelings and to make yourself feel better. What would the rest of the day be like? How productive would you be at work?

Do you respond positively to setbacks?

The rest of the day would follow this pattern. The reason for this is that you have told yourself that you were going to have a bad day. As a consequence of this you would have one. In fact, as external factors start to occur - your manager has a go at you, someone lets you down, you get a bad call – it just seems to reaffirm your original thought. The likely result is that the day gets even worse! You would sell less, offer a worse customer experience or do little productive coaching with your teams. Cognitive therapy tells us that if you think in a negative way then negative things will happen, and if you think in a positive way then positive things will happen. It's just a mindset thing.

Can customers make you have a bad day?

I have asked this question to many customer advisors and middle managers. Nearly everyone I have ever asked has answered *yes*. If this is the case though, it again suggests that external factors (in this case the customer) can determine our mood and our behaviour. I think of it as a customer physically pulling an imaginary string to make us upset, frustrated, or angry. There is no doubt that other human beings can influence our emotions, but they cannot actually make us respond in a certain way. They cannot make us confrontational. They cannot make us arrogant or sarcastic. They cannot make us storm off into the toilets and cry our eyes out. However many, many people believe that they can.

The starting point is therefore obvious.

We must change the way we think about motivation. We must accept that we are in control of our own thoughts and clearly our actions. Others can press the buttons, but we make the decision about how we respond. We can respond with enthusiasm or allow ourselves to respond with negativity. In short, motivation is internal and not external. Traditional thinkers believe that it is external. Digital thinkers believe that it is internal.

Are you motivated?

Traditional-age thinkers do not take responsibility for where they are today. If they have a bad day it is the product of someone else. It was their fault! They look for people to blame to deflect responsibility and justify their behaviour. Digital-age thinkers are forever assessing their own behaviour. They don't blame others for their behaviour but take responsibility. They are always looking to improve and will give themselves feedback. They will ask others for feedback too and will take action to improve.

Where is your thinking?

You are getting ready for work and your dog has just decided to go to the toilet on your carpet. When you clean it up, you are in a major rush and are just in time for work.

- How do you feel?
- How do you behave?

> *This scenario came up in a training session I was running. The guy it happened to blamed the dog. He then blamed customers for not buying anything. He looked at everyone except himself. Could he have got up earlier and taken his dog for a walk? Could he have been the reason the customers did not buy?*

The reality is of course that as he was riddled with frustration and anger; he was not in a state of rational control. His emotions had taken over and had a negative impact.

Alternatively, he could have followed the digital-age approach below to help him have 'a good day':

Traditional-Age Thinking	Digital-Age Thinking
Shout at the dog.	Acknowledge that you cannot do anything about it.
Have an angry rant and say *it's not fair* over and over again.	Put the event into perspective. It is not that bad!
Sulk all day and take it out on colleagues and customers.	Stay positive. Tell yourself that things are going to get better.
Let everything external make your mood worsen. Blame everyone and ignore your own role in your 'bad day'.	Tell yourself that the next call will be better. Focus on your own behaviour to make that a reality.

The reality is that you are responsible for your own day. Most days are the same. We get up and go to work. We come home and have dinner. We relax. We go to bed. That will be pretty consistent for most people's lives.

Therefore, why are some days better than others? It is true that on certain days there are more external influences on our motivation, which make it harder to respond with enthusiasm. However, we still have choices. We can let the external influence affect us to such a degree that we end up having a bad day. Or we can be rational and choose to respond with enthusiasm.

One thing we do know is that if we let external things affect us we will definitely lack motivation. We will lack energy and feel miserable and will achieve very little. If we choose the digital-age option we might just have a fantastic day. We might close more deals and have more customers thank us for our help.

Try it! Responding with enthusiasm truly can make the difference.

Summary

Creating the environment where people are internally motivated is invaluable. It reduces cost and enhances individual contribution. When people enjoy their work they do more than the bare minimum. They achieve ground-breaking results and are continually focused on improvement. They are energetic and committed to the purpose.

People must have a clear view of their purpose and the contribution they make individually. They need to be involved and managers need to create space. Managers need to ensure that people feel valued and that interesting roles are created.

People have more choice these days and vote with their feet if things are not right. Conversely they remain in the company demonstrating de-motivated behaviour that adds no value. Costs are high and customers get a raw deal. The days of motivational training courses must surely be over. They are expensive and do not provide any return on investment on their own. Creating the environment where human beings want to contribute is the key factor in progressive companies.

Practical actions to understand and learn about motivation

- Review your performance. Ask yourself, what has not gone well that you need to improve? What has gone well that you can learn from?

- Avoid negative comments about other people, departments and customers. This will help you create a more customer-centric culture.

- Consistently ask yourself if you are taking responsibility for your own behaviour. How much time are you spending looking for others to blame?

- Ask your people regularly if they enjoy coming to work. Use their responses to build in future improvements.

- Encourage your peers and leaders to become more visible and to meet people regularly face to face.

- Think about how people see you. How would you like to be remembered by your colleagues? How would you like to be remembered by your family?

- Identify what you love doing. Is it golf, holidays, reading or something else? Do it as often as you can.

- What value are you adding? What happens when you are not around? Does anyone miss you?

Understanding
measurement

*Corporate managers start off trying to manage what they want
and finish up wanting what they can measure.*

Igor Ansoff, strategy guru

Within our operational teams it is essential to challenge our
existing measures. Are they focused on continual improvement?
When we achieve success - do we review to identify our learning?
What did we do to make it happen? Were there outside influences
affecting our results? When we do well we look at internal reasons
and when we are struggling we often look at external reasons. The
more successful we are, the more that real dangers open up. In
fact, success is not always a great teacher, as we often do not stop
and review.

Many contact centres have become obsessed with the figures
available from the Automatic Call Distributor. National telecom
companies, who didn't need to worry about customers as they had
a monopoly, developed these. These figures are often used to
compare the performance of individuals, teams and sites. It is this
comparison that encourages everyone to fudge the numbers to
make his or her team/site look good. Any decent management

accountant would be able to see that these are the wrong figures to drive continual improvement.

In the digital-age world, operational managers are not clinging to the wrong numbers. They are focused on why the contact, what matters to customers, the types of calls and how many, as well as the value and how long it takes to resolve the customer problem. Whilst we know what makes the difference, we often find it hard to measure. In the absence of clear measures traditional thinkers use the ones available. These are likely to be the wrong measures but they appear scientific and easy to produce. When everyone is thinking in a digital-age way, people and teams take responsibility to continually review their own performance and the measures focus on improvement leading to a step change in performance.

Measuring to improve on a daily basis

If you have ever worked within a contact centre you will be familiar with traditional contact centre metrics. The measures can, however, be quickly devalued. Ask yourself this. Imagine that your targets - such as average handling time, after call work/wrap, and call hold time - were all achieved. If these measures were a measure of success, then it follows that your customers would be very happy. Are they?

Do you use traditional contact centre metrics to drive improvement?

Often customers are not happy. However, some planning and contact centre managers would be thrilled at reaching the set targets. They would be sending congratulatory memos to everyone. The problem is that customers might not be as elated and players in teams may remain indifferent. People who speak to customers know that these measures often hinder the customer experience. Customers and people are disconnected and planning to leave - and the managers are sending emails to congratulate teams!

Imagine the feeling you would have. A customer has contacted you and really needs help. You know you can help them but it is quite a complex issue. You need to do some investigating. You really want to help. It is a meaty issue that you can get your teeth into. However, you know that you are targeted on finishing the call within a certain amount of time. You also know that you cannot finish the work when the customer has gone and if you rang other departments to investigate, your hold time would exceed the target. You can't make outbound calls, so you can't ring the customer back.

What are your choices? You could carry on regardless and really do everything to help the customer. The customer leaves feeling great and thanks you for your help; you feel great because you know you did a great job. The problem is that you may not get any credit for your performance. You may get a pat on the back from a manager who may have been listening. However, the next day when you got your 'stats' you may well have 'under-performed' as far as the ACD was concerned. You might then be told to improve your performance. The other choice becomes much more likely now. Rather than doing everything, you would do the bare minimum. You would rush the customer and scam the system. You would get great 'stats' and probably get lots of praise. You would probably also get bigger bonuses. Then the company would build a new contact centre!

Understanding what matters to customers?

The challenge is on to ensure measures are based on what matters to customers. Everyone should understand the planned team achievements and everyone should be involved in the improvement process. Traditional budget-driven targets can remain. They just need to be measured at the back of the process by senior managers and not as the drivers for success. Planning and performance managers love the fact that they are placed directly into the front-line as performance targets. It makes their job easier if they are enforced by operational middle managers. They do not receive the criticism when customers get a poor service. But this is too simplistic.

Differentiating the customer experience cannot begin with everyone striving to 'hit' internal numbers that customers do not care about. They contact companies for help. They want a resolution and they want empathy and a polite human being. They might want to buy something! They do not want stressed robots that are trying to get them off the phone. To change requires a fundamental shift in thinking. This pseudo-scientific approach to measuring the customer experience is driven by the cost and the need to stay within the budget. It is historical and has its roots within manufacturing. It is always internally focused and is to the detriment of the customer experience. The irony is it is also less efficient than focusing on what matters to customers.

> *A former colleague of mine once told me that he was having trouble 'hitting' his performance targets. He worked in the customer service team and the nature of many of his calls meant he had to contact the delivery team. He had a call hold target of 8%. In other words, only 8% of his working day could be spent on hold.*
>
> *During a three-month period, his manager would print off his performance targets daily and put them on his desk. His call hold over three months was between 12-15%. It was circled with red pen and with an arrow pointing downwards. There was no dialogue, just circles and arrows in red pen. He was eventually placed on an action plan. The next day he achieved 7%. His manager came to see him and patted him on the back. His 'stat' sheet had a gold star on it.*
>
> *He did not feel as great as they did though. In order to achieve target he lied to customers, fobbed them off and cut them off. He had dropped them into other queues without announcing them. He used every scam he knew to hit the number. The managers were thrilled with his numbers.*

How many of his colleagues were doing the same? They were not all on action plans. Consequently, complaint letters and emails increased considerably, which prompted senior managers to become involved.

One of the senior managers visited the delivery team. It came to light that the reason the delivery team was so busy was that there were severe stock shortages. The senior managers did not know this as the delivery team were measured on the percentage of packages sent that were delivered on time. The 'packages delivered on time' figure was 98%. Unfortunately, the percentage only included the packages that were actually sent. There were hundreds of customers waiting but they were not included in the figures. The number of people in the delivery team could not cope with demand, so there was a huge internal delay.

If you waited, you were penalised. If you cheated, you were praised and got your bonus. Crazy! No one ever investigated why. They did not do this because they were entrenched in an internally-focused way of measuring performance. They were addicted to the number. People were condemned for doing a great job and customers hated it!

Are you praising the right behaviour?

These measures become a standard for everyone to adhere to. If you do meet the standard then you are doing a good job. If not, you may be a problem and will need coaching. In this environment, you would need counselling, not coaching. 'Coaching' in this scenario is a euphemism for controlling or tightly managed.

Creating the right measures has to be the first stage. Understanding the process customers go through when they contact you and then determining what 'matters to them' is key. When you measure, you are not measuring against a standard but against a clearly defined process. From the welcome through to the close, we need to engage our front-line in continually thinking about what matters to customers and always look to improve. In order for this to happen, we need some managers to change the way they think. They need to allow their people to satisfy customers.

Does good process ensure good service?

Number management can lead to crisis management. If the department has not hit target in a given day, the management team will often 'flap' about. They will attend several meetings to come up with initiatives. They do not realise that their whole approach to customer service delivery is flawed. They might improve the numbers for the following day, but the root cause will never be eradicated. Customers will never feel the improvement.

Engaging teams to become involved in improvements

Once the correct measures are in place it becomes a much more engaging process. The leaders are clear about what the measures are. The managers then become facilitators rather than enforcers. The players become heavily involved in the improvement process.

When I implemented the digital-age approach into one company the internal customer satisfaction result went down from 98% to 58%. Interestingly, the external customer satisfaction figure was at about 58%. The team were now measuring the right things but the managers were horrified. They blamed the new process. The reality is that the new process provided a true reflection of how customers were feeling.

If the real number is 58%, you have a fantastic opportunity to improve things. You accept where you are and then engage the teams in thinking of ways to improve. Ask them why customers are not happy. They challenge themselves individually and share their learning within and across the team. Everyone is just trying to improve things for customers. They are not just trying to improve the number. They are trying to improve each stage of customer contact. You are now measuring each stage of the customer contact process. The 'welcome' part of the call is at 63%. You want to improve this. You share the number with your teams and then set about making improvements. You want them to work hard at improving the welcome. You discuss ideas that could help you to achieve this. You may want to use your own name. You might want to up your energy levels. Whatever solutions you come up with, people should be given the freedom and trust to experiment.

As they do, they should be encouraged to share their experiences so that others can learn. It quickly becomes a totally engaging process where everyone is improving the right things. You might just find that the traditional numbers fall into place anyway. If they do not, there will be a reason. This approach will identify the reason quickly and improvements can be put in place to rectify it.

Are you measuring to improve or to hit target?

Reducing non-value activity

If you could work towards reducing non-value activity (activity that is because of failure or repeat contact), you could really engage your customers without constantly retrieving mistakes.

These days, why do customers ring their supplier?

How much of your customer contact is the product of failure? Increasingly, customer service companies are considering this question. Previously, they just managed the contacts on a daily basis in a very reactive way. Once the error contacts are removed, companies and teams are able to deliver an engaging experience for customers.

The role of the customer advisor will change. Rather than there being constant stress and apology, they can just spend their time ensuring that customers love the experience. This is much easier when your starting point is the customer being in an indifferent state rather than one of anger and hate!

The role of performance and planning managers

Great contact centre performance and planning managers know the exact contact patterns of the customer base and can start to predict the type of contact. This has to go beyond the all too common basic analysis of just using the 'stats' to tell us how many 'types of calls' we received. Operationally we also need to move beyond call-driver analysis. This is predominantly an operational manager-led initiative to help with internal resourcing. Its origin does not have the customer at the centre. It generally means that the customer advisors have to tick or click the generic category the contact fell into. For example, if it was a billing call, was it to do with payment or a bill query.

How much customer contact could you eradicate if you thought differently?

A lot of non-value activity is also to do with the really basic short calls. Customer advisors historically love them, but they are expensive. In the digital age, this type of contact could easily be re-directed into various technological solutions. Many companies have recognised this. As customers, we can do much more now via the Internet. Likewise, interactive voice response systems are often used so that we can get a solution to our reason for contact without having to speak to someone. Some customers prefer the human touch, but in this busy world, simple queries are surely best handled by the technology. This reduces costs and makes the transaction more efficient.

Many companies are unable to deal with the amount of traditional contact they are receiving from customers. Initially, many kept on building more centres and filling them with more people. As the world economy struggled during the early part of this century the pressure was on to reduce costs. Service companies looked to cheaper operating countries to manage the non-value contact. The strategy therefore remains the same but costs less. However, the price may well become a big one. The quality of service due to cultural differences and language barriers has made this seem like a panic solution to reducing costs. In June 2006, NPower in the UK decided that outsourcing their customer service to India had not been a great success. Apparently, the customers didn't like it and it was proving expensive as no one was looking at the reasons why customers were contacting the company in the first place. The management were focusing on call handling time and how quickly the phone was answered.

Do you focus on cost and forget the customer experience?

A lot of money could be saved through identifying your non-value contact and eradicating a huge percentage of it. You firstly need to be able to understand what failure contacts you are receiving and put process and systems in place to remove the cause. You then need to engage your managers and teams to maintain a mindset of 'what matters to customers'. Over time, everyone will train his or her mind always to put the customer at the heart of everything. This quickly makes failure, non-value and reasons for customer dissatisfaction all become incredibly transparent. This is not easy to spot when your outsourcer is in a different country and tied to a productivity-driven contract! The outsourcer was not looking to reduce contacts.

Measurements focused on the external customer experience

There is too much internal focus in many companies, resulting in the operational teams' very often losing sight of the external customer. It is amazing that this is possible within customer service companies/teams as all days are spent doing things for customers.

How much time do you spend on customer experience improvements during your working day?

What matters to customers? The best way to answer this is to put your customer hat on. What do you yourself like when partaking in the customer experience?

As a customer, it sometimes appears that we must put up with the company's way of doing things. It seems that our requirements remain of secondary importance. I am OK with companies having brand identity. I am OK with them promoting this. However, it should be kept away from the actual customer interaction.

How do you feel when you are speaking to someone reeling off a script?

In one company, the operational managers had to ensure that the customers felt the company values. Maybe as a company providing a service to paying customers we should be tapping into the customers' values and delivering an experience that is unique to them. Otherwise we are just putting them in one big 'customer pot'. If this method is used then the chances of differentiation remain incredibly slim. Some financial services companies just do not seem to understand. They insist on calling all customers by their surname, or worse, 'Sir'. Some customers want to be called by their first name. When advisors follow a script they can sound impersonal and they do not make the emotional connection.

Understanding what the customers want

What does matter to customers then? Companies need to:

- ensure that it is quick and easy to buy products or receive services.
- build trust by systemically removing failure in process.
- show that they care.
- increasingly allow customers to be involved.

The above four requirements can easily be provided through the internet. However, if the situation is complex or the customers require a conversation, a face-to-face or telephone conversation often resolves the situation.   Companies need to ensure that they answer the phone quickly, and once connected, keep waiting times to a minimum. Customers are busy human beings in a hectic world. Delays are incredibly frustrating.   In contact centres, getting through quickly is an absolute basic prerequisite. If you cannot get the basics right then forget it. Likewise, customers want to speak to someone who can actually help quickly. They do not want to have to be transferred five times to specialist teams. They do not want to be told that the department is closed and 'please, can you call back'. Customers want:

Firstly, a good transaction:

- A resolution on that contact.
- Belief that the company will do what they have said.
- To have been offered relevant products that meet their immediate needs.

Secondly, a good interaction:

- A polite and friendly human.
- To be listened to.
- Empathy.
- To be spoken to in a style they prefer.

Thirdly, if you do the above, some will want to feel special at the end of the contact. That is, to feel valued and feel that it was an enjoyable experience.

Do your customers feel special?

If these are things that matter to customers, then maybe we should measure these things. We need to measure the whole experience end to end, from the moment they consider contacting to the end of the whole cycle time for a resolution. The days of measuring success just by the budget has to go.

The customer gets a raw deal and people are left feeling disgruntled. Customers and people who are the team members do not have any loyalty. They subsequently leave. There is so much choice for both. Opportunities are truly there to differentiate. In order to do so a real leap of faith is required. If not, you will be the same as everyone else. This is, until one of your competitors gets it right. Then, where will you be?

Offering additional products to customers

We see evidence of this within sales and service. There is no doubt that this is an essential part of customer contact that can increase revenue and improve customer loyalty. Combining sales within a service environment can be a useful addition; however, it does need to be handled carefully.

> *I was in a major retail outlet a few years ago. It was January and I was spending some Christmas vouchers. As I approached the checkout, I was greeted by a very pleasant assistant who very politely and officially completed the sales transaction. It was good. Then I received the 'curve ball' - an unexpected event! She tried to sell me a half-price teddy bear with a Christmas hat on! It was obvious that she had been told to shift as many of these things as she could. They had without doubt ordered too many before Christmas and were now trying to recoup some lost revenue. I was only buying some clothes!*

This is a classic mistake companies make. Because they are often so internally focused, they try to dictate what we as customers want. They come up with campaigns to try and sell as much of a product or service as they can. They offer incentives to teams to increase commitment. The only problem is this approach can be very annoying and intrusive to customers. Some sales people explain that customers do not know what they need or want until a fact-finding discussion as part of a sales process has been undertaken. Customers are knowledgeable these days and they often *do* know what they want.

Do your campaigns and incentives lose sight of the customer?

This constant desire for 'hitting' customers with the campaign is very annoying. It causes delays for customers and it is as if we, the customers, should buy what the sales outlets want us to buy. There is another way.

Differentiating by identifying individual circumstances

The missing ingredient in the campaign/incentive approach is that no one keeps the customer in mind. Companies, in their attempt to increase revenue, quickly fail to acknowledge that all customers are different and have unique circumstances. There are many opportunities within every contact to up-sell and cross-sell but they must be handled sensitively. We must allow our teams to 'tap' into the customer's wants and needs and offer additional solutions based on this knowledge. When this is done, it ensures that customers feel like individuals. The approach is non-intrusive and it serves to strengthen relationships and loyalty. It is as if customers don't see the sell coming, because in effect there isn't one. It is a natural seamless transition into other things than can benefit the customer and make their lives better or easier.

Planners hate this of course, particularly in contact centres. They are OK with campaigns because they can ensure the operation adds a few extra words into the call. Planners can gauge how long the additional words will take and then they can 'budget' it in. The 'individual circumstance' approach is more difficult to control from a planning perspective. They get edgy that average handling time will spiral out of control. The reality is, however, that it wouldn't happen on every call. Likewise, it does serve to build loyalty with customers and increase revenue at the same time. Finally, if it is part of an overall customer-centric shift, it is destined to succeed.

Do you and your company offer additional products based on individual circumstance?

In order to offer additional products based on particular circumstance we need to trust the front-line to make decisions. They do know what the customers want and need on every interaction. They have to be allowed to be creative. They should be rewarded but not offered incentives. Incentives are a bribe. They have their origin at the beginning of the process and breed compliance. They also bring out behaviour that is often more to do with 'self-benefit' than 'customer benefit' and they soon lose their appeal.

Resolving problems for players

The role of the digital-age manager is to create the environment where players can reach their full potential. Traditional managers believe in control and tight management. Traditional managers often make all the decisions and believe that people need motivating. If something is not going well they look for a scapegoat. Try the following:

- Ask managers what they consider the role of manager to be.

- Ask customer advisors what they consider the role of manager to be.

It is difficult to predict the responses, but you will get a degree of interesting variance.

Part of the manager role is to ensure that everyone has the tools to do their job. How can they expect high performance and commitment if the basic prerequisites are not in place?

Are you spending your time ensuring that everyone has the tools to do their job?

The customer process needs to be customer friendly and systems need to work. Rules also must be kept to a minimum to prevent the constant need for managers' help. In short, managers need to resolve things for players that they cannot do themselves. Players do not need their hand holding at work. They are adults and are quite able to make decisions, without having to constantly check. The problem in the team led by a traditional-age thinker is that no one is trusted, so it is as if every decision is made by the manager.

> *In one company I worked in, there was a very friendly manager. She used to refer to her teams as 'her kids'. Everyone loved her. It sounds harsh but they loved her because she did everything for them. It was a classic parent/child relationship. In trying to encourage her to loosen the apron strings she became incredibly agitated and actually showed that her thinking was indeed very traditional.*
>
> *She wanted to ensure she did everything. She had to know everything or she felt vulnerable. She was very 'soft' but she was a traditional thinker.*

This again shows that digital age is not the 'soft' option. Digital-age thinkers create an adult/adult environment. There is lots of dialogue. Managers make decisions in their areas of expertise and players in theirs. There is no 'hand-holding'. Players take responsibility to resolve their own problems unless it is something not within their decision-making arena.

Managers must also ensure that when they take actions away, that they complete them. The problem must have existed if it was raised in the first place. It must be either affecting customers and/or the people who are paid to satisfy them and therefore is a priority. If people at the front-line have taken the time to share concerns and provide feedback, they really should receive some response. All too often I see managers go into forums and take away actions but do not visibly do anything with them.

Do you follow through with actions and provide feedback directly to the individual?

Managers may well have done something, but people don't know because they receive no update. This results in advisors losing their motivation to contribute enthusiastically. For one, it is good manners to update individuals. Secondly, it ensures that people continue to feedback improvements. Finally, if managers do not do this, it makes starting over again very difficult, as people become cynical.

Summary

The days of measuring things just because they are easy to do are over. In companies that differentiate, managers do not worry about the fact that something might be difficult to measure. They firstly identify what matters to customers and then find a way to measure it.

How many people have you made feel special today?

This is surely obvious. Why would you consider measuring how many calls a customer advisor takes, when your strategy might include *'delivering memorable experiences for customers'*? There is complete disconnection between the purpose and the measure. In other words, by achieving the calls per person target you are unlikely to achieve your purpose and may distance yourself even further!

The ACD statistics in contact centres needs to stay in planning. The measures used for planning and forecasting should not be thrust into operational areas as they drive behaviours that detract from purpose. Subsequently I see disgruntled customers, disconnected players and lots of inefficiency – generated by repeat, non-value contact.

Practical actions to understand and learn about measurement

- Look at your current measures and ask yourself whether they are designed around what matters to customers.

- Ask yourself if you are really interested in your teams and your customers. Use your own response to ascertain future plans.

- Review how committed your teams are. If you see them doing the bare minimum to get by, look at the reasons why. Try not to just blame them, and look at the work they do, the way they are managed, rewarded, etc.

- Try producing a list of ten to twenty questions about you and your leadership and ask your teams to answer them anonymously. Share the results with the teams and ask for feedback about what you could do to improve.

- Now that they know you, would your present employer employ you again? Will they miss you when you have gone?

- Review the operational measures. Are they focused on improvements or targets?

- Review your reporting. Does it add any value? How much time does it take to produce? Does anyone really use it to improve performance?

Understanding the customer

To stand out in a commoditized market, companies must understand what customers truly value. The only way to do that is to break down the traditional, often entrenched, silos and unite resources to focus directly on customer needs.

Ranjay Gulati, Harvard Business Review

Increasingly, emotion plays a key part in delivering the internal and external customer experience. When you meet people you like, you give more, you are more welcoming. They can feel this. When you love your work, you put more energy into it. When you enjoy what you are doing, you don't feel tired. If you are happy, you deliver better experiences.

> *Last year I met someone I knew. He greeted me with enthusiasm and seemed pleased to meet me. As we talked, I spotted a change in his behaviour. He appeared to change his approach almost immediately. It suddenly became a transaction - still friendly, but the warmth had disappeared. I wondered why. He was soon to tell me. At a convenient point, he said that he had initially mistaken me for someone else!*

Satisfying the internal and external customer now, with no delays, will be the challenge of the future.

In under-performing teams, measurements are often focused on the budget and not the customer. Managers can often use the measurements on a daily basis to give the illusion of being in control. In many companies, the transactions are now in the hands of the customer. Getting the transaction right is now the price of entry for many companies. Once the basics are right, companies need to concentrate on the emotional connection. It starts with ensuring that the internal environment is focused on the customer (what they want) and the development of one another.

Understanding the customer transaction and the interaction

The customer-transaction refers to the process and technological capabilities of a company and how well the company delivers what customers are asking for. The customer-interaction describes the behaviour that players use to satisfy the customer's requirements.

Interaction v Transaction

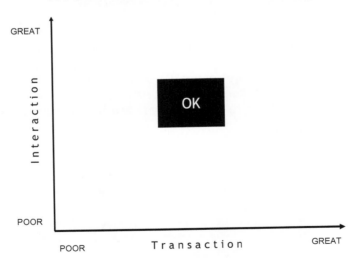

In the digital age, more and more opportunities exist for customers to have their requirements met by technology. This has proved vital to increase internal efficiency and reduce delays for customers who wish to contact companies quickly with little or no human interaction. Technological advances are frequent yet they are easily replicated. No sooner than one company installs some new technological ideas, they are copied by competitors. They are so visible, often supplied by third parties, that it is almost impossible for them to remain a secret. From a customer's perspective they can be very pleasing, as it puts them in control. They reduce delays and speed the customer service delivery process. However, due to the fact they are so visible and can be easily replicated, they are generally expected by customers.

The accurate transaction has become the price of entry. In the mobile sector, an example of the transaction would be the quality of the network. Customers expect, as the most basic prerequisite, to be able to use their phones wherever they are. If they cannot, then the company may as well give up. Customers want their data *now*.

During the mid-1990s, many of the customer-contacts within the emerging mobile telecommunications industry were to do with the poor performance of the network. Now these calls are less frequent, as the companies have recognised that this is such a basic requirement. Changes to masts and their maintenance will be almost identical within every mobile company. Similarly, internal processes and systems will be almost identical.

Consequently, the transaction cannot differentiate you from the competition for long. If the basics are not in place, you will fall behind, but having the newest technology and creative process and procedure will still leave you very similar to everyone else in the game.

Conversely, the customer interaction has been cited by many as one of the only remaining differentiators. How we engage customers is one area that we can guarantee leaving customers with an emotional feeling before, during and after the experience.

> *I sometimes shop at Asda. From a transactional sense, they are*
> *very good. The price is competitive and there is lots of choice. I*

> *can buy music, clothing and TVs. However, if I go to other suppliers, I have comparative choice at a similar price. The reason I continue shopping at Asda is to do with the interaction. I always feel that my custom is valued. They only appear to recruit customer-focused people who care about your experience. They make positive references to my purchases, always greet with a smile and they offer help with the customers' bags.*
>
> *One Christmas my wife and I were having a party and I went to buy the wine from Asda. I had many bottles in my trolley and went to a checkout (I did not have to queue!). Someone just starting her shift served me and she was very friendly and offered me help. As I started packing bottles in carrier bags a colleague on another checkout shouted over to her and let her know that there were some boxes at the end of the store that would make my packing much easier.*

This is a classic example of digital-age thinking.

The woman thought in a customer-oriented way. As a result, any given situation was seen through the eyes of the customer. She went that extra mile to leave me with a memorable experience. As she didn't have a customer at the time, she could have easily used the opportunity to have a rest. However, when you think customer-experience, your behaviour follows. It was a totally natural response from her.

> *This is very different from a scenario in a contact centre. It was incredibly busy and there were many calls queuing. As a team leader who is totally focused on customers, I jumped onto my phone and logged in to answer some calls. Other team leaders thought I was crazy. I encouraged them to do the same, but I was met with very negative responses. They seemed to think it beneath them, and that it was a job they used to do.*

The reality is, of course, that the most basic requirement in a contact centre is to understand why customers are contacting but if they do then please answer the phone quickly. If not, customers become disgruntled and may leave.

Digital-age thinkers do not need to be told to take calls; they recognise it is vital and linked to purpose and just do it automatically. They do not have to stay on the phone all day, but when the need arises, they do whatever it takes to satisfy customers. They also learn what the problems are and put forward improvements to make things better for their teams.

> *In the same scenario, I suggested to my manager that we should build 'talking to customers when it is busy' into the team leader role. This could help the transaction, I thought. It should reduce queues, increase efficiency and boost morale among the customer advisors. The manager, however, suggested that the team leaders should be coaching their teams and not taking calls. What the team leaders should be asking, of course, is 'What do you need to do your job better?' The manager also pointed out that because the team leaders were not used to using the systems and processes, then they might well increase the overall average handling time for the day!*

This is a classic example of how the customer can become a distant memory in the traditional world. It appears that hitting target was more important than delivering the most basic prerequisite of all – answering the phone quickly. Other team leaders appeared to spend much of the time coaching under-performing players or helping them to cope with the stress of the job. These team leaders had little idea of the problems that the job was causing and were busily attending disciplinary workshops to improve performance of their people. They had no idea of the real drivers of stress or the low productivity. They believed it was a people problem and spent the majority of their day dealing with the people issues that poorly designed work will bring.

In the same company, the interaction remained something that was done when it was quiet, when there was time to connect with customers. There was a script to control the call length and many people were off sick and leaving. Likewise, customer satisfaction scores were on a downward spiral.

The transaction and interaction are both essential ingredients when delivering a service. The former is the basic requirement that customers expect. The transaction can be easily copied and does not enable you to differentiate for very long at all. The interaction is very difficult to replicate. It focuses on the things that really make us, as customers, feel good and tell others about it, which does, however, require an internal culture that is supportive and involving, encouraging experiential learning and creativity. An environment of trust needs to be built, one where decision-making at the front-line is allowed.

Making the emotional connection with customers

There has been a lot of talk about making the emotional connection with customers. Sometimes referred to as 'engagement', it is widely acknowledged within companies that it is one of the only real remaining differentiating factors. With the customer transaction easily replicated, getting the customer interaction right really can build customer loyalty, increase revenue, and reduce costs. It is equally as essential within service and sales. The problem is of course that very few companies have cracked it. Their marketing and strategy are fine, but if they are not implemented in a way that results in customers receiving an engaging experience, then they have failed.

> *During 2005, I had a client based in the Netherlands and I found a taxi company that is probably the best taxi company in the world. It is a family business. It makes no difference whether Ralph, his brother-in-law or his father-in-law, picks me up. I still receive the same treatment. They arrive on time. If they are late, they ring. When it was my birthday, they knew about it and gave me a free ride. They do many little things to make the experience enjoyable. They create room for me in the rear seats by moving the front seat forward. Some of these are what you would expect, and others are truly unique. Am I emotionally attached? Yes, I am - there are many taxis but in my eyes, there is only one Ralph.*
>
> *If you need a taxi in Amsterdam try them on +31 0654243004 or www.qualityservice.nl. They will not let you down.*

Everything everyone chooses to do anywhere in the company will have an impact on the customer experience. Ultimately, it is not possible to provide consistently satisfying customer experience if employees anywhere in the company are dissatisfied, disaffected and disgruntled.

Are you creating memorable experiences for customers?

Costs have also played a part in affecting companies' attempts to engage customers. Outsourcing at home and abroad has diluted the company capacity to differentiate through making the emotional connection. Nevertheless making the emotional connection does remain on the adventurous senior manager agenda. It really can make the difference.

Recall an experience, whether it was digital, face-to-face or over the telephone, that left you feeling special. These experiences are probably quite rare, but just try to remember what happened and why you felt so great. Then think about your own company. Does your culture, measurement, leadership, etc. mean that your customer base is likely to feel like you did on that day? Customers crave emotional interaction, because human beings do.

When I talk about the customer experience, I always view the emotional connection in terms of the transaction and the interaction. The former has to do with process, system and policy. Interaction is the behavioural element that results in generating emotions in customers. The majority of customers begin the contact with a company in one of five emotional states:

Hate	Dislike	Indifference	Like	Love

We cannot influence the starting emotion too much (although by reducing the need for non-value contact we could support it), but we can certainly play a part in the leaving emotion. This will determine the lasting impression.

The vast majority of customers in a service arena start in the middle. They are generally contacting a company because they need help or want something to be done. This means that we want engaged customer advisors to see their role as not just taking calls or hitting internal targets, but as making the emotional connection and solving customer problems. If you see your role as making the emotional connection with customers, you are much more focused on the real purpose of your role. All the other stuff falls into place because you are totally focused on the customers and what they want.

Are you making the emotional connection with your customers?

In everyday life, how do you feel if you meet someone and there is no attempt being made by the other person to make a connection? They might look away and avoid eye contact. They might not acknowledge what you are saying. They might send lots of signals they are disinterested and not listening. How would you feel? Would you want to meet them again? Why is this replicated in some companies?

Measuring the emotional connection

How many companies really know how their customers or internal customers feel?

With the ongoing implementation of Customer Relationship Management there seems to be a commitment to find out as much information about customer value and their buying habits, resulting in complex segmenting and different service delivery methods. The best companies are creating the environment where the customer is placed at the heart of everything that they do. Measuring the real customer experience has to be the starting point. Devising a traditional scientific measurement approach only serves to maintain internal focus. It provides unrealistic data and leads to numbers management. The wrong numbers! The only reason to measure anything is to show what needs to improve.

There is no point improving a number/target if it really is not going to be felt by the external customer.

Identifying and implementing the customer contact process

In terms of making the emotional connection with customers companies need to connect with their teams. The teams need to be trusted and empowered to make judgment calls. They should be involved, supported and have the capacity in their roles to be creative and learn as they work.

Why would you want to make an emotional connection with your customers when no one seems to care about you?

Involving teams must happen in conjunction with changes made to the whole customer experience delivery process. Remove scripts, measure things that matter to customers and set about involving everyone in improving against the purpose. Of course, all processes have a purpose and you will know your own purpose when you engage customers.

Try this:

Agree the purpose of your customer contact process.
What outcome would you expect from the process?

Develop a customer contact process that details the stages customers go through when they contact you. Managers need to define this. An example is shown below.

It is broken into four specific areas:

WELCOME
Welcome the customer

UNDERSTANDING
Understand the reason for contact
Right Person; Right Place; Right Time
Confirm understanding of present circumstances

SOLUTION
Provide solutions to meet the customers'
requirements
Identify opportunities to develop the relationship

CLOSE and IMPROVE
Close the call
Identify opportunities to improve process of the
behaviour

When the process has been identified, then involve the teams in brainstorming the transaction and interaction elements that would contribute to a differentiated customer experience.

Look at each individual stage and agree the contents of each stage. As everyone has been involved this helps to foster commitment and everybody now understands what his or her purpose is. It is to satisfy customers, make the emotional connection with customers, and provide feedback when there have been problems for customers. Is your contact process defined?

Does your customer service delivery process breed indifference internally and externally?

If, for whatever reason, it is not possible to satisfy customers now, then it is quickly identified as everyone is always thinking about what has not gone well and what has gone well. They use the former to stimulate action and the latter to stimulate learning. Both ensure continual improvement to the customer experience. The process doesn't change but the methods will evolve as people learn.

Scripting the interaction

One of the main things that the best teams are doing is removing the seemingly constant desire to script customer interaction. The reality is that scripting makes human beings sound robotic and lacking in empathy. Outsourcing companies often script their interaction and you can feel it straight away. Secondly, managers have to create the environment where people feel able to build customer relationships and sell more products.

> *In one company I worked with, the team coach role was called Team Supervisor. It was a very apt role title. All they did all day was supervise! They would sit at their desks all day and check everyone was doing what they were supposed to do. Everyone had to follow a tight script. Any deviation meant that they would fail the call and it would affect their bonus. At worst people were put on action plans. It was thought that it would be very professional if everyone sounded the same and said the same things.*

The problem with everyone sounding the same is twofold. Firstly, not all customers are the same. The retired colonel is likely to want a different service than an eighteen-year-old student. The individual should be able to use their human skills to identify the individual requirement and deliver the service accordingly. Secondly, the whole approach is dehumanising. Customer advisors feel like zombies. They cannot use their brains for fear of failure. Likewise, customers never feel anything other than OK or indifferent and when they are ready they will go somewhere else.

Do you spend too much time checking other people's work?

In one company, the team leaders had to monitor thirty calls per day. They had not purchased any technology to help them and so if you include phone calls, e-mail and other interruptions this would take all day. In reality, all they were doing all day was checking that everyone said the same thing to customers. They were measuring against a standard that was developed by managers. It was for their benefit. The customers hated it.

Due to the fact that part of my brief was to differentiate the customer experience, I suggested not scripting the contact. I changed the team leader role to one where their predominant responsibility was coaching and identifying process improvements within teams. I renamed them team coaches. They were encouraged to sit with their teams, away from their desks. Some managers met the changes with quite a lot of resistance. Some thought it unprofessional. Others just thought that advisors and coaches would use it as an opportunity to skive or cheat. It is amazing that some managers think so little of fellow human beings.

I also focused the coaches on looking at why customers were ringing. Over 40% of the contacts were ringing again to chase things that had been promised or were not satisfactory first time. The new approach identified the inefficiencies and was now saving the company money. The customers loved it and so did the employees. Staff turnover was down and customer satisfaction was going up. The accountants liked it too!

Creating interesting roles

Digital-age thinkers believe that it is people that make things happen. Digital-age thinkers work with people and create interesting roles where people can choose to contribute enthusiastically. Most customer advisors and team leaders were thrilled with the changes that digital thinking brought about. Their roles had become mind-numbingly boring. They just went through the motions. When the change was implemented, I asked for feedback from the teams. Some comments really stick in my mind. One man said, *"I feel like the shackles have been removed."* Another said, *"I no longer feel like a robot."* This shows how powerful some changes can be. One manager said, *"This is the best thing to happen to this company in the nine years I have been here.*"

If you want to make and measure the emotional connection with customers, you firstly need to implement a customer delivery process that enables it to happen. Talking about emotional engagement is not enough if you stick to rigid and dated methods. These people wanted changes. Most were relieved that they could be human again. They also acknowledged that customers would also love the change. Sure enough, they did. Complaint letters reduced considerably, while letters and emails of praise increased.

Is it essential to like the customers?

Nearly every mission and strategy has a mention of the significance of external customers. Unless they are happy with the service, there is not a company. It seems strange that some companies become so transfixed on the internal. Some managers can spend hours talking about minute pointless details. They can become hung up on the smallest things and are forever immersing themselves in the everyday.

How many managers do you know that talk about 'our customers' in a positive way? On the contrary, many of the poor-performing companies seem to endorse slanderous comments about customers. It seems that many of us actually expect customers to be nice all the time and fit very neatly into our own internal business process. If they don't they are quickly brandished with derogatory labels.

> *In one company I worked in, I suddenly saw lots of commotion in the contact centre. The contact centre manager was taking an escalated call. Lots of team leaders and customer advisors had gathered round. This customer apparently was being 'given a taste of his own medicine' by the manager. They were right. As I observed, the manager sat back arrogantly in his chair. I could not believe the negative influence this was having. It was making customers the subject of an 'us and them' campaign. It was implying that everyone else could also be rude to customers. The manager was pressing the mute button so the customer couldn't*

> hear him while he was playing to his audience with a variety of labels and hand gestures aimed at the computer screen. The team leaders and the customer advisors loved it.

There are some difficult customers. Some of them try to wind you up; they are arrogant and sarcastic. They are, however, the minority. Most customers are people who need help.

Do you love your customers?

The problem is that there is very little talk of customers in some companies. The further up the company hierarchy, the less real customers become. How much time do you spend talking about the actual customer experience in your own management meetings? Sometimes, if they are mentioned at all, they are described in a negative light. I asked an advisor once what he thought about his job. He said, "It would be all right if it wasn't for the customers." He thought he was being funny. I thought it highlighted that he was in the wrong job. I made a point of listening in to see how he was with customers. Not surprisingly, he lacked energy and enthusiasm. He was abrupt and you could tell he considered customers an inconvenience. In another company where people seemed to like customers, customers liked them and they bought more products.

I am not suggesting advisors need to like every individual customer. I am saying that advisors must enjoy helping them. They must like talking to people and solving problems. If they do not they are in the wrong role.
How good does it feel when a customer says, "You have done a great job...thanks." I have asked this question of lots of middle managers and advisors and nearly 100% have said it feels great. It appears that in some companies the customers give more feedback than the managers do!

People who like customers experience this frequently, because they put the effort in. It keeps you going, in what can be a very isolated role. If you do not like someone in everyday life, do you think they can tell? The reality is that they will have a strong inkling. Our impact is very powerful. We send many signals both verbally and non-verbally that anyone with an ounce of emotional intelligence can notice. Therefore, if you say, 'I do not like customers', you have told your mind this. As a natural consequence, you will behave in this way too. Customers will notice the signals. You won't connect with them and they will leave the experience in an emotional state of anger, dislike or at best indifference. This will mean you can never differentiate.

Do you and your customer advisors like customers?

Leaders need to talk at length about the importance of customers. Most good ones do this already. However, this conversation tends to break down within the middle layer of the company. Too much internal focus and a culture of disliking customers see to that.

Maybe we should all remember the times that we have shown agitation when we have called a company. Think of an example and ask yourself why.

It was probably because something hadn't been done and you felt upset, disappointed or frustrated. It was important to you and you showed your frustration to the person in the shop or over the telephone. All too often, when this happens we start to feel like an inconvenience and that we have been added to the 'problem customer list'. If you like customers, you see things from their point of view. You use empathy very effectively because you care. You can imagine how they must be feeling because you are a very understanding person. That is what makes the difference.

The more we like customers the more they will feel connected to the company. If they are connected, they remain loyal and spend more and we keep our jobs!

Summary

In the digital age, the customer transaction can be easily replicated. Inefficiencies in this area are unacceptable to customers. They expect the transaction as a basic prerequisite.

Companies who are truly differentiating the experience for customers acknowledge that making the emotional connection with customers is the future.

In order for service companies to differentiate, there is a real need to create an environment focused on customers and team development. There needs to be a high degree of trust where managers allow the people satisfying customers to make decisions. This reduces customer delays but also builds customer trust and loyalty. Additionally, people feel empowered.

The environment needs to be one where customers are liked. Managers need to talk about them in a positive light and to discourage negativity. Finally, measures need to reflect the customer-centric culture and to be externally focused.

Practical actions to understand and learn about the customer

- Ask your teams if they consider it essential to like customers. Is it essential to like colleagues?

- Regularly listen in to customer-contact to understand how customers are feeling.

- Review your customer experience measurement. Does it provide a realistic portrayal of customer satisfaction?

- Try to do some analysis that will provide you with an indication of the type of customer contact you are receiving. If it is non-value contact – the outcome of failure - then build in improvements to eradicate this.

- If you currently script customer interaction, consider trying a non-scripted approach. Trusting teams to speak to customers without being told what to say is a prerequisite if you are looking to differentiate your company, and connect with your customers.

Understanding the social age

The high-value work today is in facing complexity, not in addressing problems that have already been solved and for which a formulaic or standardized response has been developed. One challenge for organizations is getting people to realize that what they already know has increasingly diminishing value. How to solve problems together is becoming the real business advantage.

Harold Jarche

If you mention 'digital' or 'social media', many people still think of these technology-related pursuits as something that is specific to younger generations. I really believe that competency in these areas will be a vital skill set required for teams, managers and companies in the future. I also believe it can be an enabler to improve customer experiences, generate wide-scale efficiencies and ultimately change the way we all work.

The approach in this chapter is not to critique how Google, Amazon or Facebook or any other digital or social organisation has changed our lives. Instead, I want to do something slightly different: discuss issues that many traditional, hierarchical organisations face today and in the coming years, and the type of *thinking* that is required to keep up in the digital world. It is clear that a new style of management is going to be needed to remain competitive in a transparent and social world, and that's where Understanding and Learning can really be embraced.

Thinking digitally, reflecting on behaviours

As the world moves more quickly than it ever has done before, there is also a stronger need to become more agile and embrace new ways of working. To be able to discuss digital or social, we must be thinking digitally!

Are you thinking digitally?

Rarely do we take time to reflect on our behaviours as consumers, and how these behaviours have transformed, particularly in the past ten years. Many of us have become so accustomed to change that it is part of our DNA to continually learn and do new things differently (think of the last time you purchased a new mobile or signed up to a new website). Industries have been turned on their heads through embracing digital and social. There are now the capabilities for new entrants who are able to think differently, be more agile and deliver quicker than competitors, whilst remaining customer-centric.

It is essential when discussing digital and social media that we consider how things were without the internet, iPhones or Facebook and then make a comparison. This will help traditional thinkers who don't believe that digital will have an impact on customers or teams and that it's simply hype.
There has been significant change in the media, music and retail sectors (and many others) as a result of the application of digital technology. These are really good examples of how digital changes are good for customers and how industries have been transformed.

Here are three examples of how digital has changed behaviours, as we go back ten years and compare....

> I would have gone to an HMV or Virgin Megastore to buy the latest albums. The process would have been initiated through a paper copy of the NME (the New Musical Express) and then a trip on a bus into the city centre. I would have then had to remember my alphabet as I would have sifted through the A to Z of CDs to find what I was after, followed by further use of my legs and brain as I would have gone to the checkout to make a payment, probably in cash!
>
> Contrast that with my behaviour today. If I hear a song on the radio, I can get out my mobile phone, use the 'Shazam' app to identify the name of the song, search and download the album. I could probably complete the initiation through to the purchase process and have the song to listen to within sixty seconds. If I wanted to I could also read the reviews or have a quick look at other related artists, all on my phone.

This industry has really changed and the way consumers buy music is almost unrecognisable when compared to historical processes. There are many new entrants including Spotify and iTunes, with Virgin Megastore and CDs pretty much ceasing to exist in the UK. With the new entrants there has been a different way of thinking and behaving, and the end-to-end process has turned from a very manual one to a whole retail process with customer feedback within seconds, which, it has to be said, is pretty impressive.

> We used to have a morning newspaper delivered before my parents went to work. Both would read it over breakfast. Every month my father would walk to the local newsagent and hand over some cash for the service. Again, this is an extremely manual process that seems a little labour-intensive from a customer perspective!
>
> Today my parents behave in a very different way. A quick use of the thumb on their smart phones or a scan of websites on their laptop and they are up-to-date with what is going on in the world. They could also turn on their

> *digital TV, go on Twitter, Facebook or take advantage on the move with mobile phone apps.*

Again, this has changed the industry, primarily as a lot of this information can be gathered for free, and like the music industry, it is also awash with new entrants and innovations. The role of a paperboy or newsagent has changed, as has the role of a newspaper. I am not an expert in this industry but you can only imagine a great deal of change has taken place!

> *It would have been a family trip to the local retail park to trial and test all the new TVs. Walking around the store, being able to see all the products, having a play around to see how it all worked. Once sorted with the chosen TV, we would pay and then drive off with a large box in the back of the car.*
>
> *Today I would go online, find the product, read and trust the reviews of people I have never met, and then find the most competitive price across a variety of retailers. Once the purchase is over with, I can also track the delivery, or if I wanted to, I could go into the store to pick it up at a time that is convenient for me.*

This is another complete change in the thinking within a retail process, and it will have changed the roles for many within this sector.

Where was your company ten years ago?

I think it's important to understand that not all customers behave in a digital way, but many do now expect to have a choice in how they contact a company. Many traditional organisations now make a large chunk of their revenue through their digital capabilities and it's because they are providing the opportunity to do so.

Making it quicker, easier and simpler!

The foregoing are quite obvious examples of how digital and social tools are changing our behaviours. There are thousands of other examples that we could draw upon to demonstrate the impact of digital:

- Watching a movie can be done online or through your television rather than going to the local Blockbuster;
- Getting the weather forecast for your exact location for the next few days on your mobile phone is now a reality, compared to having to watch the report for your entire region on the TV;
- Finding directions using location services on a smart phone via Google Maps can be compared with a paperback city A to Z;
- Tracking the distance when on a run using a smart phone app, compared to using a pedometer.

If you take advantage of such things, then they are probably making your life easier, simpler and quicker, enabling you to do more of the things that you enjoy doing!

Strong digital capabilities

I believe that if an organisation does not have strong digital capabilities, it will negatively impact on the brand and bottom line. Customers often want the choice of consuming when and how it is appropriate for them at the point of initiation. Their behaviours can change based on a whole range of external factors and desires. For example, if it's a sunny day you may choose to walk to the shops, whereas if it's raining, you may decide to buy online. This is why an integrated and complementary approach to all customer channels is important.

I was chatting with a colleague about differing banking experiences. My bank has an app for iPhone where I can transfer money and check my balance (I can't do everything online but it's better than nothing!). My colleague's bank had no such capability in place. We both concluded that as digital-age consumers, it was a basic requirement to have such tools in place and their availability could influence our choices of who to choose in the future.

I think this is intriguing. Why has one bank got this and another not? There could be many commercial reasons, but it could also be down to the management style and organisational culture why an organisation does or does not deliver digital tools.

The impact on the service sector

Many industries have been turned on their heads and one area that is very labour-intensive and costly is the service sector. Historically if you have a problem with a product or service or would like to make account changes or a payment, you would have limited opportunity to process it yourself. A lot of these activities would have been a telephone call into a contact centre with manual processing of the contact behind the scenes.

There are now tools available that encourage customers to solve their own problems themselves. Some companies proactively contact the customer so that they do not have to ring the contact centre. This could be in the form of a predictive text message within a business process, even an avatar that can provide answers to your questions, or the customer entering directly into the CRM system through automated digital processes.

Do you make it quick and easy for your staff or your customers?

The airlines sector is a good example of how digital tools have improved business processes. The end-to-end process is digitised and designed in a way that puts the customer in control and for the majority improves the experience. The email that I receive from easyJet a few days prior to departure manages my expectations, tells me exactly what I need to do and when, plus I can refer to it at my convenience when I wish, which is often when I am packing my bags!

Any questions I may have had would have probably turned to calls into the contact centre a few years ago and cost easyJet in terms of potential process failure and cost of contact. Instead, cost is being driven out of the company by using a digital capability. Airlines are really good examples of digital innovators as they are continually driving down the cost of servicing customers.

EasyJet now offer a mobile application and boast that their customers can book a flight on more than 580 routes in less than thirty seconds. Compare that to how we used to book a flight: phoning or visiting a travel agent, letting them find the right flight and most competitive rate. That seems like a lifetime ago!

The mobile application also offers other capabilities such as managing and making changes to bookings, checking flight details and even processing refunds.

What these capabilities actually mean are that customers are able to find solutions to their own problems, transact and find information relevant to their circumstances as and when they wish. These are the types of transactions that are normally managed in contact centres.

If such a tool is so easy to use, then why wouldn't you use it? The above example demonstrates how digital capabilities can be used as a strategic differentiator in a competitive market but also as a means of driving out cost from contact centre budgets.

This strongly suggests that the service sector will soon be attacked by a wave of digital and self-service innovations, if it hasn't already been.

Understanding why digital is important

Buy now I believe you understand why digital is important for all organisations and teams. As mobile phones, laptops, tablets and the software that sits on them improve, customers are finding it easier, simpler and often cheaper to use them rather than traditional methods of communications. You do not have to be an expert in IT or technology to use digital tools. The above easyJet mobile application example has been designed to be so intuitive and easy to navigate that it would be crazy not to use it!

Digital capabilities should not only impact on customer-facing capabilities. The social, collaboration and self-service tools that we see in our consumer and personal lives will be required internally as they will help organisations become more transparent, dynamic and more efficient. If you look at how Facebook and Twitter changed how we can communicate efficiently and quickly in our personal lives, then it would be ridiculous for this not to happen in a professional environment. It is difficult to envisage a modern-day workplace where poor intranets and over-reliance on email is acceptable.

This is where 'Understanding and Learning' and the digital world come together. To remain agile, to grab the ideas from teams in processes, to enable collaborative working and to be where your customers are requires a different way of thinking, culture and management. Otherwise your competitors will get there sooner and will make life easier and simpler for your customers, and disappoint your shareholders as your balance sheet gets smaller. Even if first-mover advantage doesn't derive immediate benefits for your competitors, they will have gained more learning than doing nothing.

The tidal wave of digital capabilities is coming at organisations more quickly than you can imagine. You will have those who cope and thrive within this way of thinking and those who will struggle. In ten years' time the way each one of us works and behaves will have changed because of the digital tools at an organisation's disposal. That is a lot of learning that each one of us and our teams will have to absorb to keep up!

In the digital age we can no longer be afraid of change or new technology. Every minute of being scared is a minute of learning lost.

The difference between digital and traditional thinkers

At the top end of some traditional hierarchical organisations there is often the perception that new exciting digital and social tools are a 'younger generation thing' or 'gimmicks'. Many senior management meetings often demonstrate a lack of awareness of ever improving digital capabilities and more importantly, less of a desire to even grasp what is going on in the wider digital world. Most management teams are focused on improving the service whilst reducing costs, and it is surprising that 'digital inertia' is taking place, considering most of the answers can be found in the digital landscape.

Often traditional thinkers believe that they need to know all the answers to all the questions. They need that to build their confidence. They can be secretive, closed and sometimes deceptive. Digital-age thinkers, however, are open, connect with like-minded people and collaborate with many. At the touch of a button they are kept up to date with information that interests them. Digital thinkers have moved from knowing the answers to knowing the right questions to ask.

Digital and social media solutions can be an enabler to solving many management problems but you may find that common responses to digital proposals include:

'We cannot do X, Y or Z because of technology limitations'

or

'Not everyone wants to use digital tools - what about the older generation who want to call us?'

Such counterproductive answers provide relatively simple blockers and roll off the tongue for a traditional thinker. Taking such an approach definitely stops any further creative brainstorming sessions, and there are some similarities with the command control management style.

	Traditional Age Leadership Thinking	Digital Age Leadership Thinking
Strategy	Tell	Participative
Design	Functional	Customer Focused
Information	One to one	One to many
Methods	Hard	Easy
Measurement	Backward	Predictive
Feedback	Customers	Team players
Marketing	Large Budget	Passionate Customers
Service	Call Centres	Communities of Users
Culture	Reactive	Understanding

It is wrong to assume that age alone is driving digital innovations within organisations. It is more so the ability to think in a digital mindset, having the hunger to trial and test new things to incrementally change processes in the quest for continual improvement. This can and should happen at all levels within an organisation.

I recently attended a roundtable event where a group of people gather together from different sectors. These events aim to share best practice around a specific subject in order to share learning. The latest one I attended was about social media, a relatively new area for discussion, and I was looking forward to some creative ideas and new ways of working with social-based tools, as attendees were from forward-thinking organisations.

I try not to take the lead in these sessions; I wait to see how the session goes and quickly identify how I can add value. As the session kicked off, I found myself embroiled in a conversation about controlling your customers and people whilst delving deeply into what is required in a social media policy. Whilst I accept that policies are important, I was surprised that a gathering of key industry people ended up with deciding that controlling the social world with a policy was the right approach!

The creative, innovative debate where I discovered new ways of using Twitter or online forums never materialised. The session and other attendees completely missed the point behind the social world: that you cannot control it! It is a good example of contrasting mindsets as I found myself stuck in a room full of 'traditional' thinkers whilst I think I may have been the only 'digital' thinker there. Not one to keep my thoughts to myself, I challenged them and I think they thought I was on a different planet!

We are now witnessing why open, transparent, dynamic working environments will be increasingly important as technology-driven change within teams becomes the norm in business. You will need to create the right working environments for digital thinkers to share their thoughts, to go into the unknown, to trial and test new ways of working. You will need to develop new customer propositions and ways of communicating. There is a clear link between organisational culture, the design of teams, and the ability to deliver digitally. The key will be to unleash the potential in teams to discover that the best ideas lie within teams who need the right kind of working environment to be creative. Traditional-age managers tend to arrange meetings in dark rooms to come up with the best ideas. The impact of management and mindset styles will ultimately be felt by the customers.

I recently took a train and was held outside Peterborough for well over an hour - extremely frustrating, as you can imagine. Even more frustrating when you are informed every fifteen or so minutes on a loudspeaker system that further information will provided 'when it's possible to do so'. Unfortunately, this made the train company look rather silly, as a quick search on Twitter identified a large fire outside Peterborough. Passengers were telling each other and laughing as the next customer service update repeated exactly the same thing as before. The perception

> *was that the train company were lying to customers, but it was more likely that the customer service representative just didn't know.*
>
> *It is amazing to think that as a customer you can find more up-to-date information from other customers now and not the company itself! With this in mind, you should be able to identify organisations who think in a traditional mindset and those who don't, as they should be where their customers are!*

What do we mean by traditional thinkers?

The traditional thinker is very hierarchical and structured in the way they work. You can identify a traditional thinker immediately. Here are some examples of common behaviours and outputs:

Traditional thinker behaviours	Traditional thinker outputs
Working in a functional organisational structure, focusing on keeping senior management happy.	*The workers are policed by hitting the numbers, resulting in a lack of ideas and connection with customers.*
A lot of problems are referred to as 'It's a people problem'.	*Lots of 1-1s discussing individual behaviour.*
The responsibility for resolving problems usually lies with the most senior person in the team.	*People spending hours playing company politics that results in delays making decisions whilst checking with managers.*
Owning ideas and rather than saying 'we', it is often 'I've had an idea'	*Implementing individual reward encouraging silo-based thinking in own team with little outside challenge.*

You will probably come across traditional thinkers in everyday life and you can pick up quickly whether they are hungry for change. Unfortunately, as we saw earlier on, the world is awash with vast amounts of change with industries being turned on their heads. It is inevitable that this will present challenges for those who think and behave in traditional ways.

What do we mean by digital thinkers?

Digital thinkers will think out of the box and relate things they see in the digital landscape back into the business. Digital thinkers flourish in an open, honest working environment. Ideas are allowed to be shared and more importantly, encouraged to be trialled and tested. Managers allow teams to spend time thinking about how the service could be improved and idea generation is a way of working. Quite often digital thinkers get things done. They don't necessarily develop the perfect solution or idea but are more than happy to take the learning and improve for the next time. Common behaviours and outputs may include:

Digital thinker behaviours	Digital thinker outputs
Company designed around the needs of customers with flexibility in team design and individual contribution. Issues are often about company design.	Customers being treated according to value with very few issues about the company design.
Understanding customer circumstances and amending behaviour to suit, with customers being trusted.	Improved revenue as greater focus is placed on improved experiences. Feedback and cross-functional team challenges are encouraged.
Understanding capabilities and focusing on the continual, sustainable improvement of the organisation.	Managers measuring team purpose and continually improve people, process and systems capabilities.
Problem resolutions are led by the most appropriate person.	Players take decisions in front of customers. Team play is valued as a company capability with a focus on involvement and openness.
Feedback is encouraged and learning is given a high profile in company. Challenge and innovation are encouraged, as is team play and networking.	Ideas continually come from teams. Leaders spend 70% of their meetings listening to understand, facilitating solutions from the experts.

What is next for traditional thinkers?

This is not to say that traditional thinkers are not required, but more so that there is a need for digital thinkers in every part of your business. When Sergey Brin and Larry Page (who both epitomise digital thinkers) set up Google, they brought in Eric Schmidt, a wiser, more structured character, as their CEO,. You can assume that the purpose was to provide more governance and implement more defined business processes. So there will always be a need for traditional thinkers.

Internal digital and social tools also encourage knowledge sharing and breaking down silos within business. Mix this with more informed, highly educated people arriving in business, and we may discover the traditional way of thinking is increasingly marginalised. In theory there will be a shift in knowledge from the top of the organisation to those doing the work, as those who do the work will be the most informed and armed with an abundance of ideas, given the right working culture.

When the two worlds collide it can be an extremely de-motivating experience for digital thinkers.

> *One of my colleagues worked at a telecoms company. She attended a management meeting and a part of it was a brainstorming session for a complex matter. The Director who was leading the group asked for any 'radical' ideas. There was silence as a bunch of busy, stressed managers then had to rack their brains to unearth some creative ideas to address the issue. She found the approach very traditional in the sense that you will probably not get the best ideas by asking a group of managers who are not close to the work.*
>
> *She tried to break the silence by suggesting a slightly off-the-cuff idea, pitched in a way that was slightly 'out there' and hoping to generate further ideas from others. The command control, traditionalist and extremely blunt response she received from the Director was, 'Well, that's not very radical, is it?'*

> *Not only was this in front of a group of people, which made her feel extremely uneasy, it killed any further input that she would have had for the meeting, and it clearly had the same impact on the rest of the team. It epitomised a very traditional approach as the Director then talked to the group all about his ideas, with everyone wondering why he asked in the first place! A few months later my colleague left the company. She now works for their main competitor, who has a reputation for creativity and innovation.*

The best managers in the new digital world will be those who have very little ego and create the right environment for their teams to come up with crazy, wacky ideas that may just work. If we recall 'What, Need and How', then Directors should provide direction. Managers will improve the people, process and technology capabilities. You then rely on teams to innovate and be creative. This has never been as relevant as it is today. Many people within your teams are using creative digital and social tools in their personal lives and subsequently are full of ideas that could no doubt improve your customer experience, and also save some money!

Digital and social tools allow a degree of transparency in a more dynamic sense than ever before. This could be in a social sense through Facebook or Twitter, or professionally, by simply seeing what competitors are up to. If someone in your team has an experience they are often able to demonstrate it visually to the team (through a website, text message, or posting on Twitter, for example) and it is that level of transparency that enables anyone in a team to come up with creative ideas.

> *At an industry seminar one of the participants explained to me the problem she had with a traditional-thinking Director. He had heard from one of his management team that the digital engagement team went across the company 'stealing' ideas. The Director didn't get it. He didn't understand 'learning and creating an environment of sharing' was a key part of the digital strategy and that to lead in digital we had to talk to those who were doing*

> the work rather than dreaming up ideas in a silo-based way.
>
> I was told that the traditional-thinking Director was more concerned with owning ideas than actually delivering or implementing anything. His own teams loved our approach as that enabled them to be more involved. Our approach also allowed the digital engagement team to deliver digital tools that improved roles and reduced transactional and boring types of activity, and they could see real change. Bizarrely, the traditional-age managers were trying to get lost in conversations about the ownership of ideas!

In the digital world, it must be accepted that anyone can have ideas (if you Google any particular idea it's probably been done elsewhere), and that the key bit is to make sure that it's delivered.

A lot of this thinking can only thrive within an 'Understanding and Learning' environment where there is a clear focus on enabling people to thrive and unleashing their potential. The future will be more challenging for traditional thinkers as more and more technology-driven change impacts on roles and more industries. Ensuring you're surrounded by digital thinkers may be a good strategic move!

Developing a digital strategy and the thinking required

Firstly, a good start to any digital strategy is to agree where it sits in the organisation. Most traditional organisations have silo customer service, sales, communications and IT teams. For traditional companies digital tools often lie somewhere between IT, marketing and communications, depending on the make-up of the business. If a business is truly customer-centric, then your digital team will be sat within or next to all your customer service and sales teams (people who actually talk to customers).

The reasoning behind this is twofold. Primarily, the majority of people who visit your website or use digital tools will be customers, whether new, old or existing.

Where does responsibility for digital sit?

Secondly, it's more to do with thinking and priorities. We have already identified that a different type of thinking and management are required when creating new digital propositions. If IT is leading the digital strategy then they may well also be fire-fighting and hamstrung by legacy systems or large-scale projects. Communications and marketing are more than likely trying to manage and control the brand. Both areas may well be unable to think in a customer-centric and digital way.

This requires a different way of designing an organisation for the new digital age. Unless you have extremely collaborative and customer-focused IT and communication teams, which is often rare because of the discrepant priorities, then the ability to implement innovative customer-focused propositions will be limited. Digital and social media are exciting tools that IT and communications often assume responsibility for because of historic reasons, and this state of affairs should be challenged if it has not already.

Designing a team-based collaborative environment

The importance of establishing the right creative working environment for digital thinkers to flourish cannot be underestimated. The rapid change in customer and people behaviour requires a completely different skill, management and mindset than are covered in traditional teams.

The recommendation would be for any digital strategy to be led by a customer-facing or a standalone digital group, working collaboratively next to teams that talk to customers. Having a group of people who have an awareness of technology, with a customer hat on, is probably a good start!

> *When a friend of mine worked in a retail organisation there was a significant power struggle over the management of the company website. So many different*

> *parties were involved and wanted to grab hold of it as it was an exciting area to deliver something innovative.*
>
> *The Customer Relations Director eventually assumed responsibility for it, yet the challenges didn't stop there. The IT and Communications teams could not understand why they did not have responsibility for it and this subsequently created a few problematic dynamics within the organisation.*
>
> *Over the following twelve months there were many unnecessary obstacles and challenges put in place because roles and responsibilities within the organisation were changing.*

The solution seems extremely logical, but many organisations are yet to decipher where the responsibility for digital and social sits. From previous experience, the sooner responsibilities are defined the better!

The importance of digital and social strategies

Many set off on a digital journey to develop a tool that looks good along with some snazzy technology sat behind it. In some respects they are key requirements, but it depends on your purpose for any digital tools.

This may seem like common sense, but take a moment to consider how many websites you visit and cannot do what you want to do! This happens more than you can imagine. A lot of websites are full of information yet do not always let customers fully transact, and the websites are not integrated into normal day-to-day operations.

This happens a lot because the overall purpose has not been clearly defined. often directors and senior managers get over-excited with certain ideas, involved in too much detail that moves people away from being customer-focused.

> *I have been involved in meetings where senior managers are genuinely more concerned with the images than the capability that they were providing their customers to use.*

As a customer, if you cannot do what you want, then you will either quickly move to a competitor who has the digital capabilities or create more cost within a business by calling the contact centre. Increasingly if you do not offer a good experience digitally, then customers may remark negatively about you in a social media setting.

Do you know what your customers have said about your company today?

Making everyone aware of the purpose of the website is the most important part of the strategy as it gets everyone focused on customers, capability and delivery. It also creates awareness of how digital can impact all parts of the business.

If the purpose is clearly defined and agreed, then some examples of what a customer-centric digital strategy should focus on include:

Improving the Digital Customer Experience

Any website must focus on what the customer really wants, which is quite often 'to do something' or 'transact'. Many websites just end up as a repository of knowledge and do not necessarily provide customers with what they actually require. It is really quite simple to understand what customers want, and the information already exists to quickly find this out.

Take a quick look what customers search or click on today on your website, what your competitors have on their websites and more importantly, the top ten reasons why customers call you. If you then compare top reasons for contact with the design of the home page and functionality on your website, then you will identify how customer-centric it is.

> *I contributed in a utility organisation where the vast majority of customer contact was from customers who either wanted to move home or pay their bill. We launched a customer-focused website as the old version had no transactional capabilities on it and about 700 pages of text (which everyone was particularly proud of!).*
>
> *On the old homepage there was a lot of focus on internal requirements (such as brand messages posting news stories that nobody read!) with little focus on enabling customers to do something.*
>
> *This resulted in a lot of telephone calls unnecessarily going into the contact centre, creating cost because the website didn't focus on the requirements of those visiting it.*

Increasing Accessibility

It is just as important to be where your customers are and to enable them to do things when they want. This is important from both a sales and service perspective as customers live 24/7 lives - and if they wish to do something at 4am then they should be able to!

Increasingly being able to transact with an organisation 24/7 is a basic requirement, whereas customers now also expect to be able to transact wherever they are.

Customers want to transact at their convenience. The rapid expansion of free wi-fi and 3g networks means that customers are more mobile than ever before, using a range of tools that do not have to be plugged in. As modes of engaging with customers improve, it is important to make sure customers are able to transact however and whenever they want. Social media and mobile are examples of emerging modes of customer engagement and it's where customers are. The digital and social strategy should focus on satisfying customers however they wish; otherwise they will choose someone else or a more costly mode of engagement.

> As a consultant, I was in one organisation where there was a degree of scepticism about whether there was customer demand for digital tools and whether the investment was warranted. I was continually reminded that most customers would prefer to pick up a telephone. There was no need for the challenges as within two years the numbers of customers visiting the site would have doubled with an average 60% of customers visiting the site completing a transaction.

Customers are well informed these days. A lot of customers visit websites prior to calling or visiting retail outlets. In fact more and more customers have a web browser open whilst they are talking to contact centre advisors! They will also jump from one mode of engagement to another depending on their circumstances and mindset at the+ moment a contact is provoked. Customers will also expect consistent experiences regardless of how they contact you and are often better informed than some of your own people. This means that any digital capability improvements must be integrated into all teams.

Reducing Operating Expenditure

A key purpose in any digital development must be channel shift; to encourage customers to contact and purchase through a cheaper means.

Traditionally customers would call or visit stores, which typically cost substantially more than digital transactions. In the service sector the average cost per call is about £3.00 and then the average self-service transaction costs about forty pence. Any investment in the digital landscape will provide an opportunity to reduce OPEX spend. If capabilities are customer-centric, then customers will ordinarily choose the easiest means of contact, which in this case will be the cheapest! Even if contacts come through digital means and there is some manual intervention (such as re-keying), then there is a strong chance it will be cheaper than through traditional means such as calling and writing.

If you wish to encourage customers to channel shift then make sure the top ten reasons for contact are on your homepage. The impact of implementing a transactional, customer-focused website that was structured around the top ten calls for the utility organisation resulted in a reduction of about 150k calls and significant efficiency. This is a really good example of how investment in digital with the right focus on customers can save money!

Increasing income

There are many ways that a digital strategy can increase income; whole books and university degrees discuss this in detail. Depending on the make-up of the organisation there are many opportunities to increase market share or promote different solutions to customers digitally.

The key is to be there in the first place. This is vital, so that you can learn quickly. Making it easier for customers to purchase a product is one way to increase income. From a service viewpoint, making it easier for your customers to pay and thus getting your money in quicker is another example of how to increase income.

> *A small telecoms company set off to make sure they made it easy for customers to pay their bill (it was the number one contact). For those customers where Direct Debit was not the best way to pay, the next cheapest means was online. Getting this capability in place was a basic requirement for many customers but also necessary to the company from a perspective of getting the money in as soon as possible. Within two years online payments went from zero to over $200k every year, reducing the company's costs substantially.*

Deliver quickly through trials and tests

Getting the purpose agreed and signed off is arguably the most important part of the strategy. It will ensure that any new digital capabilities tick the right boxes but it will also raise senior managers' awareness of potential impacts of digital tools.

A lot of organisations have a basic risk management process in place (and quite rightly so) to make sure there is a degree of governance. Some organisations take that a little too far and become completely risk averse in a way that hinders creativity and the ability to deliver new digital solutions quickly. For organisations to be innovative they need to trial, test and learn from new propositions.

When a company value includes 'we want to innovate', then it is often contradictory as many organisations are averse to doing things differently, particularly in the digital world. If organisations believe in innovation then surely they would be actively encouraging risk-taking in the digital landscape.

Do you test and learn, or wait?

For a business to really innovate and thrive in the digital world, action learning must take place. Take social media for example: it is where a lot of customers are today, but many organisations are not yet there. You do not 100% know what impact social or digital tools will have and writing a business case will be near impossible, so the only way to find out is to get involved through trials and tests. As your customers are already there and your people are using these tools, there is often little choice but to jump in at the deep end and take a risk.

You can plan meticulously and take months to deliver something. As the world moves extremely quickly, the learning you can get by actually doing something is probably a lot more beneficial than one or two short-term headaches and mistakes.

Historically the approach to technology has been to collect the requirements and then to deliver a solution based on those requirements. What is probably more appropriate in an agile, forward-thinking environment is to get a solution that you can quickly put in place that provides the foundations and then the ability to learn from it for future improvements. The development of cloud-based solutions has made it easier to buy a complementary system, and have it implemented within weeks rather than months.

To really embrace action learning within an organisation it requires a degree of trust within teams. They need to feel sure that if something goes wrong then the learning will be built into the next stage of the concept. That's a key reason why the 'Understanding and Learning' environment is fundamental to surviving in the digital world.

Telling customers you have new digital capabilities

Once you have got something delivered, the next stage is to tell your customers that you have good, customer-focused digital tools that are ready to be used. In my experience you will find that once you have something in place, there will always be a segment of customers who will naturally deviate towards digital, social or self-service solutions. As competitors and other sectors introduce digital tools, there will be an expectation that you will have something. The digital thinkers amongst us will want to try and do things ourselves without a huge amount of encouragement as we are keen to have a play around.

> *A good example of using a self-service tool is in supermarkets. From what I have seen, self-service check outs have not really been promoted a huge amount and a lot of customers have naturally started to use them. I discovered pretty quickly how the solution worked and how easy it was through having a play around.*
>
> *Other customers need a bit more encouragement and may need to gain a better level of understanding before they wholly change their behaviours to self-serve. Once I got the hang of it, I discovered that it's quite painful to go to the old checkout and not do it myself!*

Other segments may need educating about the benefits of being in control and self-serving. A lot of customers state that they prefer to speak to another human being. If they knew how easy some websites and self-serve tools were, they might reconsider how they engage with you. There is a degree of encouraging your customers' behaviours to change and this is where a communications team should be assisting.

> *Usually I buy train tickets online yet somehow I thought it might be quicker to buy at the station as I was passing through Kings Cross station. I found myself in an extremely long queue! I waited for ten minutes or so and estimated how much longer I would be there; probably hours! I then contrasted that with the subliminal messages dotted around the travel centre, where I was informed that I could do everything that I wanted to do online or on my mobile within seconds. I then thought to myself, why I am queuing to speak to a human being when I could go home and do this at my convenience?*
>
> *It was a good question as I left the queue. I found this fascinating as I doubt I will ever queue for train tickets again. From the train company's perspective, the fewer people they have serving customers face-to-face, the less it costs them, so this made perfect sense for them and me!*

It is really important that the communications teams understand the purpose of the digital strategy and how any communications strategies should consider how to encourage the behavioural changes amongst customers. At all customer transaction points, customers should be made aware of any digital capabilities. These touch points can include the community when your people talk to customers, over the telephone, or through traditional marketing.

A new level of listening and understanding customers

This seems a little obvious, but it's extremely important to ask customers how easy something is to do and if they would improve anything. Digital is and should be designed to make our lives quicker, easier, faster and simpler. A lot of organisations use Net Promoter Score, where they will ask you if you would recommend them. If you want to really improve and identify weaknesses in your processes, then asking how easy it was is an extremely good metric to measure. Especially in competitive environments, because if it's not easy, then customers will go somewhere it is!

If you want to improve in the digital and social age, take advantage of the fact that customers love to provide feedback, especially immediately after transacting with you. If you ask an unnecessary question in a digital process, or something is confusing on your website, then customers will point it out. It is crucial that you have capabilities in place for feedback and you ask the right question that will be an enabler for continual improvement.

> *I have been approached by many digital 'usability' consultancies that will test digital tools and also hold focus groups for feedback. Contrast that with having the right capabilities in place for customers who will give you feedback for free. It could be either through your website, in a social media forum or in a complaints team. If you do capture feedback directly from customers then you can build that into improvement plans in a more dynamic, customer-centric manner.*

Agreeing the correct measures

The best thing about the digital world is you can measure anything. There shouldn't be anything that you cannot measure. The key is to not measure too much! The purpose you are trying to achieve will then guide what to measure. You may also find that the most important statistics for the digital strategy are not in the digital team.

For example, if you're encouraging your customers to use digital and not traditional modes of engaging, then the most important measurement is the number of phone calls you receive. If you have wrapped your digital strategy around the top 10 reasons for contact, then measuring the number of phone calls and digital transactions seems fairly logical. Many organisations get lost in analysing everything but these would be the most important numbers.

If you also measure how easy the process is, then this would be appropriate to understand how the continual improvements are impacting on customers.

One key benefit of the digital world is that you have numbers that make business cases a lot more reliable. For example, if you implement an online form that is manually processed in the background then this will provide you with the right numbers for a strong benefits case for future investments in technology.

Collaborating and communicating

The majority of us have benefited hugely in our personal lives from using tools such as Facebook and Twitter. Social tools have brought about a new means of communication in not only a more open manner but also a more efficient way. We are now also seeing the emergence of even newer tools that enable more dynamic group discussions and there will be a continuation of even newer tools as digital technologies evolve.

Historically, inside and outside of work we have moved from primary use of the telephone onto texting, instant messenger and email, which was probably a big enough change to cope with for a lot of people. Now we have Facebook, Twitter and various other 'social', collaboration or messaging tools that are changing the way we behave inside and outside work.

> In my friendship group we have begun to use a tool called 'Whatsapp'. I am not sure if this is the next big thing or a fad, yet it enables friends to set up groups and collectively message one another. Perhaps an indication of how lazy I have become, rather than message all my friends individually, I now have an intuitive and user-friendly tool to message them all at once! We have used this to plan a holiday across Europe. Historically we would have sat down, discussed, planned, discussed a bit more and gone around in circles, and probably followed up with lengthy emails (this is starting to sound like a typical day for traditional thinkers at work!). Yet using a collaboration-based tool, we were able to discuss, organise a trip remotely and at our convenience.

I am sure that in twelve months' time there will be an even newer, improved tool than 'Whatsapp'. This is a good example of my friends being digital thinkers through trialling and testing new ways of communicating, but also how there is a deluge of new tools that we can use to make our lives quicker, faster and more efficient.

For example, could there be an instant messaging tool out there that could reduce the need for meetings?

If you use many of the newer forms of communicating, take a moment to consider that many businesses are dependent on email. When you get into the office in the morning to sit at your desktop computer to use an email tool it is perhaps like taking a step back in time. This has been recognised by Atos consulting who have recently decided to draw up strategies to ban email within work, replacing it with collaboration tools.

Having the right culture to maximise benefits

In your personal life you share information digitally because you want to. You feel that photographs of your holiday or posting your latest thoughts will be welcomed by your friends so they see what you've been up to. You would use tools between your friends as you feel comfortable contributing and sharing information. Transferring that into a professional environment is difficult. To implement and derive benefits from collaboration tools you need to have the right culture where sharing information is the norm.

In a command control, silo-based organisation the chances of teams wanting to share knowledge and help one another is fairly minimal. The chance of them speaking to each other is small, let alone communicating digitally!

There will be little impact from social tools when the users are concerned about the repercussions of posting something that perhaps goes against managerial agendas. The thought of teams being immediately connected requires a different type of management, where managers do not have to get involved in problem solving! In some teams where the manager is king and in control of the empire, the impact of social tools would be detrimental to the status quo.

Social tools will enable teams to be more informed and self-managing. Increasingly some teams will be more technically informed than the actual manager!

An understanding and learning environment that encourages communicating across teams will derive immediate benefits from using collaboration tools. If people are trusted and encouraged to share their knowledge, thoughts and issues, this will help imbed such tools too, in the quest to become more efficient.

Only a few organisations have highlighted that the meeting and email culture is highly inefficient and costly. As such, tools have been highly effective outside of the workplace; it is inevitable that a similar trend will take place in business to improve the way and speed in which we can work.

Behavioural changes with traditional thinkers

What is interesting with social and collaboration tools in business is the impact they will have on the command-controller management style. Those who play up to the dynamics within the business and own ideas may have to change the way they go about things. Traditionally an idea would have come from a particular person and that person would receive the plaudits. But many people have ideas, and then the real challenge is how we collaboratively work in teams, across teams, and up and down the hierarchy to get something done and implemented.

You can guarantee that your idea isn't always as innovative as you may think; often a quick search online will provide examples of similar ideas. Increasingly you will find that ideas have been done before and you will have to tweak them for your own organisation to make them better. Take Facebook, for example; Friends Reunited had a similar concept, and as others did as well. Mark Zuckerberg took an idea and made it better. It's a good example of spotting an opportunity and working extremely hard to bring it to life.

Historically you would have had an idea, run it past managers, perhaps held a workshop or customer forum and then kick-started a project. Whereas now, many ideas have been done before and you do not have to follow that process.

At the time of writing this, I have discovered the most efficient means for me to learn and keep up to date with the innovations elsewhere is on Twitter. Every day I see links to articles posted by the people I follow. I am now finding the most important part of idea generation is making sure I follow the right people on Twitter. Previously it would have been reading the right book, but now the majority of my inspirations come from following the right people! This is why collaboration and team play is ever more important. There will be ideas across teams to innovate and improve, but there will be no point having such ideas if you cannot get them implemented!

We live in exciting and revolutionary times

The next few years will definitely be exciting across all industries; why wouldn't it, as the way of serving millions of customers is about to change. One area where transformational change is about to take place and impact all of us is within the service sector. As technology capabilities rapidly advance, and many agile companies move similarly quickly, some organisations will get left behind as customers will not put up with a service that isn't quick, easy and doesn't involve them.

We are in an age where it is the norm for customer expectations and behaviours to continually change, primarily driven by digital and social changes. Such transformational change requires a different way of thinking and management style, and that's where 'Understanding and Learning' will become so important when managing teams.

To implement digital and social changes in an organisation you need to be fully transparent with your own team and others. Management need to be able to build trusting relationships across the business and also to work as quickly and dynamically as possible.

'Understanding and Learning' is a management process that enables this type of organisational culture and is fit for the digital age, ensuring that teams are customer-centric and that companies remain competitive.

What makes great teams

Tactics are important but they do not win football matches. Players win football matches. The best teams stand out because they are teams, because the individual players have been truly integrated that the team functions with a single spirit. There is a constant flow of mutual support among the players, enabling them to feed off strengths and compensate for weaknesses. They depend on one another, trust one another. A manager should engender that sense of unity.

Sir Alex Ferguson, Manchester United Manager

There are lots of research and books available to help understand what makes great teams; however there does not seem to be a universal definition. Before managers start creating a great team, they must make sure that their teams have the tools so that they can perform to their best. On an uneven surface even the best football teams can struggle.

Everyone has their own ideas and thoughts on what makes a great team. I have asked thousands of working people across Europe. I have discussed great teams with senior management and have spoken to successful leaders. I have met their teams and facilitated groups to understand why some teams are successful and some are not. The thoughts in this chapter are based on feedback received from people who have experienced success and believe that they have found the answer to what makes great teams.

From the research it does not follow that having the most talented individual players will make a great team, although having talented players certainly appears to give them a good start! However, the very best appear to take time to maintain the team spirit, develop sustainable values and recognise and understand the different contributions that individuals make to their success. They collaborate and are organised around their purpose. They nearly always contain energetic leaders that people want to follow. They have a belief and a winning attitude. An award-winning manager once told me, "A loser lives life accidentally whilst a winner has a purpose."

The leader is essential in creating the environment but maintaining it is not just a leader's responsibility. In the great teams, their efforts are focused on continually providing feedback on how the team and individuals are performing. They build loyalty with one another; they celebrate and they criticise together. In short, they succeed and fail together. There are some great teams in nearly every company. Despite the company culture, they work at creating an environment that people want to be part of.

> *Everyone wants to run for each another, everyone fights for each other and everyone is giving and if you give, you accept. This is a unique team in Europe. We are unique because, as we say in Holland 'the nose is pointed at the same direction.*
>
> *I was a bit of an individual, but the boss slowly taught me how to play together and that you get more out of your career when you work together.*
>
> *He brought this learning for everyone. If you are new you get your chances to play and slowly you think the Arsenal way. I know*

> *everyone is thinking the Arsenal way and that can make a big difference as well. Not many teams are playing the way we play.*
>
> **Robin van Persie, Arsenal following an easy 3-0 victory over Seville**

There are many characteristics that make a great team and I will explore these briefly in the following pages. However, I believe that how teams and individuals respond to failure appears to set apart the best from the rest. Many successful people have told me that along the way they have experienced disappointment and setbacks but they responded positively to the challenges that failure brings. Great teams review their successes and failures and identify how they can improve things, individually and collectively. They don't just sit about and let life get them – they change things and do things differently!

At some time in your working life you may have had the fortune to have worked with a successful group of individuals. If you have, you will remember what it was like. From my observations, there is normally a lot of emotional connectivity towards the leader and between the players. The players and the leaders put a lot of emotion into making the team a success. They are passionate about what they do. They care about one another. It's very difficult to create an emotionally charged great team but even harder to maintain it or change it. Continually renewing is the responsibility of the leader and all of the players. It is not easy and it requires patience, team focus, clear leadership and direction. Creation and renewal of great teams require four specific values. These are:

1. Trust
2. Understanding
3. Improvement
4. Purpose

Without these four values great teams are neither created nor renewed. You must have all four. You cannot have one without the others. Only the very best continually succeed and achieve ground-breaking results, year after year. What do they have that others could learn from? Thousands have helped me find the answer. With their help I have identified the key characteristics of great teams.

Great teams have trust

Trust is the cornerstone of all achievement. Without this foundation there are always conflicts and disagreements between team players. In the digital-age teams, the conflicts are about ideas and the way forward. In traditional-age teams the conflicts are often about personalities and their idiosyncrasies. Some conflict can be creative; however where there is a lack of trust, the conflict can lead to a breakdown in team dynamics and individual alienation. When trust between team players is present, players are open with one another, they face conflict and recover from it and productivity is increased. When players trust management to act and solve problems that they cannot solve themselves, they become truly connected.

Develop trusting relationships based upon respect and fairness

Understanding that all players have a view and treating them with respect at all times helps create a team spirit that can cope with failure and setbacks. All players have a contribution to make and teams find ways to ensure that each individual has the freedom to contribute, sometimes creatively, to the team's success. Every individual is different and the best teams find ways to harness the diversity and the creativity that individuals bring to the decision-making processes. The best digital-age leader works hard to maintain the spirit. They also build trusting relationships with people inside and outside their own company. Why? They know that who you know makes a big difference to your success. People with many relationships, built around respect and fairness, appear to have more opportunities to succeed.

Who would value a call from you?
When did you last speak to them?

These days there is often too much email, too many text messages and not enough conversation. Go on pick up the phone and arrange to meet someone for lunch or an evening meal.

Seek and look forward to feedback without being defensive

Digital-age teams openly share feedback. They don't bottle things up. Providing feedback to one another in a team environment helps everyone improve. Proactively looking for feedback about your performance from your team will improve you and the people around you. Players who are open to feedback help to create an environment where players can learn from one another's failure. We all fail sometimes. Some players wallow in their misfortune choosing to discuss their experiences and their difficulties. The more they discuss, the more they re-enforce the negative thoughts in their mind. The best do not waste time but review, take action and do things differently. The best are not defensive - they move forward and don't look back. Defensive players never appear to learn as they are too busy justifying their latest position to learn. Of course, giving feedback to defensive players can be difficult. The best teams help create the environment where defensive players feel that they can open up. Talk to your team about the problems of giving feedback to defensive people.

Are you defensive about feedback?

The best teams ask others for feedback on their performance. They use this feedback to improve their team and each individual. Feedback can come from many sources and it can be useful and helpful. The list can include colleagues, customers and other departments. A digital-age manager I worked with a few years ago asked this question.

He wasn't defensive, he took the feedback and made the changes, not just for himself but for the teams he worked with.

Develop trust by talking to people not about them

If a team has defensive players then players will talk about their colleagues. Defensive players do not accept feedback well and often make life difficult for the giver of the feedback. Players who have feedback have to talk to someone about the problem. Talking about people when they are not around is safe and it is normally done with people who you trust implicitly. In some companies, people talk in a derogatory way about other departments that they depend on for their success. However, it destroys teamwork, develops little cliques and destroys the trust. Eventually, someone has to sort it out – normally the team leader. At the executive level the ego gets in the way and often is only resolved by the Chief Executive. The best understand the impact of loose language on the local environment. I have asked the following question to thousands of people.

Do you want people to talk to you or about you?

Ninety-nine per cent of the people said they want people to talk to them not about them.

Yes, be open with people but be sensitive to them. Take time to think about how you might share feedback. If someone gives you feedback of a critical nature, try to learn from it and do your very best not to be defensive. Being defensive does not help you or your team to succeed. If you are defensive, people stop giving you feedback and you stop learning.

Great teams have understanding

Taking the time to understand others is a prerequisite to building lasting relationships. If you want people to understand your situation, you need them to listen to you. If you want people to listen to you the start point is to listen to them to really understand them. All you need to do is to change the way that you think. See it from their point of view not just your own. Try it at home, try it in your relationship and try it in your working life.

<u>*Listen, seeking first to understand people and situations*</u>

When teams take time to listen to one another, players develop a better understanding of the situation being discussed. The key to better understanding is not always talking. Understanding can be improved by asking questions. Take time to listen to the answer. Try not to judge the situation or circumstances until you have fully understood. Keep asking questions until you fully understand. Many conflicts can be reduced by listening first. Excellent team players and great teams do this naturally. They keep working at it.

How often do you take time to really listen to others?

<u>*Surface concerns to develop individual and team understanding*</u>

When things are going well, players often do not take time out to review how well they are doing. They are too busy having a good time! Digital-age teams systematically build in opportunities for players to raise concerns about how well or not well they are doing. They ask questions to build the understanding of one another. How do they feel individually about their achievements? What is it like to be a member of this team? Could we do better? How?

What one thing would you like me to do differently?

Great teams encourage individuals to surface conflict and they manage the conflict creatively. If they are unhappy about someone in their team or their contribution they go and talk to them. When you talk with people, seeing it from their point of view, it is often not as bad as you think. The more players listen to understand one another the more they resolve their differences. Often disagreements are merely misunderstandings. Digital-age teams focus on developing the understanding of each other, encouraging everyone to ask questions when they do not understand. When teams understand what they need to do they don't stop to ask questions during the activity - they deliver results.

Think of others, sharing concerns and support each other

Great teams welcome new players and make it easy for them to settle in. Showing empathy towards players helps everyone develop their social skills. Thinking about how others see the situation and supporting one another is seen regularly in successful teams (and relationships). Individuals are free to share their inner thoughts and this helps teams build a deeper level of understanding of one another. When you see something from someone else's point of view, really trying not to judge the situation, it is an amazing experience. You learn a lot. Try it with your best friend or at home tonight. Remember to listen first!

Do you really see things from someone else's point of view?

When individuals feel supported, valued and feel understood they relax and are more likely to listen to you.

Great teams have improvement

Assuming that teams have trust and understanding (and that is not easy) the next step is to build improvements into everything that the teams are doing. This seems easy; however it takes a special team to be able to review their performance continually. It requires individuals to be open and honest and to reveal their known weaknesses or to admit to their errors. Individuals have to take personal risks to be open about their failures. Digital-age teams review their activity in order to understand what individuals and the team did to make it work or not work. They share negative and positive feedback with one another. They challenge themselves and one another to improve.

Continually measure and coach one another to improve

In great digital-age teams, everyone measures and improves themselves. They set themselves individual targets for improvement and ask the team for feedback on their performance. They choose to make a contribution. Everyone finds time to coach players on how they can improve their performance. It doesn't take long - sometime less than five minutes. In addition, the team leader receives feedback on how they can improve their own leadership behaviour. In the very best teams, every player including the team leader, talks to the team about their individual improvement plan. Teams review the plan together every six months. In this environment, coaching and improving is continually built into the day-to-day work and not just left to the team leader.

Do you measure and improve yourself daily? How?

See things through your customer's eyes and continually improve

Creating an internal culture that is trustworthy, open to improvement, with understanding and feedback, will create an environment that players will enjoy being part of. However, it only really comes alive when the teams see things from the customers' point of view. When teams focus on what matters to customers and are continually improving the experience, impressive business results can be delivered. The team naturally share customer feedback so that improvements can be made.

What matters to your customers?

In great teams, players are interested in why customers are contacting the company. Players want to satisfy customers first time with no delays. They don't want to pass the customer on.

<u>*Take responsibility to provide feedback to motivate the team*</u>

As they contribute towards team achievements, players in the best teams give feedback to one another during the game – like players in a football team. They create the environment where everyone is expected and willing to recognise the contribution that players are making. Players don't just come in to do the work and wait for their next 1-1 or appraisal. They know that it is part of their job to give positive feedback to their colleagues. The team leader role is to help create the environment where the players closest to the work can feel comfortable to give and receive feedback. The best team leaders also receive feedback from their teams. How difficult is it to give positive feedback to a colleague?

How often do you give positive feedback to one of your team?

Hundreds have told me that it is easy to give positive feedback to others. However, only a few teams regularly put time aside to build this into their daily activities. It seems that traditional thinkers think that only the manager should motivate people.

Great teams have purpose

Trust, understanding and improvement are like three legs of a milking stool. Great teams need all three; otherwise they will fall over and not achieve what they are capable of. Trust, understanding and improvement provide the foundations to enable individuals to make the most of their potential and for the team to achieve results. They focus on succeeding as a team, continually improving themselves. Within this environment players learn a lot. It is not possible to improve if players in teams do not trust or understand one another.

Digital-age teams are fired up with a purpose and deliver results. Unless teams have a purpose they drift along, sometimes succeeding, sometimes not. When individuals have a purpose they make remarkable progress. When teams have collective purpose they can achieve much more than individuals alone.

Is your team fired up with a sense of purpose?

Take individual responsibility for circumstances, behaviour/actions

Players in digital-age teams do not blame others for how they are feeling or how they are acting. They don't blame the company. They don't blame each other. They have trained themselves always to take responsibility for the situation they are in. Once you start taking responsibility for your situation you stop wasting time and blaming others. As long as you have someone to blame – the actions are never yours. Great teams take action to improve things as individuals and as teams. They work hard to resolve their problems. They avoid the negative outlook and look forward to finding creative ways to move things forward positively. They only admit failure when they really cannot resolve a problem. Even when they cannot solve a problem great teams take responsibility to identify who they need, to help them come up with a solution.

Are you blaming someone else for your present situation?

Challenge behaviour that does not help the team achieve

This really does separate the good team from the great. When players consistently let the team down or are obviously not performing, the great team take responsibility to question the contribution of players. They do not tolerate persistent errors in individual performance. Team discipline is managed within the team and not always left to the team leader. Some great teams take time to understand why players are having problems, offering support when necessary to help them achieve. Sometimes players need to move into more suitable roles. It is not easy being part of a great team. You must keep on delivering. In this competitive world, companies cannot afford to carry any spectators.

Are you a spectator? Has anyone noticed?

In the great digital-age teams, the leader is continually reviewing the team to ensure that they have the capabilities to deliver the results not just today but into the future. They look ahead and predict what they will need in terms of the processes, the systems and the people required. They are always looking for fresh talent to bring into the team to make it stronger.

Trust each other to make individual contribution to the team

Players in great teams don't wait to be told what to do. Teams with purpose ensure that players know what they should be doing. Players document their individual contribution and review their performance regularly. Great teams expect players to make a contribution, in their area of expertise, and not sit about waiting to be asked to contribute.

What real difference have you made to your team over the last year?

High flying teams trust one another to make a difference and deliver results for their company.

Great teams have belief

Successful individuals have a belief in their own talent and continually challenge themselves to achieve. It follows that great teams must have belief that they will succeed. They can visualise what their achievement will look like. Together they believe that they can succeed.

What will you be doing in six months' time? Can you visualise it?

Great teams believe that they can change or achieve things. In all my research great teams had team players who believed that they could succeed. When others doubted and criticised them, the leaders and their teams remained resilient and continued to excel, focusing on their purpose. They don't allow the day-to-day problems and frustrations to stop them doing what they believe is the right thing to do. When the going gets tough they keep going.

If you believe you can do something, you make a start.

Summary

Building a great team in the digital age is an ongoing achievement. Giving teams a purpose, helping them understand customers and one another, building trust and continually improving is not easy but some I have met have achieved this.

In the best the leaders are emotionally charged, visible, and dynamic. They help their teams to achieve results by understanding the current problems and setting about the company to resolve them. They ask questions to assist the team in delivering results. Questions like:

What is the biggest barrier to doing your job and creating happy customers?

Great leaders want individual players to keep on learning and to succeed. The teams they lead are passionate, have strong values and together they blend the different personalities ensuring that individuals are happy and succeeding. Great teams have setbacks but believe they will succeed.

As long as individuals and teams still believe that they can achieve something, then there is no limit to what can be achieved both personally and collectively.

The moment people stop believing and think that they can't do something is the moment when they stop trying.

Practical actions to understand and learn about what makes great teams

- Agree a team philosophy based upon the statements above. Try and picture what a great team looks like - visualise it and work towards it.

- Look at the statements in this chapter and ask your team to mark out of ten where the team is against each of the statements. Use the results to open up a discussion on how they can improve.

- When things are bad - it is often not as bad as you think. Think back to a time when things also seemed bad. How are you now?

Implementing Understanding & Learning

One must learn by doing the thing; for though you think you know it, you have no certainty until you try.

Sophocles, 415 BC

If you think in a digital-age way, there are real and sustainable savings to be made. Reductions in cost and improvements in customer and people satisfaction can be realised very quickly. However, sustainable reductions only really occur through ongoing transformational change. In short, this means that strategically and tactically, digital-age thinking is being dribbled through everything across the team or better still, the company.

The ten company attributes that I have identified as being essential to the transformation need to be reflected in a digital-age way of thinking. Real sustainable advantage cannot be realised through half-measures.

The solution is not just training

The answer is not training courses away from the work. Too many of these courses are very well rehearsed and presented yet they add little sustainable benefit. They tend to be like the effect of having a cup of coffee. The caffeine 'hit' leaves you feeling satisfied, but as it wears off you tend to feel lethargic and crave another. The scenario with training is very similar. The experience may be great, but there is minimal return on investment and the only solution appears to be a repetition of the course or something similar.

How well is training being applied in the workplace?

My company 'Understanding and Learning' have created solutions that add real value to the bottom line, very quickly. The digital-age solutions connect with people, giving them the opportunity to take responsibility and resolve their own problems, bringing short-term and sustainable benefits.

The solutions do more than the first two stages of the Kirkpatrick evaluation (which you can review in the chapter on 'Understanding People Development'.) They bring about cost reduction and revenue generation. This is because they are operationally driven. The solutions have been designed to be used and integrated into the daily activity. They are never separate and have not been designed to improve people's behaviour, although this has always been an outcome anyway as people are involved in their work and trusted to make decisions. People keep learning and there exists much more team play.

Additionally, focus is on building customer loyalty through making the emotional connection and providing solutions that customers want and need. There is less desire or need to operate in silos and interdependent relationships are established, reducing time spent on game-playing and internal politics. Dialogue increases and knowledge is quickly transferred. In short, everyone understands and learns together. Subsequently, people contribute enthusiastically through choice. They are not living in fear and continually being checked. The majority will not let you down, but it requires a leap of faith and thinking differently to move into the digital-age way of doing things.

Four stages of Implementation

Implementing Understanding and Learning has benefits that can be realised extremely quickly. It can work in any environment; however, sustainable results only really occur when everyone is fully behind the changes. The length of time depends on the leadership and the actions that they take to change the team design, the process, the technology or the people who are in the way. There are four key stages for successful deployment of Understanding and Learning. Following an initial review of your organisation or your team, an agreement would need to be taken to go ahead with a need to change either the customer experience or the internal culture or both.

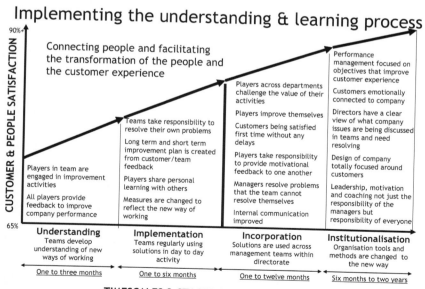

Implementing the understanding & learning process

	Understanding	Implementation	Incorporation	Institutionalisation

Connecting people and facilitating the transformation of the people and the customer experience

Players in team are engaged in improvement activities

All players provide feedback to improve company performance

Teams take responsibility to resolve their own problems

Long term and short term improvement plan is created from customer/team feedback

Players share personal learning with others

Measures are changed to reflect the new way of working

Players across departments challenge the value of their activities

Customers being satisfied first time without any delays

Players improve themselves

Players take responsibility to provide motivational feedback to one another

Managers resolve problems that the team cannot resolve themselves

Internal communication improved

Performance management focused on objectives that improve customer experience

Customers emotionally connected to company

Directors have a clear view of what company issues are being discussed in teams and need resolving

Design of company totally focused around customers

Leadership, motivation and coaching not just the responsibility of the managers but responsibility of everyone

Understanding
Teams develop understanding of new ways of working

Implementation
Teams regularly using solutions in day to day activity

Incorporation
Solutions are used across management teams within directorate

Institutionalisation
Organisation tools and methods are changed to the new way

One to three months | One to six months | One to twelve months | Six months to two years

CUSTOMER & PEOPLE SATISFACTION 90%+ 65%

TIMESCALES & STAGES OF IMPLEMENTATION

The first stage is **Understanding.** During this phase, which can take between one and three months, teams develop their understanding of a different way of working. They develop an understanding of the various solutions and begin to use them in their own teams to solve their problems and/or increase their sales.

The second stage, **Implementation**, encourages teams to further develop their understanding by regularly using the solutions and building them into their day-to-day activity. During this phase management would also be reviewing the way that they build the new measurements into the day-to-day review of performance. Most companies who have implemented Understanding and Learning have easily arrived at the end of stage two. Stage two can be completed within one and six months depending on the local leadership. During these stages, ideas and improvements are put forward to improve the customer experience and individual teams and departments can often gain enough to help them improve their own working conditions and environment.

Once stage two has been completed, leaders and managers need to incorporate the new way of working into the company to sustain the changes. This is essential as some players in teams will see the first two phases as just another initiative. Stage three is **Incorporation.** Managers integrate the solutions into the day-to-day fabric of the company. Solutions are used within and across management teams to help demonstrate commitment to the new way of working. When managers show enthusiasm for the new ways of working the progress can be accelerated. The best teams and their leaders stand out during this phase. It can take from one month to one year.

Stage four, **Institutionalisation**, sets about looking at the organisation, tools and methods to incorporate the new ways of working. The tools and methods changed include the internal communication, the performance management, the measures of success and the customer experience processes. During this stage, leaders are also identifying the individuals who are demonstrating the right behaviours and look to ensure that they are recognised and put into positions where they can influence and help accelerate the progress. Management across the organisation demonstrate full understanding and the new way of working becomes the norm. Teams develop at different speeds and this stage can take up to two years to be fully embedded.

The behaviour in Understanding and Learning environments

In successful digital-age companies all roles think differently about the contribution they make. In an Understanding and Learning environment there are only four role types. These are leaders, managers, coaches and players. Each role has quite clear responsibilities and need to work closely with other role types to create the environment where players can release their potential. I have discussed these responsibilities with teams that have implemented Understanding and Learning and have created this list of some of the responsibilities of each role. This is not an exhaustive list for each role type but does give you an idea of their responsibilities.

Leaders in Understanding and Learning environments:
- Communicate clear direction and give the team focus
- Design the company around customers with minimal hierarchy
- Focus on the customer experience across the company
- Ensure everyone knows the customer satisfaction performance
- Are visible, value their people and are involved with their teams
- Facilitate contribution of their team through challenge and teamwork

Managers in Understanding and Learning environments:
- Continually improve the people/process and systems capabilities
- Focus on what players need to implement the experience successfully
- Create roles with real purpose, with variety and improvement built in
- Solve problems that are upsetting the team and customers

- Build relationships with key dependencies across the company
- Facilitate contribution of their team through challenge and teamwork

Coaches in Understanding and Learning environments:
- Measure to continually improve the experience for customers
- Facilitate the contribution of players in a team environment
- Create the environment where the team achieve results
- Challenge out wasteful and unnecessary internal activities
- Identify the inefficiencies and delays for customers
- Focus on continually improving team and individual behaviour

Players in Understanding and Learning environments:
- Focus on how they implement the experience for customers
- Make the emotional connection with internal or external customers
- Identify and raise issues that are upsetting customers
- Have specific measures that they can continually improve
- Respond proactively to customer contacts
- Measure to continually improve the experience for customers

In addition to the above, all roles in the company need to:
- Provide customer feedback to improve process or products
- Give feedback to one another to improve their team's performance
- Take responsibility for their personal motivation and contribution
- Lead, coach and improve themselves and the team
- Share knowledge and learning with others
- Build strong relationships with everyone across the organisation

What percentage of your day do you spend on the above items?

Within all companies there are continual challenges to increase sales, reduce costs and improve customer satisfaction. When roles in teams think differently it is possible to have all three and improve the morale of the company.

The measurable benefits

Companies that take a leap of faith and implement digital thinking improve their customer experiences and benefit in the following areas:

Improving productivity
- Reduction in unwanted customer contacts
- Fewer e-mails being written/read
- Reduction in management meetings
- Reduced non-value activity and crisis management
- Reduced team meeting time
- Fewer management reports

Improving the costs to serve customers
- Reduced external/internal training budget
- Reduced incentive budget
- Reduction in employee turnover
- Less time spent on disciplinary activity
- Reduced recruitment costs
- Reduction in employee non-attendance
- Reduced cost to serve

The above are realistic improvements when the implementation is successful. In addition, you will:

- Increase the number of satisfied customers
- Improve customer satisfaction and loyalty
- Increase the number of repeat customers

The thinking needs to be built into the daily work and cannot be separated out from it.

How much money is being squandered on all the waste activities within your company?

When does it work best?

Throughout the book I hope to have given you a few ideas. However, these fifteen points act as a checklist as you make a start to implement the thinking.

1. Digital-age thinking needs to be kept on the agenda. This means that it doesn't become a one-off initiative but built into all aspects and parts of the business. Unless this happens, the effect is very much like a training course in that some initiatives are implemented and delivered and then you move onto something else.

2. Create a small team that understands the urgency to change things. This team must trust one another, lead and deliver the changes required, ensuring that they focus on the customer and their needs continually communicating the successes to the wider team on a regular basis. Without urgency change does not happen.

3. The environment that managers need to create is one that stimulates trust, ambition and creativity. Fear must be eradicated. How many people do you know who perform at their best when they are afraid of making a mistake?

4. People need to be encouraged to make the most of their potential. They may become better than you are. If this happens then you have done a great job. Give people opportunities to show what they are good at.

5. The design of the company needs to centre on what matters to customers and the product design. Break down functional structures and work hard to remove the barriers (people, process and technology) that prevent people from communicating and performing their roles to the optimum standard.

6. Improvement needs to be a daily activity. It should not just sit away with project or training resource; rather, it must be something that is part of all roles. Everyone should be focused on his or her team purpose and individual contribution. The environment should be focused on actions and learning to support the achievement.

7. People doing the work have great ideas. Listen to employees. Listen to the ones who are complaining. Make sure that people believe that their views count. Implement the ideas if possible.

8. Build involvement into the daily activity. Rather than attending assigned and pre-planned meetings, visits and forums to understand people's experiences, it is much more effective if this just becomes a 'way of doing things'. People engagement and responsibility increases considerably when people are encouraged to get more involved. Customer advisors have more to offer than just serving/speaking to customers. They should be encouraged to make the emotional connection and to feedback improvements to the transaction and interaction.

9. Create a clear customer vision and develop the strategy ensuring that clear measurements of success are defined throughout the organisation. Over-communicate the vision, ensuring that there is two-way dialogue with teams to improve the understanding. Help people believe in the service or product you are offering.

10. Identify and reward players who demonstrate the required behaviours to ensure that they are actively involved in the

change effort as the process develops. Be generous and specific in your praise towards individuals and teams.

11. Try to ensure that you create your own 'best practice' rather than rely on historical analysis based on what your competitors have done. In order to help you do this, find the talented employees and use their knowledge to help yourself and others.

12. Challenge out old ways of working and ensure that the new ways are built into the way the team operates on a daily basis. People have a tendency to go back to what they know when they come up against barriers. Keep reminding the teams of the successes of the activity.

13. Implement reviews of team performance on a regular basis. Encourage the team to be open about their successes and disappointments. Encourage others to take action and learn from their achievements.

14. This transition to digital-age thinking can be rewarding for everyone. Because the thinking preferences are at opposite ends of the spectrum, change is difficult. However, there is room for compromise through dialogue. Traditional thinkers believe wholeheartedly in their approach and why shouldn't they? Many have been incredibly successful. It was right for its time.

15. Implementing digital-age thinking requires drive, determination and commitment. Continue to focus on the purpose and find the internal motivation to keep going when you come up against difficulties. Just keep going!

Individual changes

In the perfect world, digital-age thinking would be dribbled through all aspects of a company. In one company, I worked with the Chief Executive to change the culture of the whole company with success. However, you can make a start in your own team or your own department, using the insights in this book to improve things on an individual level (personal or work-life) and at a local team level.

One of the best examples of this is a good friend of mine who, despite his company operating in a way not always consistent with digital-age   thinking,   always   maintains   his   personal   focus. Whatever goes on around him, he never loses sight of the external customer and works tirelessly, with great energy, to maintain his belief in what he considers the best way to carry out his role.   In short, he thinks and behaves in a digital   way and demonstrates associated behaviours within his leadership style.

He creates trusting, team-based, customer-focused, understanding and learning environments that add real value to the customer and people experience.

This approach enabled him to achieve and often exceed his business performance targets and engage everyone along the way.

The manager who recruited him told me that he would always recruit him wherever he was working as he naturally brings so much value to the teams that he leads.

Would you be re-employed by your manager?

Next steps for you and your team

If you want to develop your digital thinking and behaviour, then the best way is to start listening and then do something. Take action and learn through experience. This is realistically the only way anyone can change anything. As you progress, you will find others who are looking for a better way!

Start by doing something different and learn as you go!

In this uncertain world, where the future is less clear for all of us, there really is no choice but to seek new ways of learning so that everyone can make the most of their untapped potential. Be ready to adapt, anticipate, predict and search for dialogue between like-minded people you know.

Learning environments that excel require leaders and managers to design companies so that collaboration and individual creativity can naturally surface throughout the team and the company and especially in front of customers.

Enjoy your journey.

If you want to know more then please contact me.

> Richard Brimble
> Managing Director
> Understanding & Learning Limited
>
> Email: richard.brimble@understanding.co.uk
> Web: www.understanding.co.uk
> Mobile: +44 7802 950009

Digital-age thinkers across the world

I have worked with a number of people in the last few years who are experts in their fields. Some are directors and some are in various managerial roles in companies. They just make a difference wherever they have contributed. The people below had an impact on me and I could not have developed my thoughts and solutions without their feedback and support. If you need to contact any of them, please contact me and I will put you in touch with them. Although these days, some will be on Facebook, Twitter and of course many will be on LinkedIn.

Michelle Allison
A customer service trainer and coach who has an ability to implement digital-thinking solutions across teams.

Andy Boothroyd
One of the most engaged and focused team managers that I have worked with. He just believes in adding value wherever he is employed.

David Botham
David, from the Action-Learning centre at Salford University, has been a great advocate of the work within this book. His centre encourages the deployment of Action-Learning within teams to help them co-operate and solve problems together.

Richard Browning
A contact centre professional who has always provided advice and support when it has been needed. He helps operational teams understand the importance of delivering the customer experience. His unique style is motivating to me.

Kathryn Burgess
With a full understanding of digital-age thinking, Kathryn has become an expert in internal communications. She has energy and determination and her writing style is engaging and interesting. She paints pictures with her words.

Anthony Butt
The most motivational manager I know. His enthusiasm infects the people around him and he constantly creates environments where the customer is at the forefront of everyone's thinking.

Carl Dawson
An experienced project manager, who is a very clear thinker and is an expert in digital-age thinking. He has a loyal following of people who have developed with his unique style of thinking and leadership.

Chris Delderfield
Chris is an energetic and committed manager who challenges existing practice to improve experiences for people and customers.

Michelle Douglas

A very loyal and supportive digital-age thinker who is willing to stand up for what she believes in.

Theo Fietelaars

An experienced Senior Manager who understands the importance of modifying his behaviour to suit his audience and is always willing and open to give something new a try.

Ken Hills

Ken is a Chief Executive who understands the importance of the customer. He ensures that his teams are motivated to deliver their best without the hindrance of dress-down days and other such motivational approaches.

Charles Hill

Charles is an inspirational contact centre manager, with an ability to engage individuals and teams to reach their full potential. One of the top coaches I know.

Andy Hobson

A talented manager, who has a real ability to coach people to maximise their potential. A passionate advocate of digital-age thinking.

Maria Grant

A customer service professional who knows what is needed to improve customer service operations. She implements digital-age thinking with an energy that brings people with her.

David Jones

An inspirational senior manager and consultant who has a real ability to design, develop and implement training and development solutions that add real value.

Stuart Knapper

An enthusiastic and customer-focused contact centre manager who has a unique way of motivating the people around him. Stuart's customer-focused approach had an immediate impact on me and many who have met him. He is passionate about making the most of the potential of people and focuses his energy on delivering results.

Jane Lee
An enthusiastic leader who also is an expert in modifying her behaviour to suit her audience and takes the time to engage teams and coach them so that they can make the most of their potential.

Vince Muldoon
A Commercial Director, who has an ability to transform customer service operations, to increase customer and people satisfaction, reduce costs and increase revenue.

Ian Parker
A Customer Relations Director, who puts the customer at the very heart of his thinking. A Customer Management expert, who creates teams who make the emotional connection with customers for the benefit of shareholders and customers.

Stephen Peacock
Stephen is a highly talented contact centre manager. Stephen is a real people developer with a real ability to engage teams to work collectively. A brilliant coach with lots of energy to keep focused on the purpose.

Dave Pimm
Quite simply one of the best people managers and coaches I have ever come across. Many have been inspired by his approach.

Lauren Priestley
A contact centre manager who takes time to sensitively understand the people around her, contributes to the team environment and focuses her team on taking responsibility to deliver results for customers.

David Rance
A Customer Relationship expert who knows what is needed to turn companies round and has developed a software solution to measure customer-centricity, used extensively across the world.

Roeland Segers
A passionate advocate of digital-age thinking and solutions. Roeland has a real ability to implement transformational change within companies.

John Shields
John is a team leader who builds learning into everything he and his team do. He has a thirst for developing knowledge and puts passion into his day-to-day activity. He is a good advocate of digital-age thinking.

Rob Smale
Rob is a hands-on practitioner and a real guru on contact centres (both service and sales). He has been a great support when I have required advice and guidance about contact centre design and measurement.

Kees van Ek
A customer-focused IT consultant who understands the importance of technology and how it can release the potential of people. He is an excellent team player and is skilled at asking the right questions to establish the best way forward.

Elma van Vliet
An internal communications expert, who puts energy and emotion into her work and generates enthusiasm across company teams. Elma is a supportive manager who sets stretching goals for her teams and they often exceed them.

Ken Wilkinson
Ken is a customer-focused Executive Director who gives his team clear direction and freedom to deliver results. He modifies his coaching style to suit each individual, helping others to move forward positively. He builds good internal relationships and creates teams who challenge themselves to continually improve.

Mandy Wilkinson

Mandy believes in putting all her energy into making the most of the potential of everyone in the teams she leads. She has a passion for success and is the best coach I know. In fact, the best coach I have ever worked with.

Mike Yeates

He might be near the end of this list, but without him, I could not have started this journey. A truly remarkable manager who gives his teams the freedom and the space to create something special for teams and for customers. A director who provides advice and support that is always worth listening to. He knows what is needed to help companies take on the challenges of the future and just lets his teams get on with it.

Shirley Young

A dynamic and progressive HR professional who has a real passion for implementing change and people development solutions. Shirley is a truly outstanding coach and leader of teams.

Acknowledgments

I have met and learnt from thousands of people in the course of my work. Some of them have been truly inspiring and motivating. They encouraged me to document my thoughts into a meaningful format, offering me advice and guidance during the course of writing this book. There are a few special people who have always supported my work and helped me to learn more about how to bring the human factor alive in this, the digital age.

I would like to thank Martin Clark, who worked with me for three years at 'Understanding and Learning'. He added much value to the original manuscript. When I first met Martin his leadership, knowledge and coaching ability had an immediate impact on me. The more we worked together the more we realised that we could learn more together than we could alone. He brought an operational slant to this book and his practical ideas have helped thousands to improve themselves and their companies.

During the final preparation of this book I asked many people to provide critical feedback. They were all very helpful and without their input this final copy would not have been achieved. Ian Parker, former Director of Customer Relations at Orange UK, helped improve the overall structure of the book and put forward many original thoughts that I have now included. Ian is a customer-centric director and through his leadership, during the early part of this century, Orange set high standards for customer service.

Mike Yeates, a former BT Director, has been a superb coach for me over the last ten years. He gave me specific observations leading me to re-write a number of paragraphs. Elma van Vliet, an established author herself and an expert in internal communications, offered specific improvements to many chapters and put forward creative thoughts on how the book could be improved.

Carl Dawson (BT) and David Rance (Round), who have always supported the approach taken in this book, were honest in their appraisal and I have now included many of their observations and comments within this final version. I valued their support as I completed this book. In addition, David Botham (Manchester University), Kees van Ek (KPMG), Roeland Segers (Orange Netherlands), David Freemantle (author), Sarina Kessler (Verizon Business), John Maddocks (Veolia), Richard Bench (Veolia), Laura Davis (Veolia) and Maria Grant (MCI) provided additional feedback and material to improve the final version. All of the above provided feedback and encouragement when I needed it. They were critical friends and helped me to improve the original manuscript.

I couldn't have started my journey of seeing things differently without the input of David O'Brien, the former Chief Executive of National & Provincial Building Society and Karen McCormick, the Chief Executive of the Cheshire Building Society, who guided me, way back in 1991, to see a better way of working that benefits customers and unleashes the potential of players within teams.

A few years later, I met John Seddon from Vanguard Consulting and he also offered encouragement and helped me to build upon my understanding of how to change things.

I would particularly like to thank Hugh Logan, Managing Director, and all the management team at BT Mobile, Leeds, United Kingdom. During the mid-90s they gave me the inspiration to create a European award-winning environment that gave players and coaches in teams the confidence and belief that they could change things for the benefit of customers and themselves. Together, we changed things. We created a unique atmosphere where people were free to make the most of their potential and free to use their creative talents. It was an atmosphere which was totally infectious; the best people didn't want to leave. A million thanks to all of you who played your part in the transformation.

Vince Muldoon, the former Customer Relations Director at Orange Netherlands gave me much support and the opportunity to work with his directorate to help them to become more efficient, reduce unnecessary customer contact by 40%, and satisfy more customers the first time.

I would like to thank him personally for taking on my thoughts and introducing me to David Holliday, the Chief Executive, who understood the internal communication challenges he faced and allowed me to build, across his business, an inclusive culture that helped to support the brand and continue their success. Over the last few years I have had the opportunity, as a judge in the annual Professional Planning Forum innovation awards, to visit some of the most innovative organisations in the UK. I would like to thank Paul Smedley, Chairmen and Steve Woolsey, Chief Executive for their support and giving me the opportunity to learn and broaden my understanding of this industry.

In 2008, I met Chris Cope, now a digital transformation consultant at Capgemini. Chris helped me to understand how digital-age thinking could be applied in a social media and digital world. His creative thoughts and ideas inspired me to keep on learning.

Finally, I would like to thank again the many with whom I have worked. Their unique, individual talents and their collective efforts enabled them to contribute to their companies' success. Their interest and enthusiasm for understanding and learning has helped me to continue to focus on making the morale better for people within companies.

Despite all the uncertainty ahead, I remain positive about the future. The adapting organisations will create the environment where creativity and collaboration between teams is encouraged. There is huge opportunity ahead for those who take on the challenge to change.

I will continue to work with teams and companies to create environments where people, whatever their background, can make the most of their potential and release their undoubted talents because they are free and confident to do so.

Further Reading

During the last ten years and during my research for this book I have found the following books useful. Some I have read fully and for the others I have only read a few chapters. If you wish to develop your knowledge further, then have a look at any of these books.

- Managing on the Edge, Richard Tanner Pascale
- On the Frontiers of Management, Rosabeth Moss Kanter
- The Fifth Discipline, Peter M Senge
- NLP at Work, Sue Knight
- Leading Change, James O'Toole
- Please Understand Me, David Keirsey and Marilyn Bates
- Lean Thinking, James P Womack and Daniel T Jones
- The Dance of Change, Peter Senge
- In Pursuit of Quality, John Seddon
- Freedom from Command-Control, John Seddon
- 7 Habits of Highly Effective People, Stephen R Covey
- The 500 Year Delta, Watts Wacker and Jim Taylor
- Principle-Centred Leadership, Stephen R Covey
- The Power of Positive Thinking, Norman Vincent Peale
- Leading Change, John P Knotter
- Getting the Best Out of Yourself and Others, Buck Rodgers
- Crowning the Customer, Feargal Quinn
- What Customers Like About You, David Freemantle
- I'm OK, You're OK, Thomas A Harris
- Punished by Reward, Alfie Kohn

Biographies

Richard Brimble

Richard Brimble has had a successful senior management background in marketing, human resources, organisation development, internal communications and customer relations, leading and coaching teams at Reed International, N&P Building Society, BT Mobile and Veolia Water. In all these companies his teams have won international recognition for either innovation or quality. As a board member responsible for Customer Relations, he led a major change programme that was the talk of the industry. The team won international recognition for its achievements and it was once described as 'one of the top five motivated teams in the world'. In 1998 he became Managing Director of his own interim management/ consultancy company, Understanding & Learning Limited. He has worked with Chief Executives, Directors and their teams to improve organisation culture. He has advised companies in the United Kingdom, Asia, Europe and the USA on how to bring about improved communication, improved customer experiences and results through the sustained contribution of fully connected people.

His former teams are his best references, and his approach brings results in terms of customer satisfaction and improved morale, in a matter of weeks.

He is married to Julie, has two teenage sons and lives in Hertfordshire, United Kingdom. He enjoys golf, travelling and new experiences.

Martin Clark

Martin Clark is a graduate from Leeds University and has worked in a number of senior customer-facing roles over the past ten years. His main passion is facilitating the creation of an environment where people can reach their full potential. His approach is empathetic and he prides himself on adapting his style and methods to meet individual and team requirements and is equally as comfortable in the board room as he is on the shop floor.

He is married to Lucy, has a young son and daughter and lives in County Durham, United Kingdom. He enjoys most sports, particularly football, golf and cricket.

Chris Cope

Chris is currently working for a leading management consultancy specialising in digital transformation. He spent much of his earlier career working in the utility sector managing digital and customer-facing teams where he won a national managerial award for his work in digital. His professional interests include customer strategy, integrated and complementary customer experiences across all modes of engagement, social media and smart metering. He is a real believer in change, using new technologies and putting people and customers at the heart of any strategy.

He enjoys travelling, walking, playing sport, seeing as much live music as possible and supporting Nottingham Forest.